William Tatham

and the

Culture of Tobacco

William Tatham

and the

Culture of Tobacco

By G. MELVIN HERNDON

Including
a facsimile reprint of
*An Historical and Practical
Essay on the Culture and
Commerce of Tobacco*

By WILLIAM TATHAM

UNIVERSITY OF MIAMI PRESS
Coral Gables, Florida

Designed by Bernard Lipsky

Manufactured in the United States of America

Contents

I.

An Historical and Practical Essay on the Culture and Commerce of Tobacco

By WILLIAM TATHAM

London, 1800

AN

HISTORICAL AND PRACTICAL

ESSAY

ON THE

CULTURE AND COMMERCE

OF

TOBACCO.

———

By WILLIAM TATHAM.

———

LONDON:

PRINTED FOR VERNOR AND HOOD, 31, POULTRY,

By T. BENSLEY, Bolt Court, Fleet Street.

1800.

PREFACE.

An uſeful work needs no indelicate recommendation; nor can a bad one be ſupported
by it, although a ſonorous patron might happen
to help the ſale. Such as I have I give unto
the world with a heart conſcious of upright
intentions; and I candidly confeſs I am more
diſpoſed to do them real ſervice than to flatter.
If the reader find me imperfect it will be
ſome little apology that I am but a man; and
it may be a farther excuſe that I neither poſſeſs
a diſpoſition to cloak my defects under a dedi-
cation, or a party to dedicate to. This work,
being devoted to the proſperity of commerce,
bids me take my leave of compliment and attend to my ſubject.

I have been led, by mere caſualty, to trace
the hiſtory of *Tobacco* from its primitive ſource;

A 2 and

and I have perfevered in the defign of fearching out, as far as I have found it practicable,
thofe things which tend to enlighten a fubject
of novelty for the benefit of traffic. I am
compelled, by time and circumftances, to cur-
tail my book for the prefent; yet with confident hopes that the public approbation will
call for a fupplementary part, which, I truft,
will render. my defign more completely ufeful.

I beg leave to notice, on the authority of
Mr.· P. La' Bat, that the botanical term *Nicotiana*, took its origin from the perfon who firft
introduced it into France : it is a circumftance
which I do not find elfewhere recorded, that,
Jean Nicot, mafter of requefts, ambaffador from
Francis II. to Sebaftian king of Portugal, had
this honour ; and I recite it for the ufe of bo-
tanifts.

If I fhould be fo fortunate as to accomplifh
the publication of a fecond volume, it is my
intention to throw fome ufeful lights upon
the manufacture of this article ; upon its hiftory in France, Spain, Germany, Holland,

and

and other countries concerned in its culture, commerce, or manufactures; and, ultimately, to add an useful appendix of tables and prices current, in a way suited to ready reference.

THE AUTHOR.

November, 1799.

Directions

Directions to the Binder.

* Not being regularly acquainted with natural hiſtory, I find I am miſtaken in my firſt idea concerning the *eruca maxima cornuta*, p. 21. It appears to be a diſtinct inſect from the common *tobacco* or *horn* worm ; which I have ſince been ſo fortunate as to obtain the drawing of from nature, that this plate is engraved from. I am certain, however, that there is a ſimilar inſect to be found alſo amongſt the to-bacco plants.

EXPLANATION

EXPLANATION OF THE PLATES.

Plate of the Plant, p. 2.

a, A Flower Bud.

b, A Flower, the funnel fhaped corolla being cut open to fhew the five ftamina, the piftil, and capfula.

c, The Flower, as it appears when full blown.

d, A tranfverfe fection of the capfula.

e, The Leaf of the plant, having a hole in it, eaten by a tobacco worm.

Plate of the Worm, p. 21.

a, The Chryfalis.

b, The Caterpillar, or *horn worm*.

c, The fly ftate, or Moth, vulgarly called the tobacco hawk.

Plate of the Tobacco Houfe, &c. p. 29.

a, The common Tobacco Houfe.

b, Tobacco hanging upon a fcaffold.

c, The operation of prizing.

d, Infide view of a Tobacco Houfe, fhewing the tobacco hanging to cure.

e, An outfide view of public warehoufes.

f, An infide view of the public warehoufe, fhewing the procefs of infpection.

Plate of Conveyance to Market, p. 55.

a, Conveying tobacco upon canoes.

b, Conveying tobacco by upland boats.

c, Conveying tobacco by waggons.

d, Method of rolling tobacco in Virginia.

A 4   SUBJECTS

SUBJECTS OF THIS WORK.

PART I.

PART II.

PART III.

PART III. *Supplementary.*

PART IV.

PART V.

PART VI.

CONTENTS.

PART I.

ON THE CULTURE OF TOBACCO.

OF THE CULTURE OF THE CROP.

PART II.

ON THE MANNER OF HOUSING, CURING, AND VEND-
ING TOBACCO IN VIRGINIA.

Of

PART III.

OF THE PUBLIC WAREHOUSE AND INSPECTION.

                                              Of

PART III. *Supplementary.*

PART IV.

PROGRESS OF THE CULTURE AND COMMERCE OF TOBACCO.

PART V.

OF THE TOBACCO TRADE OF GREAT BRITAIN.

ABSTRACT OF LAWS AND REGULATIONS CONCERNING THE COMMERCE OF TOBACCO IN GREAT BRITAIN.

Hovering

PART

PART VI.

CULTURE AND COMMERCE ACDORDING TO
MR. ANDERSON.

State

APPENDIX.

CULTURE OF TOBACCO.

PART I.

Introductory Remarks.

HAVING lately feen a few plants of American Tobacco growing cafually in a gentleman's garden near London, and perceiving that very little is generally known in England concerning the hiftory and ordinary culture of an article of commerce which has occupied a confiderable capital in tranfatlantic traffic for about two hundred years; and indeed a plant which is peculiarly adapted for *an agricultural comparifon of climates*; without entering fo far into the fubject as to confider it a ftaple produce of the nation, I beg leave to communicate a few particulars in refpect to the hiftory and culture of this luxuriant commodity, which I am enabled to ftate from authorities, and from what

B   I recol-

I recollect to have noticed during twenty years residence in Virginia, where it is a principal export.

Botanical Definition.

The botanical account of tobacco is as follows *:—" NICOTIANA, the tobacco plant, is a genus of plants of the order of *Monogynia*, belonging to the *pentandria* clafs, order 1, of clafs v. The calyx is a permanent perianthum, formed of a fingle leaf, divided into five fegments, and of an oval figure.   The corolla confifts of a fingle petal, funnel-fhaped.   The tube is longer than the cup.   The limb is patulous, lightly divided into five fegments, and folded in five places.   The fruit is a capfule of a nearly oval figure.   There is a line on each fide of it, and it contains two cells, and opens at the top. The receptacles are of a half oval figure, punctuated and affixed to the feparating body.   The feeds are numerous, kidney-fhaped, and rugofe.

" The fpecies of this genus are reduced by Linnæus into four.   1. Nicotiana with fpear-fhaped leaves.   2. Nicotiana with oval-fhaped leaves, commonly called Englifh tobacco.   3. Ni-

* Wheeler's Botanift's Dictionary, p. 322.

cotiana

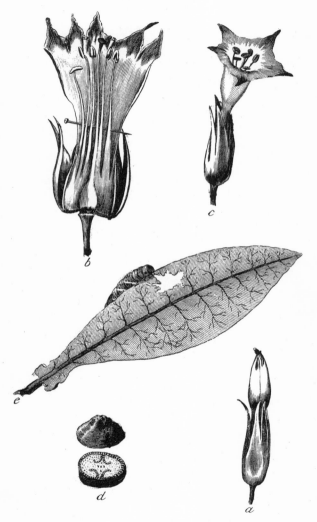

cotiana with heart-fhaped leaves, paniculated flowers, and club-fhaped tubes. 4. Nicotiana with heart-fhaped leaves, branching petals, and unequal cups.

" The firft fpecies is a native of America, and is an annual plant, propagated by feeds, which muft be fown upon a moderate hot bed in March.

" When the plants are fit to be removed, they fhould be tranfplanted into a new hot bed, of a moderate warmth, about four inches afunder. Let them be watered and fhaded till they have taken root, after which they will require air in proportion to the warmth of the feafon; they muft alfo be frequently watered, and about the beginning of May they fhould be inured to the open air; then let them be tranf-planted into a rich light foil, in rows four feet afunder, and three feet diftance in the rows. When they begin to fhew their flower ftems, their tops fhould be cut off, if they are defigned for ufe, that their leaves may be the better nou-rifhed; but if they are defigned for ornament, let them be planted in the borders of the plea-fure garden, and fuffered to grow to their full height.

" The fecond fpecies is found growing wild in many parts of England; this fort may be

propagated

propagated by fowing the feeds in March, upon a bed of light earth, and when the plants
are come up, they may be tranfplanted into
any part of the garden, where they will require
no farther care.   The third and fourth fpecies
are annual plants, and natives of Peru, and may
be propagated in the manner directed for the
firft fort."

So far with regard to the botanical definitions
of the refpective kinds of tobacco, and the
mode of culture recommended in England.   I
am perfuaded however that the ufual field culture of Virginia would fucceed in the vicinity
of London, and in the fouthern parts of England.   I fhall confine myfelf to the firft fpecies *; and fhall endeavour to give an account

of

---

* The different fpecies of the genus have been in former
days diftinguifhed in Virginia by the names of Oronoko,
fweet fcented, and little Frederic; but I have not been able
to learn from the infpectors themfelves (who I have frequently queftioned thereupon) that their botanical knowledge is fufficient to diftinguifh, at this day, one fpecies from
another of the blended mafs, by any leading characteriftic
upon which they can pointedly rely : and hence (although
the *law* affects to make a diftinction) we moft generally
find all kinds claffed in the Oronoko column of the tobacco note.

Queftion a planter on the fubject, and he will tell you
that he cultivates fuch or fuch a kind : as, for example,
" Colonel

of the method of culture, the mode of curing and vending, and of the legal regulations of this ftaple in Virginia.

Of the Choice of Ground.

So much depends upon the choice of ground fuitable for the cultivation of this plant, and fo much has this kind of cultivation been encouraged by commerce in Virginia, that this confideration has heretofore had confiderable influence on the value of eftates. Indeed this would feem to be a good criterion to decide the innate worth of foils; for it is certain that lands which do produce good crops, or full grown plants, of tobacco, will fucceed in any other branch of hufbandry. The lands which are found to anfwer beft, in their *natural ftate* in Virginia, are the light red, or chocolate coloured mountain lands; the light black mountain foil in the coves of the mountains, and the richeft low grounds. Hence has arifen the general reputation of the Virginia tobaccos,

" Colonel Carter's fort, John Cole's fort," or fome other leading crop mafter; and if the celebrated Linnæus were at this day to clafs the characteriftics of Virginia tobacco, he would probably difcover feveral divergent fpecies, in which nature and accident might feem to have cohabited fportively.

and, chiefly, the local reputations of particular
tobaccos brought to market: as, for example,
*James's River tobacco, Tayloe's Mountain quarter
tobacco, &c.* which are preferred.   The condition of foil of which the planters make choice,
is that in which nature prefents it when it is
firft difrobed of the woods with which it is naturally clothed throughout every part of the
country : hence in the parts where this culture
prevails, this is termed *new* ground, which
may be there confidered as fynonymous with
tobacco ground.   Thus the planter is continually cutting down *new* ground, and every fucceffive fpring prefents an additional field, or
opening of tobacco (for it is not neceffary to put
much fence round that kind of crop); and to
procure this *new* ground you will obferve him
clearing the woods from the fides of the fteep-
eft hills which afford a fuitable foil ; for a Virginian never thinks of reinftating or manuring
his land with economy until he can find no
more *new* land to exhauft, or wear out, as he
calls it ; and, befides, the tobacco which is
produced from manured or *cow-penned* land *,

* *Cow-penned land* is that which is manured by removing
the cattle about upon it, fo that herds are confined during
the night time to fucceffive fquares or pieces of ground at
option, until a fufficient quantity of manure is depofited.
This is effected by means of moveable fences.

is

is only confidered, in ordinary, to be a crop of
the fecond quality. It will hence be perceived
(and more particularly when it is known that
the earth muft be continually worked to make
a good crop of tobacco, without even regarding the heat of the fun, or the torrent of fudden fhowers), that howfoever lucrative this
kind of culture may be in refpect to the intermediate profits, there is a confiderable drawback in the wafte of foil. Indeed, if all accounts were fairly kept for experiment's fake,
upon three adjoining eftates of equal fize and
quality, and one of thefe were cultivated in
grain and grafs, another left remaining in
woodland, and the third cultivated in tobacco
for twenty years fucceffively, I have no hefita-
tion in believing, that either of the two firft
would yield more than the latter; or that the
drawback of waftage upon the tobacco lands
would reduce the fum total of the premifes
and net productions beneath the faleable value
of the woodland tract which had lain twenty
years neglected.

Of the Plant Beds.

The plant beds, or *plant patches* (to ufe the
local phrafe), are the places fet apart by the
crop mafter for fowing the feed of the tobacco;

and

and wherein the plants are fuffered to grow until the feafon approaches for planting the crop.

The quality of earth, and places which are univerfally chofen for this purpofe, are newly cleared lands of the beft poffible light black foil, fituated as near to a fmall ftream of water as they can be conveniently found, due attention being paid to the drynefs of the place. The beds, or *patches*, as they are called, differ in fize, from the bignefs of a fmall fallad bed, to a quarter of an acre, according to the magnitude of the crop propofed; and they are prepared for receiving the feed in March and the early part of April, as the feafon fuits, firft by burning upon them large heaps of brufh wood, the ftalks of the maize or indian corn, ftraw, or other rubbifh ; and afterwards, by digging and raking them in the fame manner of preparing ground for lettuce feed; which is generally fown mixed with the tobacco feed (the fame procefs being fuitable to both plants); and which anfwers the double purpofe of feeding the labourer, and of protecting the young tobacco plant from the *fly*; for which intent a border of muftard feed round the plant patch is found to be an effectual remedy, as the fly prefers muftard, efpecially *white* muftard, to any

other

other young plant; and will continue to feed upon that until the tobacco plant waxes ftrong, and becomes mature enough for tranfplantation.

We muft now leave the plant bed to prepare for cultivation.

OF THE CULTURE OF THE CROP.

Firft, of preparing the Tobacco Ground.

There are two diftinct and feparate methods of preparing the tobacco ground: the one is applicable to the preparation of new and uncultivated lands, fuch as are in a ftate of nature, and require to be cleared of the heavy timber and other productions with which Providence has ftocked them; and the other method is defigned to meliorate and revive lands of good foundation, which have been heretofore cultivated, and, in fome meafure, exhaufted by the calls of agriculture and evaporation.

The procefs of preparing new lands begins as early in the winter as the houfing and managing the antecedent crop will permit, by grubbing the under growth with a mattock; felling

felling the timber with a poll-axe *; lopping off the tops, and cutting the bodies into lengths of about eleven feet, which is about the cuſtomary length of an American fence rail, in what is called a *worm* or *pannel* fence †.
During

* This is a ſhort, thick, heavy-headed axe, of a ſomewhat oblong ſhape, with which the Americans make great diſpatch. They treat the Engliſh poll-axe with great contempt, and always work it over again as old iron before they deem it fit for their uſe.

† The *worm* or *pannel* fence, *originally of Virginia*, conſiſts of logs or malled rails from about four to ſix or eight inches thick, and eleven feet in length. A good fence conſiſts of ten rails and a rider, or perhaps nine rails and two riders; and the law requires a fence to be maintained good of a certain regulated height, before a proprietor can be juſtified in diſtraining cattle, damage feaſant, or ſupport an action of treſpaſs. It is called a worm fence from the zigzag manner of its conſtruction, which is as follows: The loweſt rail is laid upon the ground, then one end is raiſed up and a ſimilar rail placed under it in an oblique direction; another rail is alternately added in ſucceſſion in the ſame way, until the length of fence required is deſcribed; the ends of each rail being ſuffered to overlap each other about a foot; and theſe corners of the fence are generally raiſed upon a ſtone or ſhort block, to ſave them from decay.

The worm (as it is called) being thus laid, the ſame proceſs is repeated until the fence riſes to the height of nine or ten rails; two ſtakes (ſomewhat ſhorter than the rails will do) are then brought to each corner or interſecting angle of the rails which compoſe the fence, and one end of each being let into the ground with a hoe or mattock on each ſide
of

During this part of the procefs the negro women, boys, and weaker labourers, are employed in piling or throwing the brufh-wood, roots, and fmall wood, into heaps to be burned; and after fuch logs or ftocks are felected as are fuitable to be malled into rails, make clap-boards, or anfwer for other more partilar occafions of the planter, the remaining logs are rolled into heaps by means of hand-fpikes and *fkids**; but the Pennfylvania and German farmers, who are more converfant with animal powers than the Virginians, fave much of this labour by the ufe of a pair of horfes with a half fledge, or a pair of truck wheels. The burning of this brufh-wood, and the log piles, is a bufinefs for all hands after working hours;

of the fence, the other ends are fuffered to lean againft it, forming a crotch or crofs over the interlapping corner: into this crofs one or more courfes of heavy rails are laid (termed *riders*), which ferve to lock and keep the whole partition fecure. It is in allufion to this zigzag foundation that a drunken man is faid to be *laying out Virginia fences*.

Mr. Weld, in his plate of *an American ftage waggon*, has given a good reprefentation of a Virginia plantation; but his fence (like many other parts of his work) wants to be ftaked and ridered.

* *Skids* are two or more ftrong faplings or other pieces of long timber, upon which timber hogfheads, &c. are rolled and facilitated upon the principle of the inclined plane.

and

and as nightly revels are peculiar to the African conftitution, this part of the labour proves often a very late employment, which affords many fcenes of ruftic mirth.

When this procefs has cleared the land of its various natural incumbrances (to attain which end is very expenfive and laborious), the next part of the procefs is that of the hoe; for the plough is an implement which is rarely ufed in *new* lands when they are either defigned for tobacco or meadow.

There are three kinds of the hoe which are applied to this tillage: the firft is what is termed the fprouting hoe, which is a fmaller fpecies of mattock that ferves to break up any particular hard part of the ground, to grub up any fmaller fized grubs which the mattock or grubbing hoe may have omitted, to remove fmall ftones and other partial impediments to the next procefs.

The *narrow* or *hilling* hoe follows the operation of the fprouting hoe. It is generally from fix to eight inches wide, and ten or twelve in the length of the blade, according to the ftrength of the perfon who is to ufe it; the blade is thin, and by means of a moveable wedge which is driven into the eye of the hoe, it can be fet more or lefs *digging* (as it is termed),

termed), that is, on a greater or lefs angle with the helve, at pleafure. In this refpect there are few inftances where the American black-fmith is not employed to alter the eye of an *Englifh*-made hoe before it is fit for ufe; the induftrious and truly ufeful merchants of Glafgow have paid more minute attention to this circumftance.

The ufe of this hoe is to break up the ground and throw it into fhape; which . is done by chopping the clods until they are fufficiently fine, and then drawing the earth round the foot until it forms a heap round the projected leg of the labourer like a mole hill, and nearly as high as the knee; he then draws out his foot, flattens the top of the hill by a *dab* with the flat part of the hoe, and advances forward to the next hill in the fame manner, until the whole piece of ground is prepared. The centre of thefe hills are in this manner guefled by the eye; and in moft inftances they approach near to lines of four feet one way, and three feet the other. The planter always endeavours to time this operation fo as to tally with the growth of his plants, fo that he may be certain by this means to pitch his crop within feafon.

The third kind of hoe is the *broad* or *weed-ing*

ing hoe.   This is made ufe of during the cultivation of the crop, to keep it clean from the
weeds.   It is wide upon the edge, fay from ten
inches to a foot, or more ; of thinner fubftance
than the hilling hoe, not near fo deep in the
blade, and the eye is formed more bent and
fhelving than the latter, fo that it can be fet
upon a more acute angle upon the helve at
pleafure, by removing the wedge.   We fhall
have occafion to notice the application of this
implement under a fubfequent head of this
paper.

Of the Seafon for Planting.

The term, *feafon* for planting, fignifies a
fhower of rain of fufficient quantity to wet the
earth to a degree of moifture which may render it fafe to draw the young plants from the
plant bed, and tranfplant them into the hills
which are prepared for them in the field, as
defcribed under the laft head ; and thefe feafons
generally commence in April, and terminate
with what is termed the *long feafon in May* ;
which (to make ufe of an Irifhifm) very frequently happens in June; and is the opportunity
which the planter finds himfelf neceffitated to
feize with eagernefs for the *pitching* of his crop :

3   a term

a term which comprehends the ultimate opportunity which the fpring will afford him for planting a quantity equal to the capacity of the collective power of his labourers when applied in cultivation.

By the time which thefe *feafons* approach, nature has fo ordered vegetation, that the weather has generally enabled the plants (if duly fheltered from the fpring frofts, a circumftance to which a planter fhould always be attentive in felecting his plant patch) to fhoot forward in fufficient ftrength to bear the viciffitude of tranfplantation.

They are fuppofed to be equal to meet the impofition of this tafk when the leaves are about the fize of a dollar ; but this is more generally the minor magnitude of the leaves ; and fome will be of courfe about three or four times that medium dimenfion.

Thus, when a good fhower or feafon happens at this period of the year, and the field and plants are equally ready for the intended union, the planter hurries to the plant bed, difregarding the teeming element, which is doomed to wet his fkin, from the view of a bountiful harveft, and having carefully drawn the largeft fizeable plants, he proceeds to the next operation.

Of

Of Planting.

The office of *planting* the tobacco is performed by two or more perfons, in the following
manner: The firft perfon bears, fufpended upon
one arm, a large bafket full of the plants which
have been juft drawn and brought from the
plant bed to the field, without waiting for
an intermiffion of the fhower, although it fhould
rain ever fo heavily; fuch an opportunity indeed, inftead of being fhunned, is eagerly fought
after, and is confidered to be the fure and certain means of laying a good foundation, which
cherifhes the hope of a bounteous return. The
perfon who bears the bafket proceeds thus by
rows from hill to hill; and upon each hill he
takes care to drop one of his plants. Thofe
who follow make a hole in the centre of each
hill with their fingers, and having adjufted the
tobacco plant in its natural pofition, they knead
the earth round the root with their hands, until it is of a fufficient confiftency to fuftain the
plant againft wind and weather. In this condition they leave the field for a few days until
the plants fhall have formed their radifications;
and where any of them fhall have cafually pe-
rifhed, the ground is followed over again by
fucceffive

fucceffive replantings, until the crop is rendered complete.

Of Hoeing the Crop.

The operation of *hoeing* comprehends two
diftinct functions, viz. that of hilling, and that
of weeding; and there are moreover two ftages
of hilling. The firft hilling commences, as
heretofore defcribed, in the preparation of the
field previous to planting the crop, and it is
performed, as before explained, by means of the
peculiar implement called a hilling hoe; the
fecond hilling is performed after the crop is
planted, with a view to fuccour and fupport
the plant as it may happen to want ftrength-
ening, by giving a firm and permanent foundation to its root; and it may be effected according to the demand of the refpective plants
by a dexterity in changing the ftroke with the
weeding hoe, without any neceffity to recur to
the more appropriate utenfil.

The more direct ufe of the weeding hoe
commences with the firft growth of the tobacco after tranfplantation, and never ceafes
until the plant is nearly ripe, and ready to be
laid by, as they term the laft weeding with the
hoe; for he who would have a good crop of

C tobacco,

tobacco, or of maize, muſt not be ſparing of
his labour, but muſt keep the ground conſtantly ſtirring during the whole growth of the
crop. And it is a rare inſtance to ſee the
plough introduced as an aſſiſtant, unleſs it be
the *flook plough*, for the purpoſe of introducing
a ſowing of wheat for the following year, even
while the preſent crop is growing ; and this is
frequently practiſed in fields of maize, and
ſometimes in fields of tobacco, which may be
ranked amongſt the beſt fallow crops, as it
leaves the ground perfectly clean and naked,
permitting neither graſs, weed, nor vegetable,
to remain ſtanding in the ſpace which it has
occupied.

Of Topping the Plant.

This operation, ſimply, is that of pinching
off with the *thumb nail** the leading ſtem
or ſprout of the plant, which would, if left
alone, run up to flower and ſeed; but which,
from the more ſubſtantial formation of the leaf
by the help of the nutritive juices, which are
thereby afforded to the lower parts of the

* Many of the Virginians let the thumb nail grow long,
and harden it *in the candle*, for this purpoſe : not for the uſe
of *gouging* out people's eyes, as ſome have thought fit to in-
ſinuate.

plant,

plant, and thus abforbed through the ducts and fibres of the leaf, is rendered more weighty, thick, and fit for market. The qualified fenfe of this term is applicable to certain legal reftrictions founded upon long experience, and calculated to compel an amendment in the culture of this ftaple of the Virginia trade, fo that it fhall at all times excel in foreign markets, and thus juftly merit a fuperior reputation. I do not exactly recollect the prefent limitation by law, which has changed I believe with the progrefs of experience ; but the cuftom is to top the plant to nine, feven, or five leaves, as the quality and foil may feem moft likely to bear.

Of the Sucker, and Suckering.

The *fucker* is a fuperfluous fprout which is wont to make its appearance and fhoot forth from the ftem or ftalk, near to the junction of the leaves with the ftem, and about the root of the plant ; and if thefe fuckers are permitted to grow, they injure the marketable quality of the tobacco by compelling a divifion of its nutriment during the act of maturation. The planter is therefore careful to deftroy thefe intruders with the thumb nail, as in the act of *topping*, and this procefs is termed *fuckering*.

This

This fuperfluity of vegetation, like that of the top, has been often the fubject of legiſlative care; and the policy of fupporting the good name of the Virginia produce has dictated the wiſdom of penal laws to maintain her good faith againſt impoſition upon ſtrangers who trade with her. It has been cuſtomary in former ages to rear an inferior plant from the fucker which projects from the root after the cutting of an early plant; and thus a *ſecond* crop has been often obtained from the fame field by one and the fame courſe of culture; and although this ſcion is of a fufficient quality for ſmoking, and might become preferred in the weaker kinds of ſnuff, it has been (I think very properly) thought eligible to prefer a prohibitory law, to a riſk of impoſition by means of fimilitude.

The practice of cultivating *fuckers* is on theſe accounts not only difcountenanced as fraudulent, but the conſtables are ſtrictly enjoined *ex officio* to make diligent fearch, and to employ the poſſe commitatus in deſtroying fuch crops; a law indeed for which, to the credit of of the Virginians, there is feldom occaſion; yet fome few inſtances have occurred, within my day, where the conſtables have very honourably carried it into execution in a manner
ner

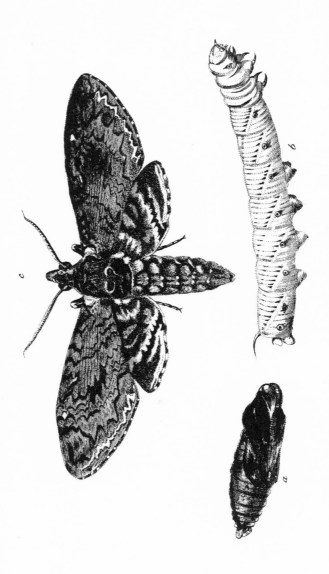

ner truly exemplary, and productive of public good.

Of the Worm.

There are feveral fpecies of the worm, or rather *grub* genus, which prove injurious to the culture of tobacco; fome of thefe attack the root, and fome the leaf of the plant; but that which is moft deftructive, and confequently creates the moft employment, is the *horn* worm, or large green tobacco worm. This appears to me to be the fame fpecies with that which Catefby has defcribed in the fecond volume of his Natural Hiftory of Carolina, p. 94, under the title of *eruca maxima cornuta*, or the great horned caterpillar.

" This caterpillar," fays he, " is about four inches long, befides the head and tail; it confifts of ten joints, or rings, of a yellow colour; on the head, which is black, grow four pair of horns, fmooth and of a reddifh brown towards the bottom, jagged or bearded, and black towards the top; on each of the rings arife fhort jagged black horns, one ftanding on the back, and two on each fide; below which is a *trachæa* on each fide; likewife the horn of the back of the laft ring is longeft: the flap of the tail is of a bright bay colour. It hath eight feet, and six *papillæ*."

There are, besides this kind, others without horns; all of them of a green colour, so far as I recollect*. And this, in Catesby's description, differs in respect to colour; this tobacco worm or *horn* worm, as the planters call it more particularly, being of a pale delicate green; an effect I apprehend which proceeds from the colour of its food when it feeds upon growing tobacco plants. The act of destroying these worms is termed *worming* the tobacco, which is a very nauseous occupation, and takes up much labour. It is performed by picking every thing of this kind off the respective leaves with the hand, and destroying it with the foot.

Of the Term " Firing."

During very rainy seasons, and in some kinds of unfavourable soil, the plant is subject to a malady called *firing*. This is a kind of blight occasioned by the moist state of the atmosphere, and the too moist condition of the plant: I do not recollect whether the opposite

---

* Marian's folio Dissertation on the Insects of Surinam contains a great variety of this genus; the green ones whereof resemble the several kinds of tobacco worm.

extreme

extreme does not produce an effect fomething fimilar. This injury is much dreaded by the planter, as it fpots the leaf with a hard brown fpot, which perifhes, and becomes fo far a lofs upon the commodity. I apprehend there are two ftages when the plant is, in a certain degree, fubject to this evil effect: the firft is whilft growing in the field, the latter when hanging in the tobacco houfe. I know of no other remedy than conftant working the ground while the feed is growing, and careful drying by the ufe of fire in the tobacco houfe.

Of the Ripening of the Crop.

Much practice is requifite to form a judicious difcernment concerning the ftate and progrefs of the ripening leaf; yet care muft be ufed to cut up the plant as foon as it is fufficiently ripe to promife a good curable condition, left the approach of froft fhould tread upon the heels of the crop-mafter; for in this cafe, tobacco will be among the firft plants that feel its influence, and the lofs to be apprehended in this inftance, is not a mere partial damage by nippling, but a total confumption by the deftruction of every plant.

I find it difficult to give to ftrangers a full

C 4   idea

idea of the ripening of the leaf: it is a point
on which I would not truft my own experience
without confulting fome able crop-mafter in
the neighbourhood ; and I believe this is not
an uncuftomary precaution among thofe who
plant it.   So far as I am able to convey an
idea, which I find it eafier to underftand than
to exprefs, I fhould judge of the ripening of
the leaf by its thickening fufficiently ; by the
change of its colour to a more yellowifh green;
by a certain mellow appearance, and protrufion
of the web of the leaf, which I fuppofe to be
occafioned by a contraction of the fibres ; and
by fuch other appearances as I might conceive
to indicate an ultimate fufpenfion of the vege-
tative functions.

Of Cutting and Gathering the Crop.

When the crop is adjudged fufficiently ripe
to proceed to cutting, this operation is affigned
to the beft and moft judicious hands who are employed in the culture; and thefe being provided
each with a ftrong fharp knife, proceed along
the refpective rows of the field to felect fuch
plants as appear to be ripe, leaving others to
ripen; thofe which are cut are fliced off near
to the ground, and fuch plants as have thick
ftalks or ftems are fliced down the middle of the
ftem

ftem in order to admit a more free and equal circulation of air through the parts during the procefs of curing, and to free the plant, as far as poffible, from fuch partial retention of moifture as might have a tendency to ferment, and damage the ftaple. The plants are then laid down upon the hill where they grew, with the points of the leaves projecting all the fame way, as nearly as poffible, fo that when the fun has had fufficient effect to render them pliable, they may more eafily and uniformly be gathered into *turns** by the gatherers who follow the cutting.

Of Gathering the Crop in.

For the better comprehending the method of gathering the crop, it is neceffary to underftand the preparation which muft be previoufly made for facilitating this part of the procefs.

In preparing for gathering the crop of tobacco it is cuftomary to erect a kind of fcaffold in various places of the tobacco ground which may happen to offer a convenient fituation. This is done by lodging one end of feveral ftrong poles upon any log or fence which

* A *turn* fignifies fuch a quantity as each perfon refpectively can carry upon his fhoulder or in his arms.

may

may be convenient, and refting the other end of fuch poles upon a tranfverfe pole fupported by forks, at about five feet from the ground; or by erecting the whole fcaffold upon forks if circumftances require it.

In forming this part of the fcaffold in the manner of joifts, the poles are placed about four feet afunder from center to center, fo that when the fticks which fuftain the tobacco plants are prepared they may fill the fpace advantageoufly by leaving but little fpare room upon the fcaffold*.

Timber is then fplit in the manner of laths, into pieces of four feet in length, and about an inch and a half diameter. Thefe are termed the *tobacco fticks*; and their ufe is to hang the tobacco upon, both by lodging the ends of this ftick upon the poles of the fcaffold which have been previoufly prepared in the field, in order to render it fufficiently pliable and in condition to carry into the tobacco-houfe, to which it is now conveyed by fuch means as the planter has in his power; and by fufpending it in the fame way in the houfe, fo

---

* This is what I apprehend to be the *formal* method; but all do not obferve regularity; many are contented with laying it upon logs and fences, and the change of weather often hurries it under cover in any way.

that

that the air may pafs through it in the procefs of curing. Inftead of this particular method, thofe who prefer to do fo, lay it a fhort while in bulk upon poles, logs, &c. in the field, before they convey it under cover.

We muft now leave the field to attend to the further procefs in the tobacco-houfe, or barn, which will form the next part, or divifion, of this fubject.

PART II.

ON THE MANNER OF HOUSING, CURING, AND VENDING TOBACCO IN VIRGINIA.

Of the Tobacco Houſe and its Variety.

THE barn which is appropriated to the uſe of receiving and curing this crop, is not, in the manner of other barns, connected with the farm yard, ſo that the whole occupation may be rendered ſnug and compact, and occaſion little waſte of time by inconſiderate and uſeleſs locomotion; but it is conſtructed to ſuit the particular occaſion in point of ſize, and is generally erected in, or by the ſide of, each reſpective piece of tobacco ground; or ſometimes in the woods, upon ſome hill or particular ſite which may be convenient to more than one field of tobacco.

The ſizes which are moſt generally built where this kind of culture prevails, are what are called forty feet, and ſixty feet tobacco houſes, that is, of theſe lengths reſpectively, and of a proportionate width; and the plate

of

of the wall, or part which fupports the eaves of the roof, is generally elevated from the groundfel about the pitch of twelve feet.

About twelve feet pitch is indeed a good height for the larger crops; becaufe this will allow four feet pitch each to three fucceffive tiers of tobacco, befides thofe which are hung in the roof; and this diftance admits a free circulation of air, and is a good fpace apart for the procefs of curing the plant.

There are various methods in ufe in refpect to the conftruction of tobacco houfes, and various materials of which they are conftructed; but fuch are generally found upon the premifes as fuffice for the occafion. And although thefe fizes are moft prevalent, yet tobacco houfes are in many inftances built larger or fmaller according to the circumftances of the proprietor, or the fize of the fpot of ground under cultivation.

The moft ordinary kinds confift of two fquare pens built out of logs of fix or eight inches thick, and from fixteen to twenty feet long. Out of this material the two pens are formed by notching the logs near their extremities with an axe; fo that they are alternately fitted one upon another, until they rife to a competent height; taking care to fit joifts

in

in at the refpective tiers of four feet fpace, fo
that fcaffolds may be formed by them fimilar
to thofe heretofore defcribed to have been
erected in the open field, for the purpofe of
hanging the fticks of tobacco upon, that they
may be open to a free circulation of air during
this ftage of the procefs. Thefe pens are placed
on a line with each other, at the oppofite
extremes of an oblong fquare, formed of fuch
a length as to admit of a fpace between the
two pens wide enough for the reception of a
cart or waggon. This fpace, together with
the two pens, is covered over with one and the
fame roof, the frame of which is formed in
the fame way of the walls by notching the
logs as aforefaid, and narrowing up the gable
ends to a point at the upper extremity of the
houfe, termed the ridge pole. The remaining
part of the fabric confifts of a rough cover of
thin flabs of wood fplit firft with a mall and
wedges, and afterwards riven with an inftrument or tool termed a *froe*. The only thing
which then remains to be done, is to cut a door
into each of the pens, which is done by putting
blocks or wedges in betwixt the logs which
are to be cut out, and fecuring the jambs with
fide pieces pinned on with an auger and wood-
en pins. The roof is fecured by weighting it
down

down with logs ; fo that neither hammer, nails, brick, or ftone, is concerned in the ftructure ; and locks and keys are very rarely deemed neceffary.

The fecond kind of tobacco houfes differ fomewhat from thefe, with a view to longer duration. The logs are to this end more choicely felected. The foundation confifts of four well hewn groundfels, of about eight by ten inches, levelled and laid upon crofs fawed blocks of a larger tree, or upon large ftones. The corners are truly meafured, and fquared diamond-wife, by which means they are more nicely notched in upon each other ; the roof is fitted with rafters, footed upon wall plates, and covered with *clap-boards* * nailed upon the rafters in the manner of flating. In all other refpects this is the fame with the laft mentioned method ; and both are left open for the paffage of the air between the logs.

The third kind is laid upon a foundation fimilar to the fecond ; but inftead of logs, the walls are compofed of pofts and ftuds, tenoned into the fells, and braced ; the top of thefe are mounted with a wall-plate and joifts ; upon

---

* *Clap-boards* are thin pieces of four feet long, riven generally out of white oak, and one edge thicker than the other.

thefe

thefe come the rafters; and the whole is covered with clap-boards and nails, fo as to form
one uninterrupted oblong fquare, with doors,
&c. termed, as heretofore, a forty, fixty, or one
hundred feet tobacco houfe, &c.

The fourth fpecies of thefe differs from the
third only in the covering, which is generally
of good fawed *feather-edged* * plank; in the
roof, which is now compofed of *fhingles* †; and
in the doors and finifhing, which confift of
good fawed plank, hinged, &c. Sometimes
this kind are underpinned with a brick or
ftone wall beneath the groundfels; but they
have no floors or windows, except a plank or
two along the fides to raife upon hinges for
fake of air, and occafional light: indeed, if
thefe were conftructed with fides fimilar to the
brewery tops in London, I think it would be
found advantageous.

In refpect to the infide framing of a tobacco
houfe, one defcription may ferve for every kind:
they are fo contrived as to admit poles in the
nature of a fcaffold through every part of them,
ranging four feet from centre to centre, which
is the length of the tobacco ftick, as heretofore

* *Feather-edged plank*, fawed ftuff fimilar to clap-boards.
† *Shingles*, wooden covering, in the method of flating.

D   defcribed;

defcribed; and the lower tiers fhould be fo
contrived as to remove away occafionally, in
order to purfue other employments at different
ftages in the procefs of curing the crop.

Of Preparations for curing the Tobacco Plant.

When the plant has remained long enough
expofed to the fun, or open air, after cutting, to
become fufficiently pliant to bear handling and
removal with conveniency, it muft be removed
to the tobacco houfe, which is generally done
by manual labour, unlefs the diftance and quantity requires the affiftance of a cart. If this
part of the procefs were managed with horfes
carrying frames upon their back for the conveniency of ftowage, in a way fimilar to that in
which grain is conveyed in Spain, it would be
found a confiderable faving of labour.

It becomes neceffary, in the next place, to
fee that fuitable ladders and ftages are provided, and that there be a fufficient quantity
of tobacco fticks, fuch as have been defcribed
heretofore, to anfwer the full demand of the
tobacco houfe, whatfoever may be its fize;
time will be otherwife loft in *makeshifts*, or
fending for a fecond fupply.

Of Hanging the Crop.

When every thing is thus brought to a point at the tobacco houfe, the next ftage of the procefs is that termed *hanging* the tobacco. This is done by hanging the plants in rows upon the tobacco fticks with the points down, letting them reft upon the ftick by the ftem of the loweft leaf, or by the fplit which is made in the ftem when that happens to be divided. In this operation care muft be taken to allow a fufficient fpace between each of the fucceffive plants for the due circulation of air between: perhaps four or five inches apart, in proportion to the bulk of the plant.

When they are thus threaded upon the fticks (either in the tobacco houfes, or, fome-times, fufpended upon a temporary fcaffold near the door, they muft be carefully handed up by the means of ladders and planks to an-fwer as ftages or platforms, firft to the upper tier or collar beams of the houfe, where the fticks are to be placed with their points refting upon the beams tranfverfely, and the plants hanging down between them.

This procefs muft be repeated tier after tier of the beams, downwards, until the houfe is

D 2   filled;

filled; taking care to hang the sticks as close
to each other as the consideration of admitting
air will allow, and without crowding. In this
position the plants remain until they are in
condition to be taken down for the next process.

Of Smoking the Crop.

From what has been said under the head of
hanging the plant, it will be perceived that the
air is the principal agent in curing it: but it
must be also considered that a want of uniform
temperature in the atmosphere calls for the
constant care of the crop-master, who generally
indeed becomes habitually weather-wise, from
the sowing of his plants, until the delivery of
his crop to the inspector.

To regulate this effect upon the plants he
must take care to be often among them, and
when too much moisture is discovered, it is tem-
pered by the help of smoke, which is generated
by means of small smothered fires made of old
bark, and of rotten wood, kindled about upon
various parts of the floor where they may seem
to be most needed. In this operation it is necessary that a careful hand should be always
near : for the fires must not be permitted to
blaze, and burn furiously; which might not
only

only endanger the houfe, but which, by occa-
fioning a fudden over-heat while the leaf is in a
moift condition, might add to the *malady of
firing* which we have defcribed in the field.

Of bringing the Tobacco in Cafe.

Cafe is a technical term made ufe of by the
planters to fignify a fpecific condition of the
plants, which can only be judged of fafely by
long experience. It is at this ftage (that is, in
a condition which will bear handling and
ftripping, without either being fo dry as to
break and crumble, or fo damp as to endanger
a future rotting of the leaf) that it is for the
firft time faid to be in cafe, and ready for farther procefs. This condition can only be diftinguifhed by diligent attention, and frequent
handling; for it often changes this quality with
the change of the weather in a very fhort fpace
of time. Thofe who have indeed a fkill in
this phenomenon have little occafion for a ba-
rometer. The method of trying it correfponds
with that by which the *quality* of the commodity is examined: it muft be ftretched
gently over the ends of the fingers and knuc-
kles, and if it is in good *cafe*, i. e. *plight*, or *condition*, it will difcover an elaftic capacity, ftretching

like

like leather, glowing with a kind of moift glofs, pearled with a kind of gummy powder; yet neither dry enough to break, nor fweaty enough to ferment.

Of Stripping and Bundling.

When the plants of tobacco which are thus hanging upon the fticks in the houfe have gone through the feveral ftages of procefs herein before defcribed, and are deemed to be in *cafe* for the next operation, a rainy day (which is the moft fuitable) is an opportunity which is generally taken advantage of when the hands cannot be fo well employed out of doors. The fticks, containing the tobacco which may be fufficiently cured, are then taken down and drawn out of the plants. Thefe are then taken one by one refpectively, and the leaves being ftripped from the ftalk of the plant, are rolled round the butts or thick ends of the leaf, with one of the fmalleft leaves as a bandage, and thus made up into little bundles fit for laying into the cafk for final packing.

Of Stowing in Bulk, and of putting farther in Cafe.

When the fmall bundles are thus made up, they are generally ftowed in bulk upon pieces of timber forming a kind of platform upon the ground, having their points all laid the fame way. In this condition they go through a fweat; and therefore care fhould be taken to examine them frequently, that this operation of nature may be affifted by fuch regulations in refpect to air, heat, cold, &c. as circumftances and experience may dictate. When the ferment in this courfe of purgation fhall have fo far fubfided as to promife a ftate of permanency in the juices, fo that the leaf will bear an elaftic kind of extenfion upon the fingers, fimilar to what has been heretofore explained, without being fo dry as to crumble or break in the act of handling, and at the fame time fo clear of the fweat as to obviate any doubt in refpect to the rifque of moulding, or rotting *even upon a paffage acrofs the Atlantic ocean,* which is the point to which the planter fhould always direct his calculations (becaufe it is of *that condition* that the public infpectors will exercife their judgment), it is confidered to be *in cafe,* and fit for further handling.

D 4

Of

Of Stemming Tobacco.

Stemming tobacco is the act of feparating the largeft ftems or fibres from the web of the leaf with adroitnefs and facility, fo that the plant may be neverthelefs capable of package, and fit for a foreign market. It is practifed in cafes where the malady termed the fire, or other cafual misfortune during the growth of the plant, may have rendered it doubtful in the opinion of the planter whether fomething or other which he may have obferved during the growth of his crop, or in the unfavourable temperature of the feafons by which it hath been matured, does not hazard too much in packing the web with a ftem which threatens to decay. To avoid the fame fpecies of rifk, ftemming is alfo practifed in cafes where the feafon when it becomes neceffary to finifh packing for a market is too unfavourable to put up the plant in leaf in the ufual method; or when the crop may be partially *out of cafe*. Hence it is that the infpectors mark in the margin of the tobacco note (which is a cer- tificate whereby crops are bought and fold without ever feeing them) the approximate proportion of the hogfhead which is of this quality:

quality: for it often happens that only one third, one fourth, half, one fifth, five eighths, &c. may be stemmed tobacco, and the remainder of the hogshead be packed in leaf according to the ordinary custom.

Besides the operation of stemming in the hands of the crop-master, there are instances where this partial process is repeated in the public warehouses; of which I shall treat under a subsequent head.

The operation is performed by taking the leaf in one hand, and the end of the stem in the other, in such a way as to cleave it *with the grain*; and there is an expertness to be acquired by practice, which renders it as easy as to separate the bark of a willow, although those unaccustomed to it find it difficult to stem a single plant.

When the web is thus separated from the stem, it is made up into bundles in the same way as in the leaf, and is laid in bulk for farther process. The stems have been generally thrown away, or burnt with refused tobacco for the purpose of soap ashes; but the introduction of snuff-mills has, within a few years back, found a more economical use for them.

Of Cafe and Bulk, preparatory to Prizing.

It will be eafily difcovered from what has been hitherto particularized, that an inftability of the feafon or variable weather may occafion a crop under procefs of curing to be often in cafe and bulk, and to be frequently fhifted and examined during that part of the procefs in which thefe changes are expected to happen; for it avails a poor labourer (to ufe another Irifhifm) *lefs than nothing at all*, if, when he has laboured hard in the culture of this commodity, he fhould blunder in this one point only, then wanted to complete a marketable ftaple, and become thus involved in a total lofs of his whole crop, and have the expences to pay into the bargain, for bringing an unmerchantable article to market, through a dreary journey, feldom lefs than a hundred miles. So ftrictly, however, has the fpirit of the tobacco laws, the profperity of the trade, and the policy of fupporting the national faith in negociating this kind of merchandize, hinged upon this ultimate point of a planter's fkill, that it behoves a crop-mafter, moft particularly at this juncture, to be vigilant; and fo fully are young practitioners now-a-days convinced

of

of it, that I believe few like to exercife their opinion without a confultation with age and experience.

Of Prizing, and its Appendages.

Prizing, in the fenfe in which it is to be taken here, is, perhaps, a local word, which the Virginians may claim the credit of creating, or at leaft of adopting: it is at beft technical; and muft be defined to be the act of preffing or fqueezing the article which is to be packed into any package, by means of certain levers, fcrews, or other mechanical powers; fo that the fize of the article may be reduced in ftowage, and the air fo expreffed as to render it lefs pregnable by outward accident, or exterior injury. than it would be in its natural condition.

The operation of prizing, however, requires the combination of judgment and experience; for the commodity may otherwife become bruifed by the mechanic action, and this will have an effect fimilar to that of prizing in too *high* cafe, which fignifies that degree of moifture which produces all the rifks of fermentation, and fubjects the plant to be fhattered into rags.

Of

Of the Apparatus for Prizing.

The ordinary apparatus for prizing confifts of the prize beam, the platform, the blocks, and the cover.

The prize beam is a lever formed of a young tree or fapling, of about ten inches diameter at the butt or thicker end, and about twenty or twenty-five feet in length; but in crops where many hands are employed, and a fuffi-cient force always near for the occafional affift-ance of managing a more weighty leverage, this beam is often made of a larger tree, hewn on two of its fides to about fix inches thick, and of the natural width, averaging twelve or fourteen inches. The thick end of this beam is fo fquared as to form a tenon, which is fitted into a mortife that is dug through fome growing tree, or other of thofe which generally abound convenient to the tobacco houfe, fome-thing more than five feet above the platform.

Clofe to the root of this tree, and immedi-ately under the moft powerful point of the lever, a platform or floor of plank is conftruct-ed for the hogfhead to ftand upon during the operation of prizing. This muft be laid upon a folid foundation, levelled, upon hewn pieces

of

of wood as fleepers; and fo grooved and perfo-
rated that any wet or rain which may happen
to fall upon the platform may run off without
injuring the tobacco. Blocks of wood are
prepared about two feet in length, and about
three or four inches in diameter, with a few
blocks of greater dimenfions, for the purpofe
of raifing the beam to a fuitable purchafe ; and
a moveable roof, conftructed of clap-boards
nailed upon pairs of light rafters, of fufficient
fize to fhelter the platform and hogfhead, is
made ready to place aftride of the beam, as a
faddle is put upon a horfe's back, in order to
fecure the tobacco from the weather while it
is fubjected to this tedious part of the procefs.
That part of the apparatus which is defigned
to manage and give power to the lever is va-
rioufly conftructed : in fome inftances two
beams of timber about fix feet long, and fquared to four by fix inches, are prepared ; through
thefe, by means of an auger hole, a fapling of
hickory or other tough wood, is refpectively
paffed ; and the root thereof being formed
like the head of a pin to prevent its flipping
through the hole, the fapling is bent like a
bow, and the other end is paffed through the
fame piece of wood in a reverfed direction, in
which pofition it is wedged. Thefe two bows
are in this manner hung by the fapling loops

4

upon the end of the prize beam or lever ; and
loofe planks or flabs of about five or fix feet
long being laid upon thefe fufpended pieces of
timber, a kind of hanging floor or platform is
conftructed, upon which weights are defigned
to act as in a fcale.   A pile of large ftones are
then carted to the place, and a fufficient number of thefe are occafionally placed upon this
hanging platform, until the lever has obtained
precifely the power which the crop mafter
wifhes to give to it by this regulating medium.

When it is intended to raife the beam of
this kind of prize, fo as to be able to take out the
blocks, or put more into the hogfhead, it is
done by tumbling the ftones off the platform,
and raifing the loofe end of the beam by
means of two forked faplings, of fufficient
length, which are placed under the beam on
each fide of it ; and the end of the beam being
lodged in the refpective forks or crotchets of
thefe props, they are raifed until they reach
the defired angle at which it is defigned to
reft the beam.

Another method of managing the lever or
prize beam is by dovetailing an upright hewn
piece of wood into a ftock of timber, laid
tranfverfely at its foot in the form of the letter
T reverfed ; and this ftock of timber being of
a convenient length, and two or three feet
.3   through,

through, forms thus, of itſelf, a ſufficient weight for the neceſſary leverage. In order to apply this purchaſe, the prize beam is mortiſed and the upright piece is put through the mortiſe. Succeſſive holes being bored croſſwiſe through the upright, two iron pins are paſſed through theſe holes, and by means of a forked lever applied under the lower pin through a twiſted grape vine, a rope, chain, or other bandage, which paſſes over the end of the prize beam; this beam or lever is brought nearer to the ſtock of timber by ſucceſſive removals of the uppermoſt pin, until it ſwings the ſtock of timber off the ground, as a weight to the end of the lever.

The lifting up of the beam is performed by another lever fixed in a fork, and communicating to the prize beam by a twiſted grape vine.

Of the Hogſhead and its Condition.

The hogſhead which is deſigned to convey the tobacco to market is regulated by law to the ſtandard of four feet ſix inches *, in length,

if

* The ambition of the planters to excel each other in heavy hogſheads has given riſe to a liberty with the legal dimenſions of the caſk, at which the inſpectors have unfortunately

if my recollection is right, but the shape and
bilge of the cask generally varies according to
the fancy of the cooper, or roughness of his
work. It is not neceffary that it should be perfectly water-tight, although it is certainly better to have it as much fo as poffible.

Tobacco, if well packed, and prized duly,
will refift the water for a furprifing length of
time. An inftance in ftrong proof of this occurred at Kingfland upon James's river in Virginia, where tobacco, which had been carried
off by the great land floods which happened
in 1771, was found in a large raft of drift wood
in which it had lodged when the warehoufes
at Richmond were fwept away by the over-
flowing of the frefhes; an inundation which
had happened about twenty years before this
cafk was found. I did not fee this tobacco

---

tunately winked. This difpofition has introduced another
evil practice of prizing too high; the confequence is, in both
inftances, very injurious to this commerce; for an over
ftraining becomes neceffary to bring fuch irregular cafks
into their proper births in ftowing the cargo; and over-
prizing produces a fatal *fea-fweat.* I am told at the king's
warehoufes, that they difcover great lofs upon the trade to
arife from thefe circumftances, and that the injury which it
retorts on the planter himfelf is of greater extent than he is
aware of: it were to be wifhed in thefe cafes, that the cultivators of tobacco would confine themfelves to *legal uniformity.*

myfelf,

myself, but it has been often mentioned to me by creditable persons, and I have no reason to disbelieve the fact. On the sixth of October, 1782, however, I myself was one of a party who were shipwrecked upon the coast of New Jersey in America, on board the brigantine Maria, captain Mᶜ Aulay, from Richmond in Virginia, and laden with tobacco. Several hogsheads which were saved from the wreck were brought round to Stillwills landing upon great Egg harbour; and amongst them some which had lost the headings of the cask, and the hoops and staves were so much shattered by the beating of the surf, that it was not thought worth while to land them, and they were just tumbled out of the lighter upon the beach, and left to remain where the tide constantly flowed over them for several weeks, so that the outside was completely rotten, and they had the appearance of heaps of manure. In this very bad condition I still persisted in trying to save what I supposed might remain entire in the interior of the lump, and at last prevailed so far over the ignorance and prejudice by which I had been ridiculed, as to effect an overhauling and repacking of this damaged commodity, and to save a proportion thereof very far beyond what I myself had expected.

E

Some

Some of the heart of this was fo highly improved, that I have feldom feen tobacco equal
to it for chewing, or for immediate manufacture ; and what was repacked was fold to a to-
bacconift in Water Street, Philadelphia, at a
price fo little reduced below the ordinary market, that the man very frankly told me, that
if he could have had the whole *drowned* tobacco in a fhort time after it was faved from
the wreck, he would have made no difference
in the price, but would rather have preferred
it for immediate manufacture, as it would have
fpared him fome little labour in a part of the
procefs. I have thought it interefting to merchants and underwriters to communicate thefe
facts, from whence they may reap fome little
information perhaps, or be at leaft induced to
make a more minute inveftigation in fimilar
cafes, and confent more reluctantly to fuftain
a total lofs.

I truft thefe motives will apologize for this
digreffion, while my recollection prompts it.

The material of which it is cuftomary to
make tobacco hogfheads is generally the beft
kind of white oak ; but Spanifh oak, red oak,
&c. are fometimes ufed, when the ufual kind
cannot be fo readily commanded. The ftaves
ought to be well feafoned, which is not always
the

the cafe; and immediately before the prizing commences it is a good method to take out the interior damp over a blaze of fhavings, or fome other light fewel. It is a misfortune alfo, which might be eafily remedied by a little attention, that the heading and hoops are too frequently made of green wood, and that on this account the hogfhead becomes readily fhattered, and its contents expofed to pilfering.

Of placing the Layers, packing the Hogfhead, and Prizing.

We now arrive at the moft tedious part of the whole procefs connected with the culture of tobacco, for this is a bufinefs which muft not be hurried over either haftily or flovenly : time is required to give each layer a proper degree of confiftency ; and neatnefs and care in pack-ing the feveral ftrata, fo as to infure the effects of keeping out the air, and of giving the ftaple a good appearance when it fhall be opened at an ultimate market.

So foon as every thing is prepared in readi-nefs at the prize-beam, the plants (being in proper *cafe*) are to be brought forth from the bulk in the tobacco houfe to the prize-beam, in fufficient quantity to lay a few layers only at each of the refpective prizings, fo that one

E 2 prizing

prizing contains but a few inches, according to
the condition of the plant, and muft be often
repeated. This repetition, however, will be
eafily underftood to be an irregular and very
uncertain part of the procefs; for as all tobacco muft be in *due cafe* when it is put into
the hogfhead, fo muft the prize-beam retain its
depreffed pofition until two diftinct ends are
attained, to wit, that of giving a compact confiftency to the cake or ftratum which is *under
prize*, and that of bringing the tobacco in cafe
for laying the next layers; over which it will
be perceived that the influence and variation
of the atmofphere muft have confiderable dominion.

In placing the layers in the cafk, the
plants are taken one by one, and are laid (not
in the manner of herrings, which they in fome
meafure refemble in fhape, but) in parallel
lines clofe to each other acrofs the hogfhead,
with the points all one way; the next courfe
or layer is reverfed with the points in an alter-
nate direction; and the interftices are filled up
with fmaller plants, laid upon a varied angle,
fo that, as far as is practicable, an even furface
may be preferved with the buts of the bundles
outwards. When this procefs is ended, fo as
to form a fufficient ftratum for that particular
prizing,

prizing, the loofe pieces which compofe the upper heading of the cafk are laid upon it; and the blocks which I have before defcribed, being then placed upon each other, two by two, tranfverfely, until they reach near enough up to the prize-beam to receive the power of the leverage upon the uppermoft block, the ftones are placed upon the platform, as before defcribed; or the power is applied in fome fimilar manner, and fuffered to remain in this pofition until the application of the next ftratum is performed according to the rules heretofore explained.

Of the Cooperage.

The cooperage, in refpect to tobacco hogfheads, is not a profeffional performance, as in other branches of the coopers' trade, but is generally an employment taken up by a cooper or carpenter upon the plantation, of which there are commonly one or two upon each eftate of tolerable fize, who ferve the occafion; or in default of fuch, by perfons of fufficient ingenuity, who are to be found in the refpective neighbourhoods where tobacco is cultivated, and who occafionally take up fuch an employment, rather as a matter of rural accommodation than as a profeffion.

E 3　　　　　　　There

There are two methods of forming the hoop of tobacco hogſheads : one of theſe reſembles the method uſed in the conſtruction of pales and tubs, called flat hooping ; and the other is of the kind uſed for hooping caſks for ordinary occaſions, called ſmart hooping.

The firſt of theſe methods is very ſlight, and ſerves only for ſuch tobacco as is to be conveyed to market by means of carts or waggons. The ſecond is a more ſubſtantial method, and will bear rolling in the mire without injury to the inſide. Every man, however, who is concerned in the tobacco trade, ſhould be more or leſs a cooper himſelf, for he will often have occaſion to put on a hoop, or to repair a ſtave, particularly on the road to market, where, in ſome modes of conveyance, this occaſion frequently occurs. He will, in any event, find an opportunity to lend his aſſiſtance in two diſtinct operations of cooperage ; one of which is while the caſk is under prize, and in heading it up for market ; and the other in the act of opening and " *turning up*"* when it comes before the inſpector in the public warehouſes. Where it happens to be neceſſary to make an allowance for the price of

* *Turning up*, ſignifies the act of replacing the caſk under the prize-beam of the public inſpection.

caſks,

a

b

c

d

cafks, it is cuftomary to eftimate two fhillings and fix pence for the cafk, and feven pence halfpenny for nails, in Virginia money, per hogfhead, which is equal to about two fhillings and fix pence fterling money of Great Britain.

Of the Conveyance to Market.

The conveyance of a crop of tobacco to market, is of five different kinds: 1. By carts and waggons. 2. By rolling in hoops. 3. By rolling in fellies. 4. By canoes. 5. By upland boats.

Conveyance by Carts and Waggons.

This kind of conveyance for tobacco, when it is intended to be carried to market, depends moftly upon the leifure of the planter, and not upon any public eftablifhment; and it is not unufual that a crop lays a confiderable time in the barn after it is ready to be taken away, becaufe it is not an eafy thing for a planter to be abfent from his domeftic concerns very of-ten upon a tedious journey. When the feafon and circumftances permit his abfence, and his horfes can be fpared, and are put in condition to encounter a long and rugged road (which formerly was in few inftances lefs than one

hundred

hundred miles from the infpection, but which
is now fomewhat reduced by increafing the
number of interior infpections), it is ufual
for feveral planters in the fame neighbourhood
to affociate together, and join their force of
horfes, &c. according to their proportions of tobacco to be conveyed to market, each waggon
taking two hogfheads.   Thus the party fet out
upon their annual, or, perhaps, biennial, expedition, taking with them their provifions,
liquors, and provender for their cattle ; and encamping conftantly in the woods until their
return, by the fide of a good *roufing* fire,
which is kindled without ceremony upon any
man's land, and with any man's fewel, without inhofpitable objections from the proprietor.
Thofe who are in more affluent circumftances,
and who have occafion to fend often to market, generally keep their own waggons in proportion to the extent of their eftates ; and there
are alfo waggons to be hired, all of them of the
fame kind, with narrow wheels, carrying each
two hogfheads ; and all purfuing the fame methods for their accommodation.   On their return, each one makes it his bufinefs to provide
for his family, and for fuch neighbours as he
can conveniently ferve, by the conveyance of
merchandize as part of their *back loads*, or
returning

returning freight. Such as are not taken up in this way, are generally occupied by merchants of the interior country, for the supply of their inland stores; and the heavy articles of salt and iron make a material part of this employment. The rates of waggonage (whereof two thousand pounds weight are usually called a load, though some waggons will carry three thousand pounds) are as follow; viz. for one hundred pounds weight, the distance of one hundred miles, the sum of four shillings Virginia money; equal to three shilling sterling*.

For one hogshead of tobacco, the distance of one hundred miles, the sum of two pounds Virginia money; equal to one pound ten shillings sterling.

For such a waggon by the day, every thing being furnished by the waggoner, the sum of twenty shillings Virginia money; equal to fifteen shillings sterling.

For such a waggon by the day, provisions and provender being furnished by the employer, the sum of twelve shillings Virginia money;

* These rates are in a general way about one third dearer than they were before the American war; and they at all times vary with the price of provender.

equal

equal to nine fhillings fterling money of Great Britain.

Carts are of courfe half the rates of waggons.

Conveyance by rolling in Hoops.

I believe rolling tobacco the diftance of many hundred miles, is a mode of conveyance peculiar to Virginia; and for which the early population of that country deferves a very handfome credit. Neceffity (that very prolific mother of invention) firft fuggefted the idea of rolling *by hand*; time and experience have led to the introduction of *horfes*, and have ripened human fkill, in this kind of carriage, to a degree of perfection which merits *the adoption of the mother country*, but which will be better explained under the next head of this fubject. The hogfheads, which are defigned to be rolled in common hoops, are made clofer in the joints than if they were intended for the waggon; and are plentifully hooped with ftrong hickory hoops (which is the toughest kind of wood) with the bark upon them, which remains for fome diftance a protection againft the ftones. Two hickory faplings are affixed to the hogf-head, for fhafts, by boring an auger-hole through them to receive the gudgeons or pivots,

pivots, in the manner of a field rolling-ftone :
and thefe receive pins of wood, with fquare
tapered points, which are admitted through
fquare mortifes made central in the heading,
and driven a confiderable depth into the folid
tobacco. Upon the hind part of thefe fhafts,
between the horfes and the hogfhead, a few
light planks are nailed, and a kind of little cart
body is conftructed of a fufficient fize to contain a bag or two of provender, and provifion,
together with an axe, and fuch other tools as
may be needed upon the road, in cafe of accident. In this manner they fet out to the infpection in companies, very often joining fociety with the waggons, and always purfuing the
fame method of encamping. This mode of
fleeping in the woods upon fuch a journey;
the red clay lands through which moft of the
tobacco rollers pafs ; the continual and unavoidable expofure to dews, muddy roads or dufty
ones ; and the diftances which they travel, contribute to add to their long beards a very
favage appearance ; and the natural confequence of this mode of living produces rough
ruftic amufements, and fimilar difpofitions.
They have hence become an object of apprehenfion to ftrangers, and a terror to the Englifh traveller, whom habit has rendered too

often

often wont to view every other country with the eyes of his own ; and who expects to find in all men thofe gradations of humble diftance to which he may happen to have been accuftomed. To thofe, in particular, who approach this (or any other) clafs of Americans, with an air of felf-important confequence, they are readily difpofed to fhew the worft fide ; and very often, under the mafk of ignorance, play fuch men many an unlucky prank, and bid them a more unpleafant welcome than even the ftory of the inhofpitable *Scotchman* exhibits in the recent travels of an *Irifh* gentleman through that well known place, the northern neck of Virginia. Let a man in a *fulky*, however, (of which they are not over fond, perhaps only from his haughty appearance) only put off his offenfive attitude of *incubation*, and accoft them like fellow mortals of the fame fpecies, and they will be the firft to do him a real fervice. The fact is, that men of great refpectability, and plentiful hofpitality when at home, think it no difgrace to fally forth upon the concerns of their crop ; and in this cafe they accommodate themfelves to manners which bid defiance to difficulty, and anfwer their ends.

Conveyance

Conveyance by rolling in Fellies.

Rolling in *fellies* is an improvement refulting from experience in the former method of rolling in *hoops*, which in long journies are found to fhatter (efpecially upon ftony roads), and very often to damage the contents, or occafion delays for a too frequent refitting of the hogfhead. Experience has fuggefted this, and practice in the expedient has rendered the invention of fellies more perfect. They confift of pieces of wood formed into fegments of a circle in the manner of cart wheels; and thefe, inftead of being formed into the rim of a wheel fupported by fpokes fixed into a nave, are fixed round the circumference of the tobacco hogfhead by means of auger holes and wooden pins driven into the bulk of tobacco, through the fellies and the ftaves of the hogfhead. By this means the ftones upon the road are greatly avoided, and the hogfhead may be fafely conveyed to a very confiderable diftance. This improvement has fuggefted another, which is now reduced to practice in the conveyance of grain, and which doubtlefs might be farther employed (if need be) in the conveyance of fluid fubftances. Wheat and other

other fmall grain is now *rolled* in many places
in Virginia, in hogfheads which are compactly
formed; well hooped with iron; the fellies
well fhod with iron wheel tire; and iron pins
for the gudgeons or axles.   There is in the
head of each cafk a fmall door or fcuttle for
receiving and delivering the grain; and I can
fee no reafon why fluids may not be as eafily
received, conveyed, and delivered, by the help
of a cock.

This is certainly a cheap and eafy-going ve-
hicle; and, when it is confidered that the
weight of a cart and its contents is thus completely relieved from the back of a horfe, and
that one horfe alone is equal to a confiderable
burden, I fhould fuppofe it worthy an experiment in many Englifh employments.

Conveyance by Canoes.

The originality of this mode of conveyance
feems to be alfo afcribable to the fertile imagi-
nation of a people, upon whom the felf-fuffi-
ciency of *doing nothing wrong*, has afperfed the
foul imputation of *doing nothing right*.

The people in the mountains far up James's
river perceived, many years ago, that the
river afforded them the means of conveying
                                          tobacco

tobacco without the trouble and expence of horfes; and that there were feafons of the year when (having little to do) this might not only be rendered a fource of clear gain, but one which afforded them fcenes of mirth and amufement.

There were, however, fome difficulties to be overcome in this inftance. The mountains were not the refidence of fhip carpenters to inftruct them; and, perhaps, few, if any, of thofe who thought of this new expedient had either feen a boat or the plan of one. They contrived amongft them neverthelefs to build two large canoes, each formed out of a folid piece of fifty or fixty feet in length, and perhaps an inch to the foot of length in the breadth of them. Two of thefe canoes were clamped together by means of crofs-beams and pins; and two pieces being again placed lengthwife upon thefe, their tobacco was rolled on upon this platform from five to ten hogfheads, which from three to five men could convey with eafe the diftance of one hundred and fifty miles to market, without the help of horfes. Another advantage refulted from this method in returning home; the canoes admitted of feparation; and as they were feldom overburdened with heavy returns, two men could manage each

canoe,

canoe, in coming home againſt the current, or in ſhooting up a narrow ſluice, in many of the rapids where there was not ſufficient water for a boat. This method is however greatly done away by the deſtruction of timber, and partly by the improvements of canal naviga‧ tion.

Conveyance by upland Boats.

The capacity of the upper part of James's river for inland navigation, and the impedi‐ ments which it became neceſſary to remove, being ſoon diſcovered by thoſe who were con‐ cerned in canoe navigation, plans were pro‐ jected for improving the navigation of that part of the river which is ſituated above the falls; and, after many ineffectual efforts by John Ballendine, Eſq. and others, at the Oc‐ tober ſeſſions of the Virginia legiſlature, 1784, an act was paſſed, whereby ſundry perſons were incorporated, and conſtituted a company for that purpoſe.

By this act a ſmall toll is impoſed upon each hogſhead of tobacco which ſhall paſs through the canal which connects the upper part of the river above the falls, with tide water, which flows to the foot of the falls, an intermediate ſpace of about ſeven miles. But this toll is nothing

nothing in comparifon with the extra waggonage which this portage formerly demanded;
and there are now a number of boats (fimilar
to thofe upon the grand trunk canal) which
carry on this bufinefs profeffionally.

This employment has very naturally called
for legiflative interpofition in refpect to the
identity of trefpaffers, and the refponfibility
of boat owners: and the following law was
accordingly paffed on the 17th of December,
1791.

" An Act for regulating the navigation of
James's river, above the falls of the faid river.

" Be it enacted, that every perfon who fhall
be proprietor of any boat or other veffel, which
fhall be employed in navigating the waters of
James's river and its branches above the great
falls at Richmond, in the tranfportation of
any produce or merchandize whatfoever, either
raifed or manufactured within this commonwealth, or imported from any other place
without the fame, fhall in the clerk's office of
the county in which the faid proprietor or proprietors fhall then live, enter the number of
each boat or veffel fo to be employed; which
number, together with the name of the county, and the name of the owner or owners of
fuch boat or veffel, fhall be written or painted

F   on

on each fide of the faid veffel, on fome confpi-
cuous part thereof, in large and plain letters,
not lefs than four inches in length.

" If the owner or owners of any boat or
veffel, which fhall be employed in navigating
the waters of the faid river, above the falls
thereof as aforefaid, fhall fail to enter in the
clerk's office as aforefaid, the name or names
of the owner or owners, the name of the
county in which he or they fhall refide, and
the number of each boat or other veffel as
aforefaid; or fhall fail to write or paint the
name or names of the owner or owners of the
faid boat or other veffel, in manner above directed, fo as to continue plain and legible as
long as the faid boat or other veffel fhall be
employed in navigation, he, fhe, or they, fhall
forfeit and pay the fum of twenty fhillings for
every day he, fhe, or they, fhall neglect to
comply with the purpofes of this act, to be
recovered by any perfon who may fue for the
fame, by warrant from a magiftrate, allowing
the faid owner or owners one month after the
firft day of April next, to attend to the requi-
fitions aforefaid."

Such are the regulations upon this extenfive
river, where the tobacco trade moft prevails.
There are fimilar regulations upon Potomack,
and

and such other rivers as have improved their interior navigation; but it is unneceſſary to recite more than this example.

The rate of conveying tobacco by theſe boats from the town of Lynchburgh to Richmond, the diſtance of one hundred and ſixty-five computed miles, is about thirty ſhillings * Virginia money, per hogſhead; equal to one pound two ſhillings and ſix pence ſterling.

We have thus far traced the culture of tobacco from the ſeed, the method of curing the plant, and of bringing the crop to market, where it is doomed to paſs through the hands of public examiners of its merchantable quality. In the next Part we ſhall proceed to the nature of public inſpections, and the intermediate proceſs previous to ſhipping.

* This price by water varies with the ſtate of the river, and demand.

F 2

PART

PART III.

OF THE PUBLIC WAREHOUSE AND INSPECTION.

WE have now gone through the feveral parts of the procefs which refpect the culture, curing, and bringing to market, of a crop of tobacco. It follows to underftand the nature of examining its quality by legal authority, previous to vending it to the merchant; for the former policy of Virginia has taken ample care to guard the moft ignorant in this commerce againft the poffibility of deception; nor is there any other door left open for it than that which is equally unavoidable in common with any other fpecies of forgery; but whereever this crime has been committed for the purpofe of vending tobacco fraudulently, I think the punifhment has been rigoroufly inflicted *.

Public warehoufes were eftablifhed under the kingly government of Virginia, for the

---

* There is faid to have been a recent exception; fee Appendix.

purpofes

purpoſes of receiving and inſpecting tobacco, at many places upon the principal rivers, below the great falls thereof; but I believe they were permitted at no place above the falls until after the American revolution, when the great increaſe of population, and the vaſt diſtance which it extended back from the former markets, rendered it neceſſary to increaſe the number of inſpections, and to diſtribute their functions and latitude to the relief of the upland people, who began to feel the oppreſſion of their many tedious journies on this account*.

They

* The change which has taken place in reſpect to the eſtabliſhment of *upland warehouſes* is to be aſcribed greatly to the aſſiduity of David Roſs, Eſq. to whoſe zealous perſeverance, enterprize, and public ſpirit, the community have often been indebted. He has been the chief promoter of *well judged amendments*, where the meaſure was dictated by the natural courſe and convenience of a thriving commerce, and *his* experiments have flouriſhed. I find proofs in the king's warehouſes, however, that fears, which I have often expreſſed in reſpect to the reſult of this precedent, were but too well founded. There is, indeed, a natural propenſity in the planter to have a warehouſe at his own door; and it is conſiſtent with the province of human vanity, to think well enough of ourſelves to become inſpectors of our own produce, without ſeeing to what a limited extent we ought to truſt that very ſelfiſh thing, called *ſelf.* Popular meaſures ſeem to have paid a poor compliment to Mr. Roſs's deſign, to their own penetration, or the true intereſt of

their

They are now extended to the river Ohio, a diftance of fix hundred miles farther into the country than they exifted under the Englifh government. They confift of a number of warehoufes, in proportion to the extent of the particular country whofe local trade they are defigned to accommodate : they are of two kinds, the one open, and the other clofe built houfes. The open houfes confift chiefly of a broad roof erected upon wooden pofts or brick pillars, forming an area of confiderable length, and this form is repeated in lines moftly parallel with each other, until the extent is fuffi-

their planting conftituents, when they indulged a *laxity of commercial principle* which the founder of *Columbia* never dreamt of introducing. It is true, that all fhoulders are not proper ones to wear the head of a David Rofs, and that a fmall part of fociety are both planters and merchants ; yet where the pecuniary motive which induces a planter to over-prize his crop, or fend an inferior quality and condition to market, prevents him from feeing that *one* fuch hogfhead rotted upon Tower-hill, will reduce the price of *ten* which he may happen to vend afterwards, it fhould certainly be the bufinefs of a wife legiflature to obferve the defects of jurifprudence, and to provide a proper remedy.

I am forry to conclude this remark with an apprehenfion of fome growing evils which threaten to fap the commercial pre-eminence of this ftaple, by transferring the credit of a well governed public infpection, to fuch a reliance upon the private planter, as would ultimately render infpections ufelefs, and annihilate the Virginia tobacco trade.

F 4   cient

cient for the propofed accommodation. The clofe-built houfes are for the purpofes of the infpection, and contain a number of rooms under lock and key: as, for inftance, the infpector's rooms, the infpecting rooms, the picking rooms, the prizing rooms, the transfer rooms, the repacking rooms, the fcale rooms, &c. But in fmall infpections fome of thefe rooms anfwer feveral purpofes, and there are, confequently, not fo many of them.

The whole of thefe buildings, with their refpective occupations and contents, are at each infpection, refpectively, under the command and direction of two refpectable officers of the government, called the *Infpectors of Tobacco.*

The premifes are generally private property, under a public eftablifhment, fubject to the control of the legiflature.

Of all thefe things we fhall learn more under their particular heads.

Of the Office of Infpector.

The office of *Infpector* is a public office conftituted by legiflative authority, for the purpofe of infpecting, and making diligent fearch, into the quality and condition of every hogfhead of tobacco which is defigned to be put on fhipboard, to the end that no impofition fhould be practifed practised in vending it to incompetent judges of the commodity; and that the best possible security may be held by the merchants in Europe, against the probability of damage arising at sea, either from the carelessness of the packer, or the too moist condition of the plant.

This office is always to be filled, at each and every inspection warehouse, respectively, by two respectable planters, being skilled in the knowledge of tobacco, who are of good repute and responsibility, and men highly respected in their neighbourhood. It is an office of high trust and importance in trade; and, to the great credit of the institution, it has scarcely produced an instance of corruption.

It is an elective office in the gift of a majority of the members present at the monthly courts of the counties respectively, where any particular tobacco inspection may happen to be situated for the local conveniency of commerce; and it is held during good behaviour, which proves generally an appointment for life. The persons (two of whom for each inspection are elected) are obliged to find ample securities, and to enter into bond for the faithful discharge of the office with which they are intrusted; but there have occurred so few instances of abuse, as to puzzle my recollection

to

to remember a cafe where this legal remedy has been reforted to.

As this is the high office of amenability, as well in regard to the due examination of the merchantable quality of the ftaple, as the cuftody and care of every man's crop, which the law has here delivered over into the public poffeffion for the convenience and fafety of commerce; fo are all other offices of the infpection inferior and fubfervient to its mandates, which are obeyed with alacrity. And it is affifted by fubordinate officers, fuch as the third infpector, the pickers, the coopers, and warehoufe attendants, of whom we fhall have occafion to take notice in their proper places.

We fhall now proceed to inquire into the feveral parts of the procefs which are obferved in the public warehoufes, from the time the tobacco is received from the planter till it is delivered to be fhipped.

Of Opening and Breaking.

The operation of opening and breaking the hogfhead of tobacco, is performed in the prefence of the infpectors, by their fubordinate officers, in the rooms or apartments called the infpecting rooms, in order to afford them an opportunity

opportunity of exercising that judgment which the law requires of them in regard to the merchantable quality of the commodity. It is to be understood that when the tobacco is brought to the warehouse by the planter, it is generally left in the warehouse yard, or rolled from thence under an open shed, as a shelter from the weather, until the inspectors have time to examine it in its turn. It is then brought forward for inspection, and the coopers (which office is generally or always united with that of picker) proceed to open the hogshead by cutting away many of the hoops without mercy, and stripping the hogshead off from the bulk of tobacco, which consists of one hard pressed loaf or cake, averaging generally one thousand pounds weight. One of the pickers or attendants then takes a large wooden wedge or spike, of about five feet in length, and one of the inspectors taking hold of the point thereof, places it against such part of the bulk of tobacco (standing then upon its end) as he chooses to examine. Another of the attendants, with a huge hand-mall, then drives the wedge or spike into the cake or bulk of tobacco till a sufficient cleft is made to raise up a smaller cake. From this cleft the inspectors take out a few bundles (or

hands,

hands, as they are termed) of the tobacco;
and they repeat this breaking in as many parts
of th. hogfhead as they think proper to take
fpecimens from, for their information concerning the fairnefs of the package, and condition of the ftaple.

Of Paffing, and of Burning.

When the infpectors have procured fpecimens of the ftaple, by means of breaking the
hogfhead, as defcribed under the laft head, it
follows to pronounce their judgment; a fen-
tence, indeed, which is of no fmall importance
to the crop-mafter, the fate of whofe whole
year's employment is now brought to the teft
of official opinion; and it refts with two men
alone to fay (in effect) whether he merits pay
for his labour or not.

If the leaf appears to be well cured, and
put up in merchantable order and condition,
they generally *pafs* the tobacco immediately on
the fpot. If the cafe is doubtful, they retire
to the infpectors' room to deliberate; and if
the tobacco plants are either the product of
fuckers, of indifferent quality, or put up in
bad order, they condemn the whole hogfhead.
In this laft cafe it is burnt; and although it is
thus a total lofs to the proprietor, and has by

4   cuftom

custom become a kind of perquisite to the warehouse attendants, yet so surprizingly has this inquisition of traffic been managed, so prudently has the authority been exercised, and so much are mankind to be reconciled to habitual losses, that I scarcely recollect a murmur against the inspectors, although I have lived several years on the premises adjoining to the tobacco kilns, where, perhaps, a thousand hogsheads have been burnt in my presence.

In the case, however, where the tobacco is passed by the inspectors without any diminution, the hogshead is immediately replaced, weighed, entered upon the public books, and a receipt or note given to the proprietor. There are also medium cases between passing and burning, which demand a specific attention. We will treat of these respectively, under the following heads.

Of Turning-up, and Weighing.

Turning-up, is a technical term which signifies the act of replacing the tobacco in the hogshead after it has passed the inquest of inspection ; and bestowing upon it, under the prize-beam, a sufficient cooperage to answer the purposes of exportation.

The process of weighing is attached to that

of

of turning-up; and for this joint fervice and nails there is a fmall allowance made, which is generally charged upon account current to the merchant, who becomes the purchafer of the crop; and he in his turn ftates this charge in the account current of the planter.

When the cooperage is finifhed, the tobacco paffes to the fcale room through the fame hands; and from this official weighing the infpector gives a voucher of *public refponfibility:* yet there are faid to be inftances lately decided, where the legiflative wifdom of Virginia has loft fight of the *ancient* maxims of its public faith, and refufed a verification of its reputed commercial fecurity*!

How far this variance of principle may comport with the interefts of her foreign credit, is a queftion which this *ancient dominion* has fubmitted to the folution of time. In fuch reference fhe clofes the mouth of an individual citizen.

Of the Warehoufe Entry, and Tobacco Note.

It has already been fufficiently explained, that the warehoufes of infpection are a public eftablifhment. It follows as a confequence

---

* See Appendix.

that

that their books are to be matter of record; but I apprehend they cannot be allowed the full and unqualified force of certain other public records, when given in evidence, becaufe they are frequently expofed openly in the office of the infpector, and cannot, upon this account, convey the fame pointed conviction to the confcience of a jury that they would do if they were lefs expofed. They are, however, lefs exceptionable in point of practice than would generally be conceived, and feem to be held in fair eftimation, as a nice equilibrium between the imperfection of fyftem, and the integrity which has preponderated in the public appointments.

The method of book-keeping in thefe warehoufes is neceffarily fpecific, and fuited to the occafion : they have the crop book, the transfer book, and fome others; and their forms are in fome inftances under legal regulations, and ruled in columns.

The crop book is the moft important concern : it contains a regular entry, in columns, of every fingle hogfhead of *crop* tobacco *

which

---

* The general average of *good crop* tobacco is rated at one thoufand pounds, but *legally crop* tobacco muft at leaft weigh
nine

which is paſſed in the warehouſe to which it
refers, from the beginning to the end of the
year ; and a ſingle line for each hogſhead reſpectively, when written tranſverſely through
theſe columns, ſpecifies the planter's mark and
number, the date when ſuch hogſhead was
paſſed and received into the public care, the
name of the proprietor, the groſs, tare, and
nett, weight in pounds, the proportion of
ſtemmed tobacco, of which the hogſhead is
compoſed, and leaves a broad margin for caſual
notes, references to the ſhipment of ſuch hogſhead, &c. From this entry a printed formal
receipt or note is filled up, ſigned by the inſpectors, and delivered to the proprietor ; and
it is by this note that all tobaccos are bought
and ſold, and circulated throughout the continent, in the ſame manner as bank notes, or
current coin : the evidence of a depoſit of
ſo much in the public warehouſes being there
certified officially upon the face of the note,
and the current value, or market price, receiving an univerſal tone from the ſpecific cre-

nine hundred and fifty nett pounds; all under that weight
are conſidered to be *transfer*, or parcels which may be transferred to make full hogſheads.

dibility

dibility of the infpection where the depofit is made *.

This note is therefore a fufficient authority in the hands of the holder, to afk, demand, receive, fue for, and recover, the tobacco or its value, which the note fpecifies to have been depofited; and when the tobacco is taken away from the public warehoufe, to be fhipped by the merchant, this note is always returned to the infpector as his voucher for the delivery. In fome inftances, however, the greater crop mafters, and thofe who are ftanding cuftomers to particular merchants, decline the trouble and rifk of taking out tobacco notes, and give a general or fpecial order for the delivery of their crop; which is equally certain, as the infpectors never fail to make an immediate entry of the weights from the fcale room.

Of the third Infpector, and of the Pickers.

The third infpector is (in this refpect) a fupernumerary officer of the infpection warehoufe, appointed in the fame way as the principal infpectors, in order that there may never

* Choice crops which have obtained a ftanding reputation will fetch an extra price.

G be

be a delay or impediment through the death, ficknefs, or reafonable abfence, of one of the principals : and any other negligence of the principals would be a mifdemeanour in office, and highly punifhable by law. One of the moft experienced of the *pickers* is generally appointed to this office, and, in any of the defaults fpecified above, he fteps completely into the fhoes of the abfentee, clothed with all his authorities, functions, and privileges.

The *pickers* are the firft gradation of fubordinate officers under the rank of infpector. Their office is alfo one of truft, and both planters and merchants might find an intereft in difrobing it of certain adopted *privileges*, at the expence of fome little fpecific equivalent. It muft be confeffed to their credit, however (for many of thefe are perfons of property and fair reputation), that more evils arife from the privilege of indulging others than any overt ufe for their own emolument ; and if, in this inftance, they fall fhort of their official obligation, this petty offence claims the fame kind of palliation which fome afcribe to be the birthright of pious perjuries. The duty of this office (befides that of cooperage, wherein it is continually occupied) refpects that medium ftate of tobacco which is neither in a condition to be paffed,

paffed, nor to be refufed : this fometimes happens from the confiderations of its being partly
bad, and partly good ; or when the whole is
good and merchantable, but prized when it
was *too high in cafe*. In either of thefe inftances it is the duty of this officer to pick and
feparate the good from the bad, and to take
away thofe parts which threaten injury to the
whole mafs at fea, in order to repack it again
in found and merchantable condition. There
are ftated rates for this fervice in a general way,
which are charged to the merchant, as heretofore defcribed ; but as the whole cafk is fometimes fo out of order as to need a complete,
laborious, and fcientific overhauling, thefe
men of experience are more amply, and very
juftly, rewarded by a fpecific agreement.

Befides this duty, all the heavy labour and
drudgery of the warehoufes fall upon this clafs,
who have feldom any other help than a few
day labourers, or negro attendants.

Of Picking, and Repacking.

Picking is, fimply, the act of feparating the
bad from the good, according to legal regulations. *Repacking*, is the act of placing and

prizing

prizing the tobacco into the hogſhead, in the ſame method which was firſt obſerved at the prize-beam of the crop maſter.

Theſe operations have both of them been, in ſome meaſure, explained under the laſt head : but it yet remains to give ſtrangers ſome farther light upon this ſubject. It ſometimes happens that the whole caſk needs to be overhauled, and put in caſe, by handling plant after plant, in a way ſimilar to that which was obſerved in the planter's tobacco houſe : to this end it is removed from the inſpection room to the picking and repacking rooms ; and it is ſometimes not only thrown into bulk, as it was originally, but is carried a ſecond time through the proceſs of hanging and drying, to which end it will be perceived very extenſive apartments, and a ſlaviſh attention of the pickers, are required.

Of transfer Tobacco.

Transfer tobacco is that collection in leaf, bundle, or hand, which ariſes from the aggregate ſtock of remnants which remain from hogſheads that are reduced by waſtage and refuſal beneath the ſtandard weight of a ſhipable,

able, or, what is commonly termed, a *crop,* hogfhead *.

It derives the name *transfer* from the practice of transferring from this aggregate ftock a fufficient parcel or quantity of this loofe tobacco into the hogfhead of another perfon, in order to make up any fmall deficiency which may render fuch cafk a refpectable hogfhead, for the purpofe of exportation ; and for this ufe it is cuftomary for the merchants to buy up, at an under price, fuch fmall or transfer notes as may have been iffued into circulation from the infpectors to the planters whofe crops or hogfheads have fallen fhort of the legal fhipable cafk of nine hundred and fifty pounds nett weight. It generally happens, however, that there annually remains a quantity of this kind of tobacco in the public warehoufes, over and above what may have been prized into crop hogfheads for exportation, and in this cafe the infpectors make a report, ex officio, to the court of their particular county, who, at their monthly fitting for the month of September, pafs an order to authorize the infpectors to make public fale of fuch tobacco for ready

* Lawfully nine hundred and fifty pounds, by cuftom underftood to average one thoufand pounds.

money;

money; and the nett produce of fuch fale, after deducting a per centage for the cafual waftage, and a commiffion of five per centum to the infpectors for management, is divided among the holders of unappropriated transfer notes, or among fuch other proprietors as may have depofited this kind of ftaple commodity with the infpectors, on the faith of their book entries.

Of Shipping, and the Manifeft.

It has been heretofore obferved that tobacco is not hawked about from place to place, and vended from one perfon to another, by means of an actual exhibition of this bulky article; but that warehoufes are erected in convenient places, as public repofitories of this ftaple; and a kind of circulating medium is iffued upon this depofit by certain officers of the government, whofe good faith and refponfibility (keeping pace with that of *Abraham Newland)* render the tobacco warehoufes of Virginia the beft banks in the ftate, and a refpectable treafury of the American nation. It will now be underftood, that this fpecies of circulation adds to the partial ufes of a circulating medium a fpecific branch of traffic, which contributes to facilitate

facilitate the means of acquifition and mutual intercourfe with the inhabitants of Europe; and which (God be thanked for the juft reward) fticks plentifully to the fingers of a Glafgow merchant.

This is an article which is wont to return profit to the induftry of the fair trader; and when he has accumulated a fufficient ftock of notes to complete his intended remittance, he tranfmits them to the infpection from whence they iffued, where the infpectors then in office, upon the ftrength of thefe obligatory vouchers, proceed to preparing him for fhipping his cargo, by fearching out for him the identical hogfheads which are fpecified in the receipts or notes of infpection by him prefented. A manifeft is then made out, fpecifying the grofs, tare, and nett, of each particular hogfhead, in columns, marked and numbered according to the inftructions of the merchant, and with the requifite references, which, being certified by the infpectors, is delivered to the merchant or his agent, as an authority to convey on fhipboard the feveral hogfheads which are therein fpecified, and deftined for exportation.

Of

Of Delivery, and Taking-off.

I apprehend the act of delivery from the inspector to the agent of the merchant, to be
perfect and complete, and the risk thereupon
to be *legally* transferred *to the full acquittal of the
inspectors*, when the several hogsheads shall
have been told off according to the manifest,
and permission given to the labourers to take
them away ; for there is necessarily a good deal
of time expended in this operation before all is
completed, and the period is as necessarily self-
existent, which transposes the tobacco and its
paper representative. I do not recollect that
the law has precisely adjusted this point ; yet
the critical juncture is essential to the spirit of
private property, and it behooves us to com-
prehend the principles upon which it changes.

It is customary in taking off tobacco to send
up some of the ablest sailors belonging to the
ship, as labourers, in this stage of the commerce ; or (which is far preferable) to employ
the negro watermen, who are adepts by experience. I have known several instances of
middle-sized negroes, who, from an habitual
flight, and practical skill, would turn three
hogsheads of tobacco upon their ends at once,
each

each hogſhead weighing one thouſand pounds
nett weight: yet I have ſeen many an over-
grown Engliſhman ſtrain hard to overcome
one hogſhead. I am aware that this account
(which has probably many vouchers among
the Virginia merchants) will be thought fabu-
lous; but a patient inquiry will render it ſomewhat more credible. The fact is, that there
is a philoſophical principle in this caſe which
the African race have pretty generally diſcovered the advantage of; and a rap upon the
hogſhead with their knuckles (which the
knowing European will aſcribe, perhaps, to
ſuperſtition) ſerves to inform them, by the
hollow ſound, which end of the caſk is heavieſt. The negro takes the benefit of the
point of gravitation; and by ſelecting caſks of
the bulkieſt bilge, with the help of a board
placed acroſs his breaſt, he puts the three in
motion at once, and aſſiſts their inclination of
preponderancy with his main ſtrength at the
critical juncture. A ſimilar principle ſhould
be obſerved in the handling of many ſolid bodies. A tree, for example, grows with the
heavieſt end downwards, and, I apprehend,
the difference of gravity would be very per-
ceptible in a ſquared log of equal dimenſions
when floating in ſtill water. Thoſe who are
accuſtomed

accuftomed to rafting timber, however, know very well the advantage of towing logs with the heavy end of the tree foremoft.

There are three diftinct methods of *taking-off* tobacco, which are practifed in Virginia; and it is generally neceffary to combine two of them before the tobacco is completely afloat: thefe are *by hand, by drays,* and *by lighterage.*

By Hand

Taking-off tobacco by hand is one of the ancient methods, for which the Virginians have the credit of fome originality; and upon this operation time and practice have afforded ufeful improvements.

Neceffity at firft compelled the joint labour, in this inftance, of both landfmen and feamen, who united in the application of manual labour to get the tobacco on fhipboard. Profit ftimulated this exertion till it extended the practice to feveral miles from the fea port; and this drudgery called forth the help of ropes and fcrews, which being fixed in the nature of traces, by fcrewing the pin into the tobacco for an axle, ferved thefe two-legged cattle for the application of accumulated force, when exigencies required it; and enabled them to

jog

jog on at an accelerated pace upon the ordinary level roads, which the lower countries
afforded. By degrees thefe traces received
the improvement of a pair of friction rollers to
relieve the rope from the chime of the cafk;
and this cuftom it feems continued partially
within the memory of fome of my acquaintances, though it it is probable that it was in a
general way abolifhed with the eftablifhment
of public warehoufes.

In refpect to taking-off, this method ftill
exifts in fome places: thofe who are moft expert, however, prefer to difpenfe with this apparatus, and manage the hogfheads with fuch
extraordinary flight of hand, that the Virginia
negroes treat a hogfhead of tobacco with as
little ceremony as a coachmaker handles a
wheel*. Both thefe methods feem to be
growing out of ufe, and the population of fea

* The warehoufes at Ofbornes, upon James's river, ftand
upon the bank of the river at the diftance of fomewhat
more than one hundred yards from the water's edge, and a
hollow road leads down an angle of about twenty degrees
from the warehoufe to the wharf. Two negroes manage,
at this place, as many hogfheads at one and the fame time
as fills up this intermediate fpace. It is done by the help of
a hand-mall, which is moved by the handle before the firft
hogfhead, which fuftains one hundred more, if need be.

port towns is found to demand a more accom-
modating conveyance.

By Drays.

Drays are but of late years introduced into
practice in the fouthern ftates of America.
The public tobacco warehoufes at Richmond,
Manchefter, and Peterfburgh, in Virginia, ftand
fome diftance from the water's edge, and the
cuftom of taking-off by hand has a long time
prevailed. Thefe towns are now growing po-
pulous, and the increafe of their commerce
has called the attention of their police to the
relief of the inconveniences arifing from rolling
hogfheads of tobacco through the ftreets by
hand, by the fubftitution of drays in the Englifh manner; this is not, however, the general
practice at all warehoufes, for many of them
continue their ancient methods.

By Lighters.

Befides the neceffity of taking-off tobacco
by the two methods herein-before mentioned,
in refpect to the land carriage, the conftant
fullage from the plough, and other wafhings
of the upland countries, have impeded the navigation,

vigation, which formerly held a better channel near the falls of the feveral rivers, but particularly James's river, where the channel is fubject to frequent changes, upon which account there is fometimes occafion to ufe a kind of flat-bottomed lighter or *fcow*, which draws but a few inches water, and will take off from ten to twenty hogfheads or more, and convey them to veffels in the channel which frequent the river trade, of which notice will be more particularly taken hereafter. Thefe lighters are very convenient for this purpofe, being built with flat bottoms, upright fides of about two feet fix inches or three feet, and floped up at each end fo as to ride over the waves with lefs refiftance than a fquare or blunt end would permit. A fimilar kind of boats are ufed for the ferries in Virginia; thefe admit a waggon and team to drive in at one end of them, which is driven out at the other when the boat arrives at the oppofite fhore; and this method is found capable of confiderable accommodation and difpatch.

Of Depredations.

Of all the commercial articles which traverfe the ocean, there are none, perhaps, which

which are more fubject to waftage by depredations than the commodity we are fpeaking of.
It is continually expofed to pilfering, even
from the time it is cut from the field, and
through the whole procefs of curing; and until it is conveyed to market it is indeed fubjected to fimilar injury. But the greater loffes
are fuftained after it is delivered into the public
warehoufes: it feems proper to fpeak of thefe
fpecifically.

Of Depredations privileged by Cuftom.

I have intimated under the general head
that depredations upon tobacco are committed
from the moment it is firft gathered into the
barn; but there are of thefe fome privileged
by cuftom from the inftant *curing crops* become
fit for ufe; and the chewing, fmoking, and
fnuffing depredators of the country, find illicit
means enough to effect an imperceptible reduction by littles, fuch as few perfons care to notice. As this fpecies of making common property has perhaps fome hofpitable and bene-
volent principles attached to it, I fhall let it
alone, and more efpecially as the prefence of
the proprietor may be faid in moft cafes to give
a tacit approbation. But when the crop is
once

once delivered into the public warehoufes, and an officer of the government is charged with a refponfibility for its forthcoming, there can be no *proprietary* prefence (in the general nature of the tranfaction) from whom an affent can be received for the exercife of fuch privileges as are *malum in fe*, and are not a whit the more qualified becaufe cuftom has led men to practife them in open daylight. It fhall be the bufinefs of this work to ftate thefe facts impartially, to point out the inftances of mal-feafance which are overlooked; and it refts with thofe to whom it more appropriately be-longs to remedy the evils which may be dif-covered.

Now it is cuftomary with moft planters to weigh the bulk of tobacco with the fteelyards, when it is firft packed into the hogfheads; and from this weighing they are enabled to give their merchant an approximate affurance of the quantity he may expect from them; for it is generally a cuftom in the tobacco trade for the merchant to deliver the planter his goods upon account current through the year, and to credit him by the amount of his crop, an-nually, when it is carried to market. It is here received into the care of a public officer; but

if

if there happens to be a glut of bufinefs, fo that
the turn of infpection is procraftinated, it remains openly in the warehoufe yard, or, perhaps at moft, only rolled under an open fhelter, until the infpectors can find leifure to
attend to it.   During this period it is expofed
to the firft ftage of *public privilege*; for every
man thinks himfelf privileged to take a handful as he paffes, for the purpofe of chewing or
fmoking, *according to eftablifhed cuftom*, dream-
ing little perhaps that the example is fo often
repeated as to deceive the merchant's expectations very perceptibly; for as the hogfheads
are pretty generally fhattered in bringing to
market, there is no want of fufficient apertures
through broken ftaves and deficient heading,
which afford an eafy admiffion to the too
greedy hand of the privileged plunderer of a
produce for which others have paid the fweat
of their brow.

Such is the ftate of depredation during the
intermediate ftage which occurs between the
delivery of the crop and the act of infpection.
But it is after this operation, and during its
procefs, that the great harveft of cuftomary
plunder commences.

The attendants upon the warehoufe operations,

tions, and their illicit receivers, are the moſt benefited of all men, by a practice which has become a kind of calculable privilege through its frequent indulgence; though all who paſs are admitted partakers, in a certain degree, without much ceremony. The firſt, however, have grown into a kind of formidable profeſſion, who are not only in the open habit of vending other people's tobacco, *by privilege*, in twiſts and rolls for home conſumption, but are the principal merchants who ſupply ſailors and ſmall adventurers for exportation. Nay, I believe, it would not be hard to prove, that negro attendants at the Richmond warehouſes have been honoured with applications from England for the choiceſt chewing tobacco; that this privilege has in other inſtances extended itſelf to caſks; and I ſhould not think it an exaggerated eſtimate upon the aggregate of this commerce, to calculate its loſſes by privilege at many thouſand pounds of tobacco per annum.

The rejected tobacco has been heretofore another privileged ſource of conſiderable depredation; and I preſume the items of ſnuff and ſoap aſhes have yielded reſpectable profits. I underſtand that late laws have abated the rigour of this inquiſitorial penalty, and that a planter is now clearly permitted to take away

H and

and make the beft of an inferior commodity.
If not, it would certainly be an equitable amendment to let the rejecting infpectors affign the
inferior degree of ufe for which the plant might
be fuitable, to the profit of him alone whofe
induftry was applied in cultivating, and bringing it to an unfortunate market.

Of fucceffive Depredations by cafual Expofure.

Hitherto I have noticed only thofe depredations which are confidered under the idea of
privileges, and fanctioned in fome degree by
the tacit affent of the crowd who may be
looking on. It remains yet to notice various
depredations by petty thefts, which cannot be
confidered to be much lefs injurious to proprietors.

The practice of roguifh planters ftealing
from other men's tobacco houfes, has been in
feveral inftances detected, profecuted, and punifhed, as the judicial records of the country
teftify; and as the laws on this head have
made ample provifion to punifh the offence,
there feems to be no other remedy than examples of moral rectitude, and vigilance, to fee
them duly enforced. Hogfheads of tobacco
which are fometimes left expofed on their way
to

to market, which may be occafioned by the breaking down of waggons, the tiring of horfes, or the lownefs of water conveyance during droughty feafons, are cafualties which cannot be fo well guarded againft; and I believe cafes have happened in this inftance, where the hogfhead has been ftolen with impunity. To this fpecies of depredation, however, as well as that committed by privilege, we find tobaccos moft of all expofed in the public warehoufes, and in taking off with defective headings and ftaves, for it is fuch opportunities as thefe which are moft likely to fhelter villains from detection, and particularly in the dark deeds of the night. It is from thefe thefts that the peddling commerce of the country and the adventures of feamen are often augmented; and the remedies merit confideration among thofe who are injured.

Of the Crop Mafter, Overfeer, and Hands; and of their refpective Shares, Functions, and Privileges.

The propenfity which the people of England feem to have, too generally, to impute the odium of a flave trade upon the inhabitants of a country on whom their own thirft after foreign lucre has beftowed the hated evil, induces

H 2   me

me to notice *this worſt condition of its exiſtence* in any part of the American continent which lies northward of the indigo culture: though I confeſs myſelf at preſent to be imperfectly prepared to write upon a ſubject which is now accidentally taken up, after ſeveral years abſence from the ſcene of action, and on which account my memory feels conſiderably weakened. I will, neverthelefs, attempt a conciſe ſtatement of what occurs, leaving my deficiencies to the amendment of thoſe who may be more immediately acquainted with the ſyſtem of apportioning American crops, or who may find leiſure and inclination to inveſtigate ſuch a topic to enrich the annals of agriculture.

The *crop maſter* is generally the proprietor of the land which he cultivates, and always he is underſtood to be the tenant in poſſeſſion: more technically, he is the maſter of the eſtate, who generally underſtands the whole proceſs of the culture, and gives inſtructions concerning the various operations, though perhaps he does not attend perſonally to their execution: he furniſhes all the neceſſary proviſions, utenſils, and apparatus; is lord of the ſoil, and receives a proportionate profit of its productions in kind, whether he tills the ground with his own ne-

groes,

groes, with hireling labourers, or with independent cultivators, termed *croppers*. In any
of thefe events, when the crop is gathered, he
receives his proportion of it in fhares according
to *cuftom of the country*. An idea of this cuftomary arrangement may be conceived by
ftrangers from the following example, which
prevails in fome places, but varies in others:
If A (for inftance) furnifhes the land, and finds
every thing neceffary to its cultivation, and B
undertakes the labour of the culture, A will
fhare two parts, and B will fhare one. If, on
the contrary, A finds the land only, and B furnifhes the labour and neceffaries of cultivation,
A will fhare one third part, and B will take
two. It follows from thefe proportions, that
the rent of the land is valued at one third of
the whole produce; the furnifhing of the provifion and materials at one other third; and
that the other one third part is to compenfate
for the manual labour beftowed. Now it is
this labour which is divided among the labourers who perform it: as, for inftance, a hand
of medium capacity will perform one fhare of
the aggregate labour; a hand of extraordinary
capacity will perhaps perform a fhare and a
quarter, or a fhare and a half of fuch labour;
a woman will perform three quarters of a fhare;

H 3 a boy

a boy half a fhare, &c.   And in this way the
fhares are ultimately fettled in, what is termed,
dividing the crop.

The *overfeer* is a kind of fubordinate f+eward (for upon large eftates there is a fteward
who intervenes between the mafter and many
overfeers), who overfees and fuperintends the
management of the crop, and is much, or altogether, with the hands during the hours of
labour, which continue from daylight until
the dufk of the evening, and fome part of the
night, by moon or candlelight, during the
winter.   Overfeers are generally white men of
fome experience and refpectability ; and there
are fome of the profeffion of high characters
and good intereft.   There are, neverthelefs,
negroes upon many eftates who rife by their
merit to this degree of promotion ; and there
are generally upon large eftates very truft-
worthy *foremen* among the negroes, who officiate in their overfeer's abfence, and fave him
much trouble by their management.   It is remarkable, however, that black overfeers are
more fevere tafk-mafters than the white ones,
and are more dreaded by their fellow-flaves.
The employment of an overfeer never ceafes,
from the feed to the harveft : he muft be always and every where prefent (as it were), and
fhould

should know every thing which paffes till he has taken his crop to market. He is the re-fponfible perfon for all tranfactions upon the eftate, and his intereft is generally interwoven in one common web with that of his employer, and of the labourers, to be ultimately divided into fhares; but there are, neverthelefs, fome exceptions where mafters give their overfeers a ftanding falary in lieu of their fhares. An over-feer partakes, in the ordinary cafe, of every fpecies of crop which is cultivated, according to the rate of his agreement, which will per-haps extend to a fhare and a half, two, three, or more fhares, according to his reputation, experience, and merit. And this compenfa-tion is feldom feparated from the joint ftock, but more generally fold in the aggregate, and accounted for by the employer upon fettle-ment; yet this is a point which is optional with the overfeer. In many cafes the over-feer is allowed to keep a horfe or two of his own, a few hogs, cattle, &c. and thefe feldom fhame their keeper, as they range at large upon free coft.

The *hands* are moft generally flaves belong-ing to the eftate; and thefe in fome inftances are attached to it, and defcend with the land to the next heir: in others they are confidered

H 4   perfonal

perfonal property, according to the nature of the cafe, and the local regulations of the particular legiflation; for each ftate in the union retains its diftinct and feparate *fovereign* rights, and the boafted fupremacy which an Englifh-man is wont to afcribe to Congrefs is more qualified than it is generally conceived to be. The fons, however, of many planters work in the crop equally with the negroes, nor is there any material practical diftinction obferved between them. There are alfo white hirelings who cultivate tobacco, efpecially upon the footing of *croppers*, but thefe are more generally found among the Irifh and German planters, than among the Virginians, and their fare is in common with the family. Confining the idea of *hands* to negroes who compofe the majority, their mafter is compenfated for their labours in the crop, by an allowance of their proportionate fhares. In return for this he generally furnifhes them with coarfe clothing; a negro quarter refidence, or a private houfe of their own, if they choofe to build one out of his materials; as much land as they think proper to cultivate at leifure hours, rent free; a regular allowance of corn and falt provifions, or falted fifh; the privilege of cultivating cotton, melons, potatoes, vegetables, flax, hops, fruits,

fruits, &c.; of rearing as many ducks, geese,
dunghill fowls, and turkies, as they can manage : in some instances this indulgence is extended to a small stock of swine ; and I have
known many slaves who kept their own
horses, and lived comfortably and respectably
upon the surplus of their time.

It is true, indeed, that the policy of the
law has invested the master with an absolute
authority to tyrannize ; but this is rarely exercised, and especially since the American revolution. There are, however, some whose
avarice is found to stimulate them to acts of
severity and penury, but such are justly ab-
horred, and the perpetrators of those cowardly
cruelties are seldom without the penalty of
their demerit, in the conspicuous contempt of
their neighbours. When it is considered, indeed, from how many social cares and duties
negro slavery is exempted ; that the master is
obliged to provide for them in all events ; that
prudence often elevates their circumstances
above the industrious labourer of Europe ; that
the mitigated condition of their present shackles, renders the name of the thing more horrible than the restraint, it may (though not to
be voluntarily sought after) be a more enviable
                                    situation,

fituation, in the eye of found philofophy, than
the pompous bondage of the pageant great.
At any rate, I have known negroes who have
reafoned againft emancipation ; and have been
credibly informed of others who have petitioned to return to their former flavery ! Happily for myfelf, I neither am, nor ever fhall
be, a flave-holder,

Of

Of various Methods of cultivating Tobaccco in America, according to the Practice of former Times, which have occurred since the Commencement of this Work.

THE Reverend Mr. Hugh Jones, Minister of James's town in Virginia, who has written a short and faithful account of that country, published in London in 1724, gives us the following particulars with regard to the culture of this article.

" When a tract of land is seated *," says he, " they clear it by felling the trees about a yard from the ground, lest they should shoot again. What wood they have occasion for they carry off, and burn the rest, or let it lie and rot upon the ground.

" The land between the logs and stumps they *hoe* up, planting tobacco there in the spring, enclosing it with a slight fence of cleft rails. This will last for tobacco some years if the land be good, as it is where fine timber or grape vines grow.

" Land, when hired, is forced to bear tobacco by penning their cattle upon it; but cow-

* H. Jones's Present State of Virginia, p. 39, printed in London, 1724.

penned

penned tobacco taftes ftrong, and that planted in wet marfhy land is called *non-burning to-bacco*, which fmokes in the pipe like leather, unlefs it be of a good age.

" When land is tired of tobacco it will bear Indian corn or Englifh wheat, or any other European grain or feed, with wonderful in-creafe.

" Tobacco and Indian corn are planted in hills, as hops; and fecured by *worm fences*, which are made of rails fupporting one another very firmly in a particular manner.

" Tobacco requires a great deal of fkill and trouble in the right management of it. They raife the plants in beds, as we do cabbage plants, which they *tranfplant* and *replant* upon occafion after a fhower of rain, which they call *a feafon*. When it is grown up they top it, or nip off the head, fuccour it, or cut off the ground leaves, weed it, hill it, and, when ripe, they cut it down about fix or eight leaves on a ftalk, which they carry into airy tobacco houfes; after it is withered a little in the fun, there it is hung to dry on fticks, as paper at the paper mills; when it is in proper cafe (as they call it) and the air neither too moift, nor too dry, they *ftrike it*, or take it down, then cover it up in *bulk*, or a great heap, where it

lies

lies till they have leifure or occafion to *ftem* it (that is, pull the leaves from the ftalk), or ftrip it * (that is, to take out the great fibres), and tie it up in *hands*, or *ftraight lay it*, and fo by degrees prize or prefs it with proper engines into great hogfheads, containing from about fix to eleven hundred pounds; four of which hogfheads make a tun, by dimenfions, not by weight; then it is ready for fale or fhipping.

" There are two forts of tobacco, viz. *Oroonoko*, the ftronger, and *fweet-fcented*, the milder; the firft with a fharper leaf like a fox's ear, and the other rounder and with finer fibres: but each of thefe are varied into feveral forts, much as apples and pears are; and I have been informed by the Indian traders, that the inland Indians have forts of tobacco much differing from any planted or ufed by the Europeans."

A gentleman of Holland, in a private treatife, which he has lately written in the German language, for the inftruction of profeffional tobacconifts, has fpoken of a method of culture in Virginia, which is unknown to me,

---

* The terms, *ftem*, and *ftrip*, are here tranfpofed; probably by an overfight of the firft printer,

but

but which may have been practifed, perhaps, by the Dutch adventurers to that country, whofe goods were fecured to them by the four-teenth article of the treaty of furrender to the Commonwealth of England, executed at James's city in Virginia, on the 12th day of March, 1751. And as the method defcribed may probably afford fome agricultural lights worth notice, I have been at fome pains to render it correctly into Englifh by the help of a gentleman fkilled in the original tongue.

" In fpring," fays he, " *red* feed, in prefer-ence to the white, is put into a clean pot; milk or ftale beer is poured upon it, and it is left for two or three days in this ftate; it is then mixed with a quantity of fine fat earth, and fet afide in a hot chamber, till the feeds begin to put out fhoots. They are then fown in a hot-bed. When the young plants have grown to a finger's length, they are taken up between the fifteenth and twenty-fecond of May, and planted in ground that has been previoufly well manured with the dung of doves or fwine. They are placed at fquare diftances of one and a half foot from one ano-ther. In dry weather, they are now to be watered with lukewarm water foftly fhowered upon them, between funfet and twilight.

" When

" When thefe plants are full two feet high, the tops of the ftems are broken off, to make the leaves grow thicker and broader. Here and there are left a few plants, without having their tops broken off, in order that they may afford feeds for another year. Throughout the fummer the other plants are, from time to time, pruned at the top; and the whole field is carefully weeded, to make the growth of the leaf fo much the more vigorous.

" In the month of September, from the eighth to the fixteenth day, and between the hours of ten in the morning and four in the afternoon, the beft leaves are to be taken off. It is more advantageous to pluck the leaves when they are dry than when they are moift. When plucked they are to be immediately brought home, and hung upon cords within the houfe, to dry, in as full expofure as is pof-fible, to the influence of the fun and air; but fo as to receive no rain. In this expofure they remain till the months of March and April following; when they are to be put up in bundles, and conveyed to the ftore-houfe, in which they may be kept, that they may be there ftill more perfectly dried by a moderate heat.

" Within eight days they muft be removed
to

to a different place, where they are to be fpa-
ringly fprinkled with falt water, and left till
the leaves fhall be no longer warm to the feel-
ing of the hand.   A barrel of water with fix
handfuls of falt are the proportions.   After all
this the tobacco leaves may be laid afide for
commercial exportation.   They will remain
frefh for three years."

So far for the method related by the gentleman from Holland.   I find fome farther particulars concerning the early methods of cultivating and managing this plant, related in the
very fcarce and interefting voyages of Peere
Le Bat, written in the French language, which
I have caufed to be tranflated ; but as it would
mutilate his account of the fubject, if I were
to feparate the particulars of the culture from
the reft, I prefer to give a fuller ftatement in a
feparate part of this work, to which I muft
beg leave to refer the reader ; and I have hopes
that the obftinacy of habitual practice, and
the trodden paths of our anceftors, will prove
no obftacle to thofe experiments, and compari-
fons, which may be helpful to agricultural
knowledge, efpecially in Virginia, where nature has afforded a wide and bountiful field, if
men would but truft themfelves a little way
beyond the leading-ftrings of their forefathers.
I fhall

I fhall add to this a few particulars concerning the methods of culture, and of curing tobacco in Maryland, and in the northern parts
of Virginia.

*Method of Raiſing and Curing Tobacco in Mary-
land, as communicated to the Committee on
Agriculture in Boſton*, 1786. See American
Muſeum, p. 135, 1787.

" Tobacco is raiſed and cured, in this ſtate,
nearly according to the following proceſs.

" In March, a bed is prepared in ſome rich
ſpot on the plantation, by burning a large
quantity of bruſh-wood * upon it, and raking
the ſurface fine. About the firſt of May the
ſeeds are ſown in it broad caſt, and generally
mixed with aſhes, in order to diſperſe them
more equally. The young plants are cleanſed
of weeds in the ſame manner as ſeedling onions
or cabbage plants ; and, like the latter, are
fit to be tranſplanted when about two inches
high.

" The ground to receive them, when ſet out
or tranſplanted, is prepared with a narrow hoe,
by digging holes of about a foot ſquare, and as

* *Bruſh-wood*, ſignifies the loppings of trees, ſuch as in
ſome places in the north of England are called *chatts*.

I   deep,

deep, three feet apart every way, in rows. This is termed *holing*: the earth about the hole, and that which came out of it, is next formed into a hill, over the hole, like cabbage hills, only larger: this is termed *scraping*.

" The hills being thus prepared, the first fucceeding rain which wets the ground fufficiently, the plants are drawn from the beds, and planted in the fame manner as cabbages, and are filled up in the fame manner by replanting thofe hills where any fail.

" When the plants are well fixed, and begin to grow, they muft be kept very clean from weeds with broad hoes, which reduce the hills quite down. The next hoeing is to bring up the hills again, round the ftalk; and this weeding and hilling fucceed each other during the whole growth. The plant muft be topped when the flower ftalks begin to appear; and this is performed by breaking off the top with the finger and thumb, leaving from fix to ten leaves, according to the apparent ftrength and vigour of the plants.

" Every week or ten days during this growth, it puts out fuckers between the ftalk and every leaf. Thefe muft be conftantly broken off with the fingers as they appear. About

i   the

the firſt of September, and from that till froſt comes, the tobacco ripens, and muſt be cut. There is ſome difficulty in deſcribing it in this ſtate, ſo as to be certainly known : however in general it is known to be ripe by the leaf putting forth yellowiſh ſpots, pretty thick over it; and having attained a conſiderable ſubſtance and richneſs. It is then cut down, near the ground, and let lie till the ſun has ſoftened it from its brittle ſtate, and it may be houſed without the leaves ſnapping off. It is then pegged, and hung up in a houſe in the man-ner that bacon generally is, only ſo thick that the plants generally touch each other, and in tiers one above another, from within a yard of the ground floor to the ridge of the houſe; the peg is drove through the ſtalk, and the hanging is on ſticks about four feet long, laid from beam to beam. It hangs in the houſe about ſix or eight weeks, to dry; and in damp weather a gentle fire is made under it to pre-vent its moulding.

" Many of the planters give the fine *kite foot* a colour, by curing it altogether with hickory fires under it conſtantly, until it is dry. When cured, as they term it (or dry), it can only be handled in damp weather, called *ſeaſons*. In ſuch weather it is taken down and ſtripped;

this

this is performed by holding the butt-end of
the plant in your left hand, and with the
right cutting off the firſt leaves (leaving the
ſmaller, or thoſe of a different quality, which
are commonly on the ſame plant), until you
have enough gathered to form *a hand of tobacco*
(or bundle); then you lap one leaf round the
ends of the ſtalks, gathered neatly together in
the hand, by beginning at the extremity with
the little end of the leaf, and turning it round
and round, forming a head of about two
inches and a half long; then the end of the leaf,
with which you have moulded the head, is
tucked into the bundle; and the tobacco being
ſtripped and ſorted into different qualities, is
packed up in bulks, as the planters term them,
which is only laying the hands even upon one
another (as bricks are piled) to any convenient
height; from whence at any other *ſeaſon* (or
damp weather) it is taken and packed in hogſheads.   This operation is performed in the following way: the packer gets into a hogſhead,
placed under a prize, fixed in a poſt like a ci-
der prize, and a perſon outſide hands him the
tobacco, which he begins to pack away in the
bottom of the caſk, with the heads next the
ſtaves all round, and then acroſs the caſk,
until the caſk is about one-fourth filled, with
the

the weight of the packer fitting on it.   Boards,
or falfe heading, are then laid evenly on it, and
blocks, one upon another, up to the prize.
This quantity will prefs down to about three
inches thick in the bottom, becoming a firm
and folid cake.

" The prizes remain on it, until it is firm,
which will take feveral hours; during which
time the planter packs other cafks, or goes
about other bufinefs.

" Thefe packings and prizings are thus repeated until the hogfhead is filled up to the
top, quite folid.   The weight of a hogfhead is
from feven hundred and fifty pounds to one
thoufand one hundred and fifty pounds nett in
Maryland: in Virginia much heavier."

I have noticed in the early part of this work
fome of the fpecies of injuries which arife from
over-prizing.   It is a great injury to the
James's river trade that the planters are fo difpofed to excel each other in this particular.   I
remember to have purchafed a crop at South
Quay in 1778, which was made at Moore's Ordinary in Prince Edward's county, Virginia,
which (if my memory is right) weighed from
one thoufand four hundred to one thoufand
feven hundred pounds per hogfhead, of the
cuftomary fize.   In the northern parts of Vir-

I 3   ginia

ginia they appear to approximate the Maryland
method of culture and treatment, as will be
feen by Judge Parker's following paper.

*The Method of Cultivating and Curing Tobacco
in that part of Virginia which borders upon
Maryland, as practifed by Judge Parker, and
communicated to the American Mufeum in
1789.*

A man who wifhes to make fine tobacco,
fhould be very particular in the choice of his
feed; I mean as to the kind. I do not know
a greater variety of any kind of vegetable than
of tobacco; from the fweet-fcented, the beft
fort, to the thick-jointed, a coarfe kind of tobacco; but of which I think the moft can be
made. I would recommend to a gentleman
who would wifh for the reputation of a good
planter, to cultivate the true fweet-fcented.

When he has chofen his feed, let him prepare the beds, in which he intends to fow it,
very fine; when thus prepared, they muft be
burned with corn-ftalks, in order to deftroy
the feeds of weeds and grafs, which, even
when he has done the beft with his beds, he
will find very troublefome, and difficult to ex-
tirpate. The beft time for fowing the feed is

as

as early after Chriftmas as the weather will permit. When fown in beds, prepared as above directed, which fhould be done as foon as poffible after they are burned, inftead of raking-in the feed, the beds fhould either be patted with boards or gently trodden with naked feet. This being done, the next care is the covering them warmly with cedar or pine brufh, to defend the young plants from the froft.

After all his trouble and care, the planter's hopes are often blafted by a little fly, which frequently deftroys the plants when they firft come up, and very often when they are grown to a moderate fize ; no certain remedy againft them has as yet been difcovered. I have heard, indeed, that fulphur will deftroy them ; and I believe it will ; but it muft be often repeated, and will be too expenfive. I have thought, although I never have tried it, that a pretty ftrong infufion of faffafras, root or bark, fprinkled frequently over the beds, would de-ftroy thofe infects ; and I judge fo, becaufe I have experienced its effects upon the lice, a kind of fly, that infefts cabbages. Drought will alfo deftroy your plants, even where they are large in the beds ; the planter fhould, there-fore, before the drought has continued too

I 4

long, water his plants night and morning, until he has a good rain. You will fee then,
from thefe enemies to plants, the neceffity of
having feveral beds differently fituated, fome
convenient to water-fwamps, and fome on
high ground, well expofed.

These plants, at a proper fize, as opportunity offers, are to be tranfplanted into hills at
three feet diftance.

Here it may be neceffary to give fome directions as to preparing the ground to receive
the plants, and to inform you what kind of
foil is beft adapted to tobacco. The fame kind
of land, I think, that is proper for wheat, is
fo for tobacco, neither of them delighting in
fandy foil. I do not think a clayey ftiff foil
will fuit tobacco; however, let the foil be ftiff
or light, it ought to be made very rich, by
cow-penning it on the fward, or by fpreading
your farm-yard manure over it. I would recommend that the hills fhould be made in the
autumn, and at about the diftance of three
feet, or three feet and a half in the row and
ftep; by this means it has a larger furface expofed to the froft, which will affift in the pulverizing and fertilizing it. A good hand may
very well tend from ten to twelve thoufand
hills of frefh light land; or from fix to ten
thoufand

thoufand of ftiff land; and I believe where the planter depends upon manuring his land for a crop, he will find it difficult to get even five thoufand hills properly manured.

If the planter has time to turn over, in the month of February, the hills which were made in the fall, he will find his advantage in it; but I fcarce believe that time will be found.

If the tobacco feed has been fown early in good beds, and thofe beds properly attended to, you may expect to plant your hills from them in May.

The earlier your tobacco is planted, the better, as it will not be fit to cut in lefs than three months; by planting early, your tobacco will be houfed in Auguft, a month by far the beft in the whole year to cut it, as it then cures of a fine bright nutmeg colour, and will have a much better fcent than later tobacco.

When you perceive your plants large enough to fet out, you muft prepare your tobacco hills by re-working them, breaking the clods very fine, and then cutting off the top of the hill, fo as to have it broad and low; you then clap your hoe upon the top of it, which breaks the fmall clods.

Having turned as many hills as you think you can plant with convenience at one time,

you

you are to wait until a rain comes, ever fo little
of which, at this feafon of the year, will be
fufficient, provided you can draw your plants
from the beds, without breaking. The plants
will more readily extend their roots if fet out
after a moderate rain, than if planted in a very
wet feafon. Remember that you never prepare more hills than you can plant the next
feafon; as frefh turned hills are beft for the
plants. In this manner you are to proceed
until the whole of your crop is planted. You
may continue to plant every feafon, until the
laft of June; but I think you have very little
chance of making good tobacco if you have
not your whole quantity planted by that time.
After your crop is *pitched*, or planted, in the
manner directed, it will require your clofeft
attention. Your tobacco has at this period a
very dangerous enemy in a fmall worm, called
the ground-worm, which rifes from the
ground, and makes great havoc among the
young and tender plants, by cutting off and
eating the leaves quite into the hill. It fometimes happens that you will have your crop to
replant five or fix times before you can get it
to ftand well. You are then to watch the
firft rifing of the worm; and every morning
your whole force is to be employed in fearching

ing round each plant, and deſtroying this worm. When your tobacco begins to grow you muſt carefully cut down the hills ſhelving from the plants; and take every weed and ſpire of graſs from around the plants, without diſturbing the roots. They will, after this weeding, if the weather be ſeaſonable, grow rapidly. When they have ſpread over the hills pretty well, and a little before they are fit to top, about four of the under leaves are to be taken off; this we call *priming*; and then the tobacco muſt have a hill given to it.

As ſoon as it can be topped to ten leaves, it muſt be done, and this by a careful hand, well uſed to the buſineſs. He is to ſuffer his thumb nails to grow to a conſiderable length, that he may take out the ſmall bud from the top, without bruiſing, leaving ten leaves behind in the firſt and ſecond topping, or until it grows too late for the plant to ſupport ſo many leaves; then to fall to eight, and even to ſix; but this the ſkilful topper will be the beſt judge of, as it can be only known from experience. You are now to be attacked by another enemy, as dangerous and as deſtructive as any; it is the *horn-worm*, of a green colour, which grows to a large ſize, and if ſuffered to ſtay on the plant will deſtroy the whole. The firſt *glut* of
them,

them, as the planters call it, will be when the tobacco is in the ftate above mentioned; and your hands muft be almoft conftantly employed in pulling them off, and preventing their increafe; but if you have a ftock of young turkeys to turn into the field they will effectually deftroy thefe worms. You are again to hill up your tobacco, and lighten the ground between the hills, that the roots of the tobacco may extend themfelves with eafe. Immediately after topping, your tobacco begins to throw out fuckers between the leaves, where they join the ftalks: thefe fhould be carefully taken off, for if they are fuffered to grow, they greatly exhauft the plant. Not long after the firft glut of worms, comes a fecond, in greater quantities than the former, and they muft be treated in the fame manner.

Tobacco, thus managed, will begin to ripen in the month of Auguft, when it is to be cut, as it ripens, in order to be houfed: but you fhould have a very fkilful fet of cutters, who know well when tobacco is ripe; for if it be cut before it is full ripe, it will never cure of a good colour, and will rot in the hogfhead after it is prized. The tobacco, when ripe, changes its colour, and looks greyifh; the leaf feels thick, and if preffed between the finger

and

and thumb will eafily crack: but experience alone can enable a perfon to judge when tobacco is fully ripe.

I think the beft time to cut tobacco is in the afternoon, when the fun has not power to burn it, but only caufes the leaves to be fupple, that they may be handled without breaking. It fhould then remain on the ground all night: the next morning after the dew is off, and before the fun has power to burn it, it muft be picked up; but there fhould be no appearance of rain the preceding night; for fhould a heavy rain fall upon the tobacco, when lying on the ground, it will injure it greatly, by filling it with grit, and, perhaps, bruifing it. Tobacco is, indeed, generally cut in the morning, but in this cafe it muft be watched very narrowly, and picked up, and put in fmall heaps on the ground, before it begins to burn; for if it be fcorched by the fun it is good for nothing.

There are different methods taken in the management of tobacco, immediately after being cut, and fufficiently killed by the fun for handling. Some hang it upon fences until it is nearly half cured before they carry it to hang up in houfes, built for the purpofe; but this mode I do not approve of, as the leaves are

are too much expofed to the fun, and are apt
to be injured.   A much better method is, to
have fcaffolds made clofe to the houfe you in-
tend to cure your tobacco in ; and having a
fufficient number of tobacco fticks of about
four feet and a half long, and an inch thick,
you bring in your tobacco from the field, and
putting from ten to fourteen or fifteen plants
upon a ftick, you fix the fticks upon this fcaffold, about nine inches the one from the other;
there the tobacco remains until the leaves turn
yellow.   By this method you prevent the fun
from coming to the leaves, and the rays only
fall on the ftalks.   After remaining a fufficient
time, you remove the fticks, with the tobacco
on them, into the houfe, and fix them where
they are to remain, until the tobacco be fully
cured.

The houfes built for the tobacco are from
thirty to fixty feet long, and about twenty feet
wide : the roof has wind beams about four
feet diftance, to fix the fticks on, and contrived
at proper fpaces to receive the whole of the
tobacco, until the houfe is full, fo that there
be a fpace of fix inches between the tails of the
upper plants and heads of the lower, for the
air to pafs through.

If a perfon has houfe-room enough I would
advife

advife that the tobacco fhould have no fun, but be carried into the houfe immediately after it is killed, and there hung upon the fticks. But, in this cafe, the plants fhould be very few on the fticks, and the fticks at greater diftances from each other ; for tobacco is very apt to be injured in the houfe, if hung too clofe in a green ftate. If a crop could be cured in this way, without fun, its colour would be more bright, and the flavour finer ; the whole juices being preferved unexhaled by the fun.

When your tobacco is fully cured in the houfe, which may be known by the colour of the leaf, and the drynefs of the ftem, it may be then ftripped from the ftalks, when it is in a proper ftate ; that is, in feafon, which moift-ens it fo as it can be handled. As foon as the tobacco is fo pliant that it can be handled without breaking the leaves, it is to be ftruck from the fticks, put in a bulk until it is ftrip-ped from the ftalks, which, in the earlier part of the year, fhould be immediately done, left the ftalks, which are green, fhould injure the leaf. If the tobacco is *too high in cafe* when it is ftruck, it will be apt to rot when it gets into a fweat. One thing fhould be particularly at-tended to, and that is, it fhould be ftruck as it

firft

firſt comes into caſe; for if it hangs until it is too high, or moiſt, and you ſhould wait until the moiſture dries away to the ſtate I adviſe it to be in when you ſtrike it, it will moſt certainly, when in bulk, return to its full ſtate of moiſture; and, therefore, it ſhould hang until it is perfectly dry; and you are to wait till another ſeaſon arrives to put it in proper caſe.

The next thing to be done, after the tobacco is ſtruck, as I have ſaid, is to ſtrip it, and here you are to be particularly attentive. All the indifferent leaves are firſt to be pulled from the ſtalks, by ſorters well acquainted with the buſineſs, and tied by themſelves to be afterwards ſtemmed. The plant, with the leaves, is to be thrown to the ſtrippers: they are to ſtrip off the leaves, and tie up five leaves in a bundle with one of equal goodneſs. When you have got enough for a hogſhead, which I adviſe not to be more than a thouſand weight, it ſhould be immediately packed up with very great care, and prized. Your hogſheads ſhould be made of ſtaves not exceeding forty-eight inches long; and the head ought not to be more than from thirty to thirty-two inches in diameter. No directions can be given here for the packing, it can only be
learned

learned from practice.   If more tobacco than
I here recommend be prized into a hogſhead
it will be apt to be bruiſed : a circumſtance
which ſhould be carefully avoided.

PART IV.

PROGRESS OF THE CULTURE AND COMMERCE OF TOBACCO.

Of the firſt Knowledge of the Tobacco Plant.

IT is generally underſtood that the tobacco plant of Virginia is a native production of that country; but whether it was found in a ſtate of natural growth there, or a plant cultivated by the Indian natives (whoſe very origin is yet doubtful, and is daily becoming a matter of learned inquiry), is a point of which we are not informed, nor which ever can be farther elucidated than by the corroboration of hiſtorical facts and conjectures *.

I have been thirty years ago, and the greateſt part of my time during that period, intimately acquainted with the interior parts of America; and have been much in the unſettled parts of the country, among thoſe kinds of ſoil

---

* See Pere La Batt's account on the ſubject, tranſlated from the French.

which

which are favourable to the culture of tobacco ;
but I do not recollect one fingle inftance where
I have met with tobacco growing wild in the
woods, although I have often found a few
fpontaneous plants about the arable and trodden grounds of deferted habitations.

This circumftance, as well as that of its being now, and having been, *cultivated* by the
natives at the period of European difcoveries,
inclines towards a fuppofition that this plant
is *not* a native of *North* America, but may pof-
fibly have found its way thither with the earlieft migrations from fome diftant land.   This
might, indeed, have eafily been the cafe from
South America, by way of the Ifthmus of Pa-
nama*; and the foundation of the *Chaɕtaw*
and

* * *

* *Lionel Wafer*, who publifhed his travels upon the Ifthmus of Darien in 1699, fays, in page 102, " Thefe Indians
have *tobacco* amongft them.   It grows as the tobacco in Virginia, but is not fo ftrong, perhaps for want of tranfplanting
and manuring, which the Indians do not well underftand ;
for they only raife it from the feed in their plantations.
When it is dried and cured they ftrip it from the ftalks, and
laying two or three leaves upon one another, they roll up
all together fideways into a long roll, yet leaving a little
hollow.   Round this they roll other leaves one after another, in the fame manner, but clofe and hard, till the roll
be as big as one's wrift, and two or three feet in length.

Their way of fmoking when they are in company together is thus : a boy lights one end of a roll and burns it to a
coal,

and *Chickasaw* nations (who we have reasons to consider as descendants from the *Tlascalians,* and to have migrated to the eastward of the river Mississippi, about the time of the Spanish conquest of Mexico by *Cortez)* seems to have afforded one fair opportunity for its dissemination.

The first knowledge which the *English* may be supposed to have of this plant, seems to be deducible from the report of Sir John Hawkins in July 1565 [*], who says, that " The Floridians, when they travel, have a kind of herb dried, which, with a cane and an earthern cup in the end, with fire and the dried herbs put together, do sucke thorow the cane the smoke thereof, which smoke satisfieth their hunger, and therewith they live foure or five

coal, wetting the part next it to keep it from wasting too fast. The end so lighted he puts into his mouth, and blows the smoke through the whole length of the roll into the face of every one of the company or council, though there be two or three hundred of them. Then they, sitting in their usual posture upon forms, make with their hands held together a kind of funnel round their mouths and noses. Into this they receive the smoke as it is blown upon them, snuffing it up greedily and strongly as long as ever they are able to hold their breath, and seeming to bless themselves, as it were, with the refreshment it gives them.

[*] Hakluyt's Voyages, p. 541.

dayes

dayes without meat or drinke, and this all the
Frenchmen ufed for this purpofe : yet do they
holde opinion withall, that it caufeth water
and fleame to void from their ftomacks." It
is not clear to me, however, that this fumid
preparation was tobacco, as Mr. Hakluyt has
fet it down ; for the Indians fmoke much of a
bark which they fcrape from the *killiconick*, an
aromatic fhrub, fomewhat refembling the willow ; and have alfo a preparation made with
this and *fumach* leaves, or fometimes with the
latter mixed with tobacco.

There is, however, a very particular account given of the tobacco of Virginia, by
Mr. Thomas Harriot, who made a voyage thither in 1586, and reported as follows:

" There is an herbe which is fowed apart by
itfelfe, and is called by the inhabitants *uppowoc* :
in the Weft Indies it hath divers names, according to the feveral countries and places
where it groweth, and is ufed : the Spanyards
generally call it *tobacco*. The leaves thereof
being dried and brought into powder they ufe
to take the fume or fmoke thereof, by fucking
it through pipes made of clay, into theyr fto-
mack and head : from whence it purgeth fuperfluous fleame and other groffe humours, and
openeth all the pores and paffages of the body :
by

by which means the ufe thereof not only pre-
ferveth the body from obftructions, but alfo (if
any be, fo that they have not beene of too
long continuance) in fhort time breaketh
them : whereby theyr bodyes are notably preferved in health, and know not many grevious
difeafes, wherewithall we in England are of-
tentimes afflicted.

" This *uppowoc* is of fo precious eftimation
amongft them, that they thinke theyr gods are
marveloufly delighted therewith : whereupon
fometime they make hallowed fires, and caft
fome of the powder therein for a facrifice : being in a ftorme upon the waters, to pacifie
theyr gods, they caft fome by into the ayre
and into the water : fo a weare for fifh being
newly fet up, they caft fome therein and into
the ayre : alfo after an efcape of danger, they
caft fome into the ayre likewife : but all done
with ftrange geftures, ftamping, fometimes
dancing, clapping of hands, holding up of
hands, and ftaring up into the heavens, uttering therewithal, and chattering ftrange words
and noifes.

" We ourfelves during the time we were
there, ufed to fuck it after theyr manner, as
alfo fince our returne, and have found many
rare and wonderfull experiments of the vertues

K 4   thereof :

thereof: of which the relation would require a volume by itfelfe: the ufe of it by fo many of late, men and women of great calling as elfe, and fome learned phyficians alfo, is fufficient witneffe *."

The editors of Hall's Encyclopædia, publifhed by Mr. Cooke in 1789, have given the following account of tobacco under the head of *Nicotiana.*

" There are *feven fpecies,* of which the moft remarkable is the *tabacum,* or common tobacco plant. This was firft difcovered in America by the Spaniards about the year 1560, and by them imported into Europe. It had been ufed by the inhabitants of America long before, and was called by thofe of the iflands, *yoli,* and *pæ-tun,* by the inhabitants of the continent. It was fent into Spain from Tobaco, a province of Yucatan, where it was firft difcovered, and from whence it takes its common name. Sir Walter Raleigh firft introduced it into England about the year 1585, and was the firft who taught them how to fmoke it. Tobacco is commonly ufed among the oriental nations, though it is uncertain by whom it was introduced among them. Confiderable quantities

---

* Harriot's Voyage to Virginia, 1586. Hakluyt, p. 75.

of

of it are cultivated in the Levant, on the coasts of Greece and the Archipelago, in Italy, and the island of Malta.

" Among all the productions of foreign climes introduced into these kingdoms, scarce any has been held in higher estimation than tobacco.   In the countries of which it is a native it is considered by the Indians as the most valuable offering that can be made to the beings they worship.

" They use it in all their civil and religious ceremonies.   When once the spiral wreaths of its smoke ascend from the feathered pipe of peace, the compact that has been just made is considered as sacred and inviolable.   Likewise when they address their Great Father, or his guardian spirits*, residing as they believe in every extraordinary production of nature, they make liberal offerings to them of this valuable plant, not doubting but they are secured of protection."

So far in regard to the origin of a plant which has given such wonderful employment to the people of Great Britain during these

* I have more generally understood these offerings to be to the *devil*: the Indians always say (I think) that their *God* is a good being, who will do them no harm; but that they think it necessary to appease an evil and mischievous spirit.

two

two laſt centuries (of which one is juſt ex-
piring) : an employment which occupies an
immenſe capital in trade ; and from which
many affluent fortunes have ariſen.   It will
afford a curious, and perhaps ſatisfactory entertainment, to reiterate the progreſs of this
commerce, and the improvements which have
been ſucceſſively made in it from the earlieſt
periods of untutored nature to the preſent perfection of ſcientific manufactures.

Of the primitive Commerce in Tobacco.

According to the foregoing accounts we
may conclude the firſt commerce in tobacco to
have commenced in 1585 or 1586 ; Mr. Harriot's account is dated in 1586 ; and he was
one of Sir Walter Raleigh's party.

The firſt thirty years which ſucceeded this
period of diſcovery were greatly interrupted by
quarrels among the Indian natives, as we learn
from the hiſtories which remain ; and it is
highly probable that ſome of the earlieſt written accounts of this commerce have periſhed
with the parties who were maſſacred.

The earlieſt *official* accounts which I have
been able to find, are contained in the public
records of Virginia, which I have been permitted

mitted to tranfcribe, and from which I have extracted much certain and interefting matter by means of an amanuenfis: the earlieft of this goes back to the twenty-fifth of July, one thoufand fix hundred and twenty-one, which is thirty-five years later than the firft *certain* knowledge of the plant by the Englifh nation.

On the twenty-fifth of July, 1621, the London Company, ftiled, *The Right Honourable the Earl of Southampton and others the Lords with the reft of the worthy Adventurers of the Virginia Company*, wrote to the governor and council of ftate refiding in Virginia in the following words:———" With great difficulty we have erected a private magazine, men being moft unwilling to be drawn to fubfcription to be paid in *fmoke*. If therefore you expect for the future any fuch place; it muft be your principal care that the Cape merchant be not conftrained to vend his commodities at any fet price; and in particular not to be enforced to take *tobacco at any certain rate*, and that you be aiding as well to this as to the former magazine for the return of debts. We require that the market be open for all men, that the charitable intention of the adventurers be not abufed and turned into private gain. Therefore we defire you to have principally in your

care

care that a ſtrict proclamation be ſet out to prohibit ſuch engroſſing of commodities, and foreſtalling the market, thereby to vend to poor people at exceſſive rates. Such oppreſſion and grinding of the poor we in our hearts abhor, and require you ſeverely to puniſh: aſſuring you nothing can be more pleaſing to us than the puniſhment of ſuch monſters as devour their brethren by this wicked and barbarous practice; eſpecially if ſuch wickedneſs ſhould be exerciſed by men in place of authority."

Theſe inſtructions were ſigned by the Earl of Southampton, Mr. Deputy Farrer, Sir Edwin Sandys, Doctor Anthony, Doctor Gulſton, Doctor Winſton, Mr. Nicholas Farrer, Mr. Gibbs, Mr. Wrote, and Mr. Wroth. And on the twelfth day of the next month, Auguſt, they again wrote as follows.

" We cannot but condemn the uſe that is made of our boats, that are only employed in trading in the bay for *corn*. Almoſt every letter tells of that trade, which we only approve in caſe of neceſſity; for we conceive it would be much better for the plantation, and more honour for you and our nation, that the naturals ſhould come for their proviſion to you, than you to beg your bread of them. We

We fhall with a great deal more content hear of ftorehoufes full of corn of your own growth, than of a fhallop laden with corn from the bay. We pray you therefore that a larger proportion of ground be affigned to every man than formerly hath been ; and that the fevereft punifh-ment be inflicted upon fuch as dare to break your conftitutions herein ; and that officers be not fpared, nor their tenants nor fervants dif-penfed with.   Our magazine is fuddenly to follow this fhip, wherein there are much greater proportion of things fent than were in the laft : and though our factor of the laft magazine was either by importuning perfuaded, or by conftraint inforced to part with his goods at under rates, *to be paid in tobacco* at three fhillings per pound (which here, charges de-ducted, was fold for lefs than twenty pence per pound), yet will not the adventurers be fo in this refpect, for they are determined to ac-cept of tobacco at no certain price, nor will fell their commodities upon truft till that wick-ed phrafe and council be rooted out of the mouths and hearts of the planters, that *any thing is good enough for the merchants.*   How worthy we are of this attempt we appeal to yourfelves; yet hath it not been refented by you, nor the infolence punifhed.   But feeing

                                                    our

our care and charge is repaid with fuch monftrous ingratitude, we defire you to give notice
to the colony, that after this year they expect
no farther fupply of any neceffaries to be ex-
changed with them for their *darling tobacco.*
We have given them a year's notice before
hand, that they may fall upon fome other
courfe ; and being fenfible of the great lofs the
adventurers ftill fuftain by your *roll* tobacco,
made up with fillers (as they term it), it is by
us and the adventurers ordered, that the Cape
merchant accept of none but leaf tobacco. We
pray you to publifh this our order throughout
the colony, that they may be provided to exchange with our Cape merchant none but leaf;
and fuch as willingly tranfgrefs, thus having
notice, if they fuffer for it, it fhall be no part
of our care"

From the confiderations contained in thefe
two laft recited official inftructions, it appears
extremely clear, that fuch was then the prevalent fafhion of ufing tobacco in England, and
upon the continent of Europe (probably coun-
tenanced to encourage the fpirit of adventure
which had befpread the atlantic ocean in the
foregoing century), that the colonifts were al-
lured by the extraordinary price of three fhillings per pound, to abandon the chief objects

of

of their migration into thofe fruitful regions, for the profpect of exorbitant lucre which this commodity held out ; and that on this account they fo difgracefully fubmitted to an impolitic dependence upon the natives for bread, as to put the adventurers to their fhifts to fupport the neceffary independence of colonization ; and, very juftly, to merit their fevere reprehenfion.

We learn, however, that it was deemed neceffary to follow up thefe remonftrances very ftrenuoufly ; and to check this monftrous propenfity to a miftaken policy in the extenfion of this culture, by requefting the interventions of jurifprudence for fome degree of legal reftraint, as we find the company of adventurers again writing on the eleventh day of the next month (September), as follows :———" We defire you by whofe wifdom and integrity we expect a general redrefs, to be by all lawful means and juft favours, aiding and affifting to the bufinefs itfelf, and to our factor· Mr. Blaney, that both his perfon and the goods may be fafely and conveniently provided for, and accommodated ; and that the felling and bartering of them be left free to his difcretion, and according to the prices and inftructions he hath here given unto him by the adventurers ;

whofe

whose unanimous resolution, and charge is, not to accept of tobacco at *three shillings* the pound, finding, besides all former losses, that near forty thousand weight sent home last year for the general company and magazine, the better half hath not yielded eighteen pence per pound; and the rest not above two shillings: to which prices there is no possibility that they should arrive this next year. So that there must be an abatement of the price of tobacco; neither can we yield (which is by some persons pronounced), but by the whole company (not merely the adventurers of the magazine) it is denied, to continue the old rate of three shillings per pound, and to overvalue as much in the goods sent hence, as the tobacco is esteemed less worse than that rate. For although for matters of profit it might go current much alike, yet thereby we should maintain the colony in their overweening esteem of their darling tobacco, to the overthrow of all other staple commodities; and likewise continue the evil will they have conceived there, and the scandalous reports here spread of oppression, and exactions from the company's selling all their commodities for three times the value of what they cost. Upon which fond and unjust surmises, they think it lawful to use all man-

ner

ner of deceit and falsehood in their tobacco that they part with to the *magazine*. This is the next thing wherein we desire your care and favour, being assured from our factor in London, that, except the tobacco that shall next come thence, prove to be of more perfection and goodness than that was which came home last, there is no hope that it will vend at all : For albeit it be passed once, yet the wary buyer will not be again taken. So we heartily wish that you would make some *provision for the burning of all base and rotten stuff, and not to suffer any but very good to be cured, at least to be sent home*; whereby, certainly, there would be more advance in the price than loss in the quantity."

To these instructions and remonstrances the governor and council returned the following answer :———" It is a thing very well liked of that you have left the price of tobacco at liberty, since that it is a commodity of such uncertain value by reason of the great difference thereof in goodness ; and howsoever much of the tobacco of the last crop hath not proved very good by reason of the unseasonableness of the year, and of the want of time for the curing of it, yet we desire that no precedent may be made thereof; especially of that brought home

L   by

by the marines, whofe bringing of bad as well as good we could not at this time remedy; but have taken order, as much as in us lieth, to prevent it for the time to come. For the drawing off the people from the exceffive planting of tobacco, we have by the confent of the general affembly reftrained them to *one hundred plants the head*; *upon each of which plants there are to be left but only nine leaves*, which proportion, as near as could be gueffed, was generally conceived would be agreeable with the hundred weight which you have allowed. By which means, as alfo by the courfe which we have taken, for the keeping of every man to his trade, we doubt not but very much to prevent the immoderate planting of tobacco. But nothing can more effectually encourage all men to the planting of corn in abundance, and fo divert them from plantng of tobacco, than, that you would be pleafed fince it is your defire that great quantities of corn be planted here, as well for fuch multitudes of people as you hope yearly to fend over, as for our own ufe, to allow us a merchantable rate."

About this period we find the intervention of war with the Indians, and the cares of the colonial government as well as that of the company of adventurers, fo much occupied with

4   the

the means of defence againſt the enraged natives, whoſe horrid maſſacres threatened to
depopulate the European ſettlements, that the
correſpondence between the two countries is
moſtly filled up with accounts of the military
tranſactions of the times ; and the ſtaple of
tobacco was left more to the courſe which
chance might dictate.   We learn ſomething,
however, of the ſtate of that culture from a
letter from the governor and council of Virginia, dated at James's city, January 20, 1622,
wherein it is related to the adventurers, that
there had been as many *private* adventurers
recommended to them that year as it would
require five times the crop of that year to ſa-
tisfy ; " *there being not made above three ſcore
thouſand weight of tobacco in the whole colony.*"

Notwithſtanding this contraſt between the
ſupply and demand, we find frequent complaints on the part of the colony, of want of
ſtrength, and danger of famine.   Yet ſo great
was the inducement of *three ſhillings per pound,*
given about this period for tobacco in England,
and ſo much greater muſt have been the number of mercantile adventurers than that of actual ſettlers, that the latter were ſtimulated
by the proſpect of gain to hazard every thing
in favour of this lucrative plant : inſomuch

indeed,

indeed, that the company of adventurers found it neceſſary to reſtrain the plantations to ſixty pounds weight per head of their population; and the impoſition of his majeſty's cuſtoms (as ſtated in the adventurers' letter to the governor and council, dated at London, the 2nd of May, 1623,) was ſtill continued at the (then reduced) rate of nine pence per pound.

Such, however is the unaccountable diſpoſition of infatuated man, that neither theſe precautions, nor the after endeavours of the adventurers, aided by the vigilance of the public councils, could reſtrain this ill-judged and inordinate thirſt for a very precarious traffic; although the pitch to which it had arrived endangered the very exiſtence of thoſe concerned in it, and at that time bid fair to annihilate an enterprife which has opened to the world *an inexhauſtible ſource of commercial riches.*

Of the firſt Legiſlative Interpoſition in Regulating the Culture and Commerce of Tobacco.

We find it recorded, that after the hurry of war was a little over, and the advancing progreſs of population led to an organization of the colonial government, and convened a legiſlative authority at James's town, that one of of their very firſt acts went to a more ſerious regulation of this growing abuſe than the company had been hitherto able to effect. I cannot give a better picture of the times than the following, which I have been permitted to copy from their original record.

" *At a Grand Aſſembly ſummoned the ſixth of January, 1639 *.*

Preſent,

Sir Francis Wiatt, Knight, Governor, &c.

Captain John Weſt	Mr. Argoll Yeardley
Sir John Harvey, Knt.	Mr. George Menife
Capt. Sam. Mathews	Capt. Th. Willoughby
Captain Peirce	Captain Henry Brown
Mr. Rich. Kemp, Sec.	Capt. William Brocas
Mr. Roger Wingate, Treaſurer	Mr. Ambroſe Harmer
	Mr. Richard Bennett

" The names of the burgeſſes for the ſeveral plantations returned by the ſheriffs being as followeth, viz.

---

* A ſtranger will not, perhaps, perceive the immediate relation of *names* to the *hiſtory of tobacco*; but as many of theſe were founders of families occupying the ſame premiſes at this time, it affords a conſiderable hiſtoric light.

L 3

For

For the Country of Henrico {
Capt. Tho. Harris
Mr. Chrift. Branch
Mr. Edwd. Tunftall
}

For the County of Charles City {
Capt. Francis Epps
Capt. Tho. Pawlett
Mr. Edward Hill
Mr. Jofeph Johnfon
}

For the County of James's City
Chicohominy Parifh }

The upper Chippokes and Smith's Fort }

The lower Chippokes, Hogg Ifland, and Lawn's Creek }

Martin's Hundred to Keeth's Creek }

Farloe's Neck to Warone's Ponds }

Johnfon's Neck, Archer's Hope, and the Neck of Land }

For the County of Warwick River {

N. B. This part of the original record is defaced and imperfect.

Mr. Zachary Crip

For

For *the County of Charles's River*
{ Mr. Williams
  Mr. Hugh Gwyn
  Mr. Peregrine Bland }

For *upper Norfolk County*
{ Mr. Randolph Crew
  Mr. John Gookins
  Mr. Triftram Norris }

For *the County of Lower Norfolk*
{ Capt. John Sibfey
  Mr. John Hill }

For *the Ifle of Wight County*
{ Capt. John Upton
  Mr. Anthony Jones
  Mr. John Moone
  Mr. James Tuke }

For *the County of Eliza-beth City*
{ Mr. Thomas Oldis
  Mr. Peter Stafferton }

For *the County of Ackow-mack*
{ Mr. Obed. Robins
  Mr. John Neale }

" Whereas the exceffive quantity of tobacco of late years planted in the colony, and the evil condition and quality thereof being princi-pally occafioned thereby, have debafed the commodity to fo vile efteem and rate ; unlefs fome fpeedy courfe be eftablifhed therein it will be altogether impoffible for the planters to re-ceive any reliefe or fubfiftance thereby, or be enabled to the raifing of more ftaple commo-dities, or to difingage themfelves of fuch debts

L 4   as

as they are already plunged into. For the more timely redrefs whereof, as alfo for the advancement of the price of tobacco, the principal merchants and moft confiderable number of adventurers to the colony have made tender of thefe propofitions following, and fignifying their confents under their hands to the conditions therein expreffed, viz. That in cafe all the tobacco planted this prefent year 1639 in the colony of Virginia be abfolutely deftroyed and burned, excepting and referving fo much in equal proportion for each planter as fhall make in the whole the juft quantity of twelve hundred thoufand pounds of tobacco, the abfolute beft of the faid tobacco and no more, fo as the faid twelve hundred thoufand pounds of the faid beft tobacco have all the ftalks ftripped and fmoothed; in confideration whereof they the faid fubfcribers are content to accept and receive forty pounds of the faid beft tobacco fo ftripped, fmoothed, and ferved; in full fatisfaction of every hundred pounds of tobacco now due to them or any of them for any goods fold untill or before publication hereof in Virginia. Provided the faid forty pounds for every hundred pounds of tobacco be paid unto them and every of them, their and every of their affigns at fuch feveral times as the faid

tobacco

tobacco fhall grow due unto them and every of them.

" Provided alfo that in two years next enfuing, viz. in the year 1640 and 1641, fuch reftraint be had in planting as that there be planted and made twelve hundred thoufand pounds of the like abfolute tobacco, and no more; and if in cafe there be any tobacco over and befide the faid quantity of twelve hundred thoufand pounds, that it fhall yearly, be abfolutely de-ftroyed, for and in confideration of the abate-ment aforefaid, which faid fubfcribers are like-wife confenting and agreeing as appeareth by a teftimonial under the hands of the governor, and divers of the council, and others, that if it fhould happen through the late arrival of their faid propofitions the faid ftripping and fmoothing which is principally defired cannot this year be effected, then, if the tobacco of this year, 1639, be reduced to the quantity of fifteen hundred thoufand pounds without ftrip-ping and fmoothing, they would be willing to receive fifty pounds of tobacco for one hundred pounds debt, provided that the colony be re-gulated for thefe two enfuing years to the quantity of twelve hundred thoufand pounds per annum ftripped and fmoothed as aforefaid.

" Now the governor and council together
with

with the burgeffes of this grand affembly
having weighed the aforefaid propofition, and
taken into confideration the vaft quantity of
tobacco both in England and all other places
where the commodity hath been formerly
vended, to which, if all the tobacco of this
year's growth fhould be added and no reftraint
of planting to be made for the future (whereas
it is now moft defpicable) it muft (then) bring
affured lofs to all who fhall be dealers therein ;
both to the planters of their labours, and to the
merchants of their adventures ; have therefore
thought fit upon mature advice to comply with
the faid merchants' and adventurers' requeft;
and, to condefcend upon the aforefaid conditions and confiderations, to deftroy the tobacco
of this year, to proportion and to reftrain and
ftint the planting of tobacco for thefe two years
next enfuing, in fuch manner and form as in
this act is hereafter expreffed.

" Firft, That all tobacco of this year's growth
fhould be reduced to the proportion of fifteen
hundred thoufand pounds weight without ftrip-
ping and fmoothing, which in fo unfeafonable
a time of the year could not be effected : It is
thought fit, and eftablifhed, that in and for the
feveral limits and precincts hereunder mentioned, there be yearly chofen and appointed
men

men of experience and integrity for the care-full viewing of each man's crop of tobacco. The viewers of this year (being nominated and appointed by the aſſembly) are as followeth, viz.

" The viewers of this preſent year are, as hereunder, named commiſſioners; being joined to ſee the due execution.

For Henrico County.

1. From the World's End to Henrico { Mr. Chriſt. Branch
Roger Chapman
Tho. Oſborn

2. For Henrico, Coxon Dale, Varina, and Four Mile Creek { Mr. John Cookeney
John Baker
Samuel Almond

3. For Curles, Brome, and Turkey Iſland { Mr. Richard Cock
Bryan Smith
Ambroſe Cobb

4. For the North Side of Appomattor River { Mr. Wm. Hatcher
Thomas Shippy
Richard Johnſon

5. For Conicoke { Mr. John Baugh
Joſeph Bourne

Charles's

Charles's City County.

1. From the City to Bicker's Creek
{ Mr. Edward Hill
James Warredine
John Woodward

2. From the north side of Appomatter River
{ Mr. Cheney Boice
Anthony Wiatt
Nath. Tatham

3. For Merchant's Hope
{ Mr. Rice Hoe
Richard Tifdall
Richard Craven

4. For Weftover, Buckland, and up to Turkey Ifland
{ Mr. Walter Afton
Edward Sparfhot
Roger Davis

5. From Wianoak to David Jones's
{ Mr. Hen. Canterell
John Gibbs
Wm. Lawrence

6. From Maycox downwards to Mr. Claye's
{ Mr. John Fludd
John Glipps
George Place

7. From John Wall's his houfe to the utmoft extent of Wianoke Parifh downwards
{ Mr. Jofeph Johnfon
William Murrell
John Wall

James's

James's City County.

1. From the easterly side of Chippoke's Creek to Mr. Fludd's
{ Mr. Ben. Harrison
William Gapin
Edward Minter

2. From Mr. Fludd's Plantation to Mr. Gray's
{ Capt. Hen. Browne
John Garey
Henry Carman

3. From Smith's Forte to Grindon's Hill
{ Mr. Thomas Swann
John Bishop
William Mills

4. From Grindon's Hill and both sides of Lower Chippoke's Creek
{ Mr. Tho. Stampe
Stephen Webb
Erasmus Carter

5. For Lawn's Creek and Hogg Island
{ Mr. William Spence
Robert Latchett
John Dunston

6. For Sandy Point and Chicohominey Parish
{ Mr. Bridges Freeman
William Frye
William Morgan

7. For Thomas Harves, Pasby Haies, the Maine, and James's City
{ Mr. Rt. Hutchinson
Edward Oliver
Christ. Lawson

8. For the Neck of Land
{ Mr. David Mansell
George Malen
Edward Wigg

9. For

9. For the Gleab Land, Archer's Hope, Jockies Neck, and the Rich Neck

> Mr. Ro. Brewſter
> John Davis
> John Thompſon

10. For the eaſterly ſide of Archer's Hope Creek to Warome's Ponds

> Cap. Hm. Higginſon
> Nicholas Cummins
> Thomas Browne

11. From Warome's Ponds to Peter Ridley's

> Mr. Fer. Franklin
> Reynold Jones
> Ralph Looney

12. For the weſt ſide of Keith's Creek

> Mr. Thomas Cauſey
> William Shute
> John Hayward

Warwick River County.

1. For the upper part of Warwick River ſo far as the Pariſh of Denby extendeth, and down to the upper ſide of Bachelor's Hope Creek, and Standley Hundred

> Capt. Wm. Peirce
> Francis James
> Ro. Symonds

2. From the lower ſide of Batchelor's Hope Creek down to the upper ſide of Water Creek

> Mr. Tho. Barnard
> Tho. Rainſhawe
> Francis Rice

3. For

3. For the Parish of { Mr. Tho. Harwood
Mulberry Island and { Ro. Burtt
Keith's Creek { Wm. Whittaker

4. From the lower side { Mr. Zachary Cripps
of Water's Creek to { George Stratton
the lower part of the { Thomas Moore
County

Isle of Wight County.

1. From Lawne's Creek { Mr. Wm. Barnett
to Castle Creek { Rd. Jackson
{ Wm. Lawson

2. From Castle Creek to { Mr. Justice Cooper
the Alps. { Henry King
{ William Ellis

3. From the Alps to { Mr. Peter Hull
Basses Choice and the { Lawrence Ward
Indian Field { John Sparkman

4. From the Indian Field { Mr. Arthur Smith
to the Level and so on { Joseph Cobb
both sides the Creek { Robert Boyde

5. From the Road Point { Mr. Jos. Salmon
to the Head of Pagan { John Mills
Point Creek { George Rawles

6. From

6. From   Hampſtead } Mr. John Lewin
   Point to Mr. Robert } William Crannage
   Pitts   } William Lewis

Upper Norfolk County.

1. From Mr. Bullock's } Mr. Tho. Burbage
   Houſe to Newman's } James Knott
   Point   } John Parrott

2. From   Newman's } Mr. Tho. Drewe
   Point to the head of } William Parker
   the River and Tuck- } William Tucker
   er's Neck   }

3. From Mr. Gookin's } Mr. John Hill
   to the weſternmoſt } John Benton
   branch of Matraver's } Francis Moulde
   River   }

4. From Samuel Grif- } Mr. Olive Spry
   fin's to Mr. Raye's } Tho. Emmerſon
                       } Peter Johnſon

5. For the weſtern ſide } Mr. William Eyers
   of Chuck-a-tuck from } Rd. Preſt
   the Ragged Iſlands to } Epaphroditus Law
   the head of the Creek }

Lower

Lower Norfolk County

1. From Capt. Wil-
loughbys to Daniel
Tanner's Creek
{ Capt. T. Willoughby
William Ship
Robert Jones

2. From the Weftern
Branch to Elizabeth
River
{ Lieut. Fran. Macon
Henry Cattelyne
Thomas Wright

3. For Danl. Tanner's
Creek and the eaftern
branch on both fides
{ Mr. William Julian
John Gater
George Fawden

4. For the fouthern
branch on both fides
{ Capt. John Sibfey
Thomas Meeres
Robert Martin

5. For the Little Creek
and Eaftern Shore
{ Mr. Henry Sewell
Robert Hayes
Chrs. Burrowes

6. For the fouth fide of
the River
{ Mr. Edw. Windham
John Stratton
Thomas Keeling

Ackowmack County.

1. From Hungars
{ Capt. Wm. Stone
Armeftrong Fofter
John Mayor

M   2. From

2. From Mr. Bugley's to the King's Creek
{ Mr. Wm. Andrews
John Webſter
Jas. Barnaby

3. From the King's Creek to the Old Plantation Creek on that ſide
{ Capt. Wm. Roper
Elias Hartree
Jonathan Gibbs

4. From Mr. Neal's upwards to Mr. Littleton's
{ Mr. Nath. Littleton
Luke Stubbins
Henry Wade

5. From Mr. Littleton's and all on that ſide
{ Mr. Wm. Burdett
Henry Bagwell
Wm. Berryman

Elizabeth City County.

1. From Harris's Creek to Far Hill, and to Hampton River
{ Mr. Leonard Yeo
John Branch
Sam. Parry

2. For the ſouth ſide of the Back River
{ Mr. John Arundall
John Robinſon
Nicholas Brown

3. For the Old Poquoſon, from the beginning of the Damms to Mrs. Pureſies
{ Mr. Peter Stafferton
Gilbert Perkins
George Hull

6

4. From

4. From Mrs. Purefies's to Mr. Eaton's { Mr. Symon Purefie
Wm. Armstead
Thomas Burges

5. From William Parry's houfe to the utter-moft end of the County { Mr. Thomas Culey
Samuel Jackfon
Danl. Tanner

Charles's River County.

1. From Back Creek for the fouth fide of Capt. Wormeley's Creek { Mr. John Chew
John Lilley
Abraham Englifh

2. From the weft fide of Capt. Wormeley's Creek upwards as far as the Parifh extends { Capt. Rd. Townfend
Nath. Warren
Wm. Nottingham

3. For the weftern fide of Queen's Creek { M. Hugh Gwyn
Anth. Parkhurft
Jof. Crofhaw

4. From the lower fide of the Parifh to the eaftern fide of Capt. Utye's Creek { Capt. Nich. Martin
William Sayer
Nich. Stillwell

5. From the weftern fide of Cap. Utye's Creek and eaftern fide of Queen's Creek and the Middle Plantation { Mr. William Pryor
Rd. Davis
John Harwell

M 2   6. For

6. For the north fide of the new Poquofon River

- Capt. Jnᵒ. Cheefman
- John Jackfon
- Arthur Makeworth

7. For the fouth fide of new Poquofon River

- Mr. Tho. Curtis
- George Saphur
- Robert Lucas

The Oath of the viewers to be as followeth :

" *You fhall fwear diligently to view, and faith-fully, without favour, malice, partiality, or affec-tion, to burn all rotten and unmerchantable tobacco according to your beft judgment, which fhall be fhewn to you within your limits ; as alfo you fhall fwear faithfully and duely to obferve and keep the act of affembly concerning burning of half the good tobacco which fhall be, or be known to be, within your limits.*

" Which faid viewers being fworn according to the abovefaid oath, upon viewing of any man's crop of tobacco, what they fhall find ground leaves, rotten, or any otherwife unmer-chantable, are to fee it burned ; and what they fhall find good and merchantable they the faid viewers fhall feal with the feal appointed for meafuring of barrells, and inferted in the mar-gin. And to avoid all connivance that may be ufed by one viewer towards another, it is thought fit that the commander of every county

fhall

shall make choice of some able persons to be also sworn by the commander, who upon viewing of the tobacco belonging to the viewers are to do and execute as aforesaid. It is further enacted that if any viewers which now are, or which hereafter, shall be appointed, shall be neglectfull, remifs, or shall use delay in the executing of their office, that each viewer in case of such neglect, remission, or delay, shall forfeit five pounds sterling per day : the one moiety whereof shall be and come to the king, and the other to the publick use. Provided always, that it shall be free and lawfull for the said viewers or any of them to follow their own occasions, and respite the execution of their office two days in every week, notwithstanding any thing in this act to the contrary. Provided also that the planters shall have several days respite after publication hereof, to sort their tobacco : in which time the viewers are to provide themselves with seals. And it is ordered, and enjoined, that if any planter or person whatsoever, shall pay, receive, or put on board any ship or ships, any tobaccos before the same have been viewed and allowed by the viewers to be good and merchantable, and sealed with the aforesaid seal : he or they so offending shall forfeit double the quantity so

M 3   shipped

ſhipped and delivered ; the one moiety whereof ſhall be to the king and the other to the viewer of that precinct from whence the tobacco was firſt paid, and to the informer. And to prevent all neglects of this ſervice, which may be occaſioned either through ſickneſs or death of any of the viewers, the commander of the county ſhall have power, and is hereby authoriſed to appoint, and to give oath to ſome able perſon or perſons. And becauſe by ſuch burning only of the bad tobacco as aforeſaid, it cannot be preſumed that the tobacco will be reduced to the deſired quantity of fifteen hundred thouſand pounds in the whole of this year's growth : It is further enacted by this general aſſembly that all the tobacco be forthwith viewed and ſealed as aforeſaid ; and it ſhall not be lawfull for any perſon whatſoever to export or lade on board any ſhip or ſhips any quantity of tobacco either in leaf or rolls, before the viewers from whence the tobacco is to be ſhipped be acquainted therewith ; who are to adminiſter an oath to the owners or agent of or for the tobacco to be ſo ſhipped, viz. ſuch of the ſaid viewers as are qualified thereto by the place of comiſſioner, that he ſhall account to them for the full and entire quantity of his tobacco within the ſaid limitt ;

and

and if any perfon or perfons whatfoever fhall
conceal any part or parcell of tobacco fo intended, or which fhall be fhipped, from the
knowledge of the viewers, and of fuch conceal-
ment fhall be lawfully convicted, he or they
for fuch offence fhall forfeit double the quantity thereof, half to the king, and the other half
to the viewers of that limitt from whence the
tobacco is fhipped, and to the informer; and
befides fhall fuffer the punifhment due for per-
jury according to the laws of England.   And
the faid viewers are hereby authorized and required to fee and caufe to be burned in their
prefence half the tobacco which fhall be fhewn
to them upon oath as aforefaid, either belonging to any perfon or perfons in England, or
within the colony, or elfewhere, provided always that it fhall be lawful for any perfon
having fundry parcells of tobacco in one and
the fame county, to burn a number of hogfheads of tobacco remaining in one place; and
having a certificate from the viewers of the
limitt that he hath clearly burned fo many
hogfheads of tobacco, viz. without any allowance of a half not to be burned, in fuch cafe
it fhall be lawfull for the viewers of another
limitt within the fame county, to fpare him
the like number of hogfheads without burning

half

half of them, fo as the parcell which it is defired to be fpared from burning exceed not in
weight the parcell entirely burned in any confiderable quantity which muft be cleared and
known by fuch certificates as aforefaid. And
to the intent to remove all obftacles and dif-
couragements which may flacken the endeavour and care of the viewers in the execution
of their office, viz. as well in burning all the
bad and ill conditioned tobacco as half the good
and merchantable; all commanders, and all
other officers, and all his majefty's fubjects, are
required to be aiding and affifting to them
therein, as they will anfwer the contrary. And
in cafe any perfon fhall refufe to fhew his tobacco to the intent the fame may not be viewed
and the bad tobacco burned, as alfo half the
good deftroyed and burned, by locking it up:
in fuch cafe where no other means will prevail
(perfuafion being firft ufed and the perfon ftill
perfifting refractory), it fhall be lawful for the
viewers to break open the doors of any houfe
wherein in likelihood the tobacco of fuch perfons may be concealed, to be for the better
execution of their offices therein, to which
this act doth authorize them without further
warrant on that behalf. And whereas the
fubfcribers do further propound that for thefe

two

two enfuing years the colony may be regulated to twelve hundred thoufand pounds of tobacco per annum, and no more; and that likewife to be ftripped and fmoothed, in confideration whereof they are content to accept of forty pounds of tobacco for one hundred due to them for goods fold, untill or before publication : which is conceived by the affembly to be intended before publication of the act; provided the faid forty pounds of tobacco for every hundred be paid unto them, or every of them, or their, or every of their affigns, at fuch feveral times as the faid tobacco fhall grow due unto them. Notwithftanding which faid provifo which doth ftreightly engage the debtor to pay his debt at the date of his fpecialty, upon forfeiture in cafe of failing of the forefaid abatement of fixty pounds in the hundred; it appeareth by teftimonial under the hand of the governor and divers of the councill and others, that it was not intended by the fubfcribers, neither is it conceived that the faid abatement fhould be forfeited, in cafe payment be made of two thirds of the proportion to which they are reftrained within the time of two years next enfuing: which is intended to be for two crops after this prefent crop of tobacco. It is therefore enacted as near as may be to cor-

3   refpond

refpond with the propofitions of the faid fubfcribers, that no perfon or perfons whatfoever,
within the colony, for thefe two enfuing years,
fhall make above the proportion or quantity of
one hundred and feventy pounds of tobacco
per poll.   Which faid proportion of one hundred and feventy pounds of tobacco per poll,
doth amount (by computation according to
the lift) to the quantity of twelve hundred
thoufand pounds of tobacco; in the whole
thirteen hundred thoufand pounds of tobacco;
which faid overplus of one hundred thoufand
pounds of tobacco the affembly doth think fitt
to add to the twelve hundred thoufand pounds
of tobacco, to defray all public charges and impofitions, being after the rate of twenty pounds
per poll : in refpect they conceive it a burden
no way tolerable for the inhabitants to dif-
charge all tolls and impofitions neceffitated upon them, fuch as falaries for publick offices,
and fupport of public buildings, to which his
majefty's inftructions enjoin them out of the
faid quantity of twelve hundred thoufand
pounds of tobacco, being but after the rate of
one hundred and fifty pounds per poll.   Neither doth the affembly conceive that they fhall
exceed the rate propounded by the fubfcribers,
by fuch overplus, in refpect of the great lofs of
weight

weight and fhrinkage known to happen to tobacco in paffing fo long a voyage by fea. Provided always, notwithftanding any thing in
this act to the contrary, that if any monopoly
or contract be impofed upon the commodity
that this act is to be void and of none effect.

" Whereas fundry perfons upon knowledge
had of the great quantity of tobacco planted
this year within the colony may be prefumed
to be covenanted and agreed with merchants
and others dealing in fhipping to lade certain
tons of tobacco aboard their fhips at a rate conditioned by them, or to pay dead freight or
fome other forfeit in cafe of their non performance : whereto by this courfe of burning and
deftroying the tobacco they may in all likelihood, to their great damage and prejudice, be
difabled. Be it therefore enacted for the better
relief of all fuch perfons, who by juft proof
fhall make it appear that they are materially
difabled by this act of burning the tobacco, to
perform their conditions, and not from any
other caufe or ground, viz. that they had provided ready in cafk, the proportion of tons
agreed upon, one half whereof was deftroyed
according to order, that in fuch cafe fuch perfons fhall not be obliged to perform above half
the

the tenor of his condition, and so proportionable in the like cases.

Whereas divers persons by reason of the late proclamation prohibiting (untill further orders from this assembly) all trade and commerce for tobacco, have been enforced to supply the necessity themselves, and their servants, to engage themselves for the payment of money for commodities taken up by them which they are not to perform. Be it therefore enacted, that in such case the merchants shall rate commodities as low as they cost them the first purchase in England with petty charges; and the debtor shall lade in the name of the creditor, on board such ship as he shall like and approve on, so much tobacco as shall be satisfactory for his debt at the rate of three pence per pound, as also so much tobacco at the rate of three pence per pound as shall satisfy the merchant or creditor for his adventure at the rate of thirty pounds per ct.; and if it shall happen that the tobacco shipped as aforesaid shall produce any overplus to the principal debt as aforesaid, the rate of thirty pounds per ct. being likewise satisfied, that then the creditor shall be accomptable for the same to the debtor. But in case the tobacco shipped as aforesaid shall not produce the sum satisfactory as aforesaid,

said, that then the debtor shall satisfie the same the ensueing year, with an allowance after the rate of eight pounds per ct. for forbearance. Provided that this act shall not extend to any other debt made and due in money, but to such ones as have arisen and become due since the date of the proclamation prohibiting all trade and commerce for tobacco as aforesaid. Provided also, that notwithstanding any thing in this act to the contrary, it shall be lawfull for any debtor to pay and satisfie the creditor, or to compound his debt by any other way and means than by such course set and expressed in this said act. Provided also, that it shall be lawfull for the debtor to consign his tobacco to any friend in England, who upon payment of the debt and charges within twenty days after the unlading of the ship at the port of London, is to receive the same. Whereas also since the publishing of the aforesaid proclamation prohibiting trade and commerce for tobacco during a time therein limitted, divers persons have bargained for commodities upon condition to pay for the same in tobacco as it shall be rated by this assembly : it is thought fit that in such cases tobacco shall pass at the rate of three pence per pound, and likewise the remainder that

shall

ſhall be in the hands of the planters after their debts are ſatisfied ſhall not be difpoſed of under three pence per pound at the firſt penny.

" To prevent the exceſſive rates of freight and tonnage for goods exported from the colony, it is enacted, that no perſons whatſoever, after publication of this act, ſhall give above the rate of ſix pounds for freight per ton, the ton to conſiſt of four Virginia hogſheads according to the ſize ; neither ſhall any merchant, maſter of a ſhip, or any other perſon dealing for ſhipping exact above the rate of ſix pounds per ton, upon ſuch penalty and cenſure as ſhall be thought fit by the governor and council ; provided that this act or the penalty thereof ſhall not extend to ſuch perſon or perſons who before the publication of this ſaid act had bargained and agreed for a greater price per ton.

" Be it alſo enacted, that if any perſon having debts due unto him in tobacco ſhall not demand the ſame before the tenth of May next enſuing, after which date, if the creditor ſhall lawfully tender the ſame before witneſs, and the debtor ſhall notwithſtanding refuſe to receive it, that in ſuch caſe it ſhall be lawfull for the debtor to call the viewers for the ſaid plantation or limitt, upon whoſe certificate to any

court

court or courts, within the colony, of the goodnefs of the faid tobacco, and of the quantity equal to the debt in queftion, the debtor fhall be difcharged of the faid debt, provided he do not convert the faid tobacco to any other ufe, and that he be carefull to preferve the fame from damage or fpoiling: neither is it intended that the faid debtor fhall ftand to all hazards of fire, or other accidents for the fame.

" Whereas it is thought fit as aforefaid, that the quantity of one hundred thoufand pounds of tobacco overplus, befides the twelve hundred thoufand propounded by the fubfcribers, be planted per annum for three enfuing years, being after the rate of twenty pounds per poll ; by which addition the proportion of one hundred and fifty pounds per poll, amounting by computation to twelve hundred thoufand pounds of tobacco, is augmented and enlarged to the proportion of one hundred and feventy pounds per poll; which faid twenty pounds per poll is for the defraying as aforefaid of all public charges and impofitions.

" It is now thought fit by the affembly to order and difpofe of the faid twenty pounds per poll to the ufes hereunder mentioned, viz.

" To the minifters for their duties ten pounds of tobacco per poll for every titheable perfon, perſon, out of which proportion the miniſters to maintain their clerks and ſextons.

" The muſter maſter general three pounds of tobacco per poll for every tithable perſon ; to be collected and paid by the ſeveral ſheriffs.

" To the captain of the forte, for his entertainment and maintenance, and for the procuring and maintaining of ten guarders for the forte, three pounds of tobacco per poll for every tithable perſon ; to be collected and paid by the ſeveral ſheriffs as aforeſaid.

" And whereas upon conſideration of the repairing of the forte, it was conceived by the aſſembly to be a vain and fruitleſs endeavour in regard of the apparent decay of the foundation, it is therefore thought fit that there be levied the next year by the ſheriffs two pounds of tobacco per poll for every tithable perſon, toward the making and erecting of a plattforme at Point Comforte, whereon to mount the ordnance, and alſo for the building of a convenient houſe for the ſaid captain, which ſaid two pounds of tobacco per poll is to be paid by the ſheriffs to ſuch ſurveyor or officer as ſhall be appointed by the governor and council to overſee the work : That there be alſo levied the next year by the ſheriffs as aforeſaid two pounds of tobacco for every tith-

able

able perſon throughout the colony, for and towards the building of a ſtate houſe, which is
alſo to be paid by the ſeveral ſheriffs to ſuch
ſurveyor or officer as ſhall be appointed by the
governor and council to overſee the work ;
Which ſaid ſeveral levies, or any other,
amounting in the whole to
pounds of tobacco per poll being paid, it is
thought fit that the remainder be deemed an
overplus of one hundred and fifty pounds per
poll, which raiſeth the quantity of twelve hundred thouſand weight to be deſtroyed and
burned (drinking tobacco excepted).

" Whereas through the great debts and deep
engagements of divers of the inhabitants it
may be preſumed they cannot pay and ſatisfie
the ſame this preſent year, and will alſo be
diſabled to diſcharge them theſe two enſuing
years, as the regulation of tobacco to ſo ſmall
a proportion muſt of conſequence bring a great
calamity and diſtreſs upon divers poor men,
even to the loſs and hazards of liberty and live-
lyhood unleſs ſome courſe be taken for redreſs
therein.

" Be it therefore enacted, for their relief in
the premiſes, that all ſuch perſons being at the
publication hereof engaged to pay debts beyond their abilities to ſatisfie their creditors

N   this

this prefent year, fhall not be compelled to pay or fatisfy more than two thirds of their debts for this prefent year, and for the two enfuing years ; nor any farther than two thirds of their crop of tobacco ; but that it fhall be lawfull for them to referve the other third for and towards their neceffary fubfiftance, without any moleftation by or from their creditors ; to which end and purpofe it is farther eftablifhed that no execution fhall pafs againft the bodies or eftates of any debtors as aforefaid, for or concerning the faid third during the time of the two enfuing years.

" Be it alfo enacted for the better advancement of the price of tobacco, that no perfon or perfons whatfoever fhall barter, fell, or put away any of the tobacco of the growth of the enfuing year within the colony under the full value and rate of twelve pence per pound, upon the penalty or forfeiture of his or their whole crop or crops of tobacco ; the one half whereof fhall be to the informer, and the other to the public ufe. And that no perfon fhall barter, fell, or put away any of the tobacco of the growth of the following year, viz. anno 1641, under the full value and rate of two fhillings per pound ; and under fuch penalties as aforefaid.

Hence

Hence we learn the rude and imperfect state of those inspection laws which the progress of time and experience has so amply improved and concentrated; and it appears to be about this period that tobacco was introduced in lieu of specie, as a kind of circulating medium, and as the measure of price and value in Virginia negociations: a local practice of that country where a man is as well understood when he says *I will give you ten hogsheads of tobacco for your horse*, as if he offered you one hundred guineas or pounds.

We perceive in this law, that the custom of passing tobacco current in payments had so far obtained ground, that the parson made no scruple of receiving this luxurious article for preaching; or the clerk for bawling out amen! And that the military officer thought it no way dishonourable to his profession to draw his pay in this specific article of traffic. At the general assembly of the succeeding year we are furnished with the following specimen on a larger scale of public payments; and we may here also discover one of those early instances of right honourable reconciliation to private interest which palliated this traffic in the hands of a colonial governor, and ultimately involved the supreme executive, and the whole legion

N 2

of

of taxes in the commerce of Virginia, until a very recent period.

Even the tavern keepers were compelled to exchange a dinner for a few pounds of tobacco: for their rates were fixed in this specific commodity at this subsequent assembly. But a still more striking evidence of its general currency will be found in the following act.

" Whereas it appeareth to the assembly that the colony standeth engaged for arrears due to several persons the quantity of thirty-nine thousand two hundred twenty-three pounds of tobacco ; whereas also many important occasions nearly concerning the public weal of the colony, do necessarily require the agency of some persons of quality and experience in the affairs of the country, which, besides the care and pains of the said agents, must, of consequence, be accompanied with great and extraordinary expence and charge : the persons to be nominated by the governor and council, and the instructions given by them. It is therefore thought fit, that for a reward and recompence to such persons for their care and pains, and for the defraying of the charges there shall be levied this year four pounds of tobacco per poll for every tithable person throughout the colony ;

lony ; amounting in the whole to eighteen thoufand five hundred eighty four pounds of tobacco. Whereas likewife it is thought fit that there be levied four pounds of tobacco per poll for every tithable perfon throughout the colony, for the ufe of the governor, as a free and voluntary gift from the colony, amounting as aforefaid to eighteen thoufand four hundred eighty-four pounds of tobacco.

" It is therefore enacted that there be levied this year by the fheriff for the difcharging of the aforefaid payment, feventeen pounds of tobacco per poll for every tithable perfon throughout the colony, which faid payments are to be made by the feveral fheriffs to the perfons, and for the ufe hereafter mentioned, viz.

Pounds of Tobacco

" That the fheriff of Warwick County fhall pay unto Captain Samuel Mathews 5219
" The fheriff of Lower Norfolk County unto the faid Captain Mathews . . . 5610
" The fheriff of Elizabeth County unto the faid Captain Mathews . . . 5541
" The fheriff of the Ifle of Wight County unto the faid Captain Mathews 4752

" Which faid feveral fums, amount-

N 3   ing

Pounds of
Tobacco

ing in the whole to twenty-one thousand twenty-three pounds of tobacco, are arrearages due to the said Captain Mathews 21023

" That the sheriff of Upper Norfolk shall pay unto Captain William Peirce and George Menifie, Esq. 8000

" Which said eight thousand pounds of tobacco is due to them the said Captain Peirce and Mr. George Menefie for demurrage of the ship Revenge, anno 1635, formerly discharged aud satisfied by them.

" That the sheriff of Elizabeth City shall pay unto Captain Robert Falgate five hundred pounds of tobacco for his charges in his employment as muster master 500

" That the sheriff of Charles's City shall pay unto Mr. John Neale . . . 8976

" That the sheriff of the Upper Norfolk shall pay unto the said Mr. Neale   224

" Which sums in the whole amount to the quantity of nine thousand two hundred pounds of tobacco, and is for so much disbursed by him, and was for-

8   merly

merly to be paid out of the levy of
twenty-fix pounds per poll 9200

"That the fheriff of Ackowmack
fhall pay unto Richard Smith for two
drums for the publick fervice 500

"That the fheriff of Charles's River
fhall pay unto fuch perfon as fhall be appointed by the governor and council for
the ufe of the agents 13073

"The fheriff of Henrico 3876

"Which faid feveral fums make in
the whole feventeen thoufand four hundred and forty-nine pounds of tobacco,
being after the rate of four pounds of tobacco per poll as aforefaid 17449

"That the fheriff of James's City fhall
pay unto the governor 13787

"That the fheriff of Ackowmack
County fhall pay unto the governor . . 4797

"In the whole eighteen thoufand five
hundred and eighty-four pounds of tobacco, as a voluntary and free gift from
the colony as aforefaid 18584

N 4   "That

Pounds of
Tobacco

" That the fheriff of Charles's County fhall pay unto Mr. John Corker, clerk of the affembly, one thoufand pounds of tobacco, out of the arrears of the laft levy 1000

(Signed)

Vera copia,

RICH. KEMP, *Secretary*."

This law for the regulation of payments in this fpecific ftaple is the firft of the kind which I have been able to find recorded. It bears date in the year 1640, and is cotemporary with a proclamation of the governor and council, which is founded upon the act of the colonial legiflature, paffed at James's Town the preceding year, 1639, concerning the reftraint and burning of tobacco, which its purport is to carry into execution. We learn from thefe laws how much the fubject of this ftaple was interwoven in the fpirit of the times; and how nearly the hiftory of the tobacco plant is allied to the chronology of an extenfive and flourifhing country, whofe meafures contribute greatly, even at this day, to give a tone to the affairs of the American union.

4   Shortly

Shortly after this period we find the records of that country fo copioufly filled with military tranfactions, that there feems to be little other notice taken of tobacco than what refpects the payment of guards and engineers, and the builders of batteries and fortifications. Probably the revolutionary fpirit of the approaching times occupied more of their attention, for we find them recorded to have held out loyally, and to have furrendered honourably.

Neither the articles of their capitulation with the Englifh republic, nor the act of indemnity which accompanies it, throw any particular light upon this fpecific hiftory, except what is to be inferred from the conciliatory tenor of thefe inftruments; but as they are the moft concife ftatement of the times which can be given, and may be new to fome perfons; and, more particularly, as they exhibit the picture of times in which the Solomons of the age were wont to run mad after a tobacco plant, I fhall be pardoned for inferting a tranfcript of this agreement from the archives of the prefent Virginia government.

Articles agreed on and concluded at James's Cittie in Virginia, for furrendering and fettling of that plantation under the obedience and government of the Commonwealth of England, by the Commiffioners

Commiſſioners of the Council of State, by autho-
ritie of the Parliament of England and by the
Grand Aſſembly of the Governour, Council and
Burgeſſes of that Country.

" 1. It is agreed and confented that the
plantation of Virginia, and all the inhabitants
thereof, fhall be and remain in due obedience
and fubjection to the Commonwealth of England, according to the laws there eftablifhed,
and that this fubmiffion and fubfcription be
acknowledged a voluntary act, not forced nor
conftrained by a conqueft upon the countrey,
and that they fhall have and enjoy fuch free-
domes and prevelidges as belong to the free
borne people of England, and that the former
government by the commiffions and inftructions be void and null.

" 2. That the grand affembly, as formerly,
fhall convene and tranfact the affairs of Virginia, wherein nothing is to be acted or done
contrarie to the government of the Commonwealth of England, and the lawes there eftablifhed.

" 3. That there fhall be a full and totall re-
miffion and indempnitie of all acts, words, or
writeings, done or fpokin againft the parliament of England in relation to the fame.

" 4. That Virginia fhall have and enjoy ye
antient

antient bounds and lymitts granted by the char-
tirs of the former kings, and that we fhall feek
a new chartir from the parliament to that purpofe againft any that have intrencht upon ye
rights thereof.

" 5. That all the pattents of land granted under the colony feale by any of the precedent
governours, fhall be and remaine in their full
force and ftrength.

" 6. That the privilidges of haveing ffiftie
acres of land for every perfon tranfported into
that colony fhall continue as formerly granted.

" 7. That ye people of Virginia have free
trade as ye people of England do enjoy to all
places and with all nations, according to ye
lawes of that commonwealth, and that Virginia fhall enjoy all privilidges equall with any
Englifh plantation in America.

" 8. That Virginia fhall be free from all
taxes, cuftoms, and impofitions, whatever, and
none to be impofed on them without confent
of the grand affembly; and foe that neither
ffortes nor caftles bee erected, or garrifons maintained without their confent.

" 9. That noe charge fhall be required from
this country in refpect of this prefent ffleet.

" 10. That for the future fettlement of the
countrey in their due obedience, the engagement

ment fhall be tendred to all ye inhabitants according to act of parliament made to that purpofe, that all perfons who fhall refufe to fubfcribe the faid engagement, fhall have a yeare's time, if they pleafe, to remove themfelves and their eftates out of Virginia, and in the mean time dureing the faid year to have equall juftice as formerly.

" 11. That ye ufe of the booke of common prayer fhall be permitted for one yeare enfueing with referrence to the confent of ye major part of the parifhes, provided that thofe things which relate to kingfhipp or that government, be not ufed publiquely, and the continuance of miniftirs in their places, they not mifdemeaning themfelves, and the payment of their accuftomed dues and agreements made with them refpectively, fhall be left as they now ftand dureing this enfueing yeare.

" 12. That no man's cattle fhall be queftioned as ye companies, unlefs fuch as have been entrufted with them, or have difpofed of them without order.

" 13. That all ammunition, powder, and armes, other than for private ufe, fhall be delivered up, fecuritie being given to make fatisfaction for it.

" 14. That all goods allreadie brought hither

ther by ye Dutch or others, which are now on fhoar, fhall be free from furprizall.

" 15. That the quittrents granted unto us by the late kings for feven yeares be confirmed.

" 16. That ye commiffioners for the parliament fubfcribing thefe articles, engage themfelves and the honour of the parliament for the full performance thereof: and that the prefent governour, and ye councill, and the burgeffes, do likewife fubfcribe and engage the whole collony on their parts.

RICHARD BENNETT.   Seale.
WM. CLAIBORNE.   Seale.
EDMUND CUSTIS."   Seale.

Thefe articles were figned and fealed by the commiffioners of the councill of ftate for the Commonwealth of England, the 12th day of March, 1651.

An Act of Indemnitie made at the furrender of the Countrey.

" Whereas by the authoritie of the parliament of England, we the commiffioners appointed by the councill of ftate authorized thereto having brought a fleete and force before James's cittie in Virginia to reduce that colonie under obedience

obedience of the commonwealth of England, and findeing force raifed by the governour and countrey to make oppofition againft the faid ffleete, whereby affured danger appearinge of the ruin and deftruction of ye plantation, for prevention whereof the burgeffes of all the feverall plantations being called to advife and affift therein, upon long and ferious debate, and in fad contemplation of the greate mifferies and certaine diftruction which were foe neerely hovering over the whole countrey; We the faid commiffioners have thought fitt and condefcended and granted to figne and confirme under our hands, feales, and by our oath, articles bearinge date with theife prefents, and further declare that by ye authoritie of the parliament and commonwealth of England derived unto us theire commiffioners, that according to the articles in general wee have granted an act of indempnitie and oblivion to all the inhabitants of this coloney from all words, actions, or writings, that have been fpoken, acted, or written, againft the parliament or commonwealth of England, or any other perfon from the beginning of the world to this daye.   And this wee have done that all the inhabitants of the colonie may live quietly and fecurely under the commonwealth of England.

land. And we do promife that the parliament and commonwealth of England fhall confirme and make good all thofe tranfactions of ours. Witnefs our hands and feales this 12th day of March, 1651.

RICHARD BENNETT. Seale.
WM. CLAIBORNE. Seale.
EDM. CUSTIS." Seale.

Of the more modern State of the Tobacco Trade.

Thus far we have reviewed the culture and commerce of tobacco from the earlieft knowledge of the plant. I lament that I am compelled to leave a kind of chafm in my defign to have given a regular and uninterrupted detail of this trade from the period at which we are here arrefted in our progrefs for want of document; for I have not been able to procure a copy of the Virginia laws in London, and feel the deficiency of many other interefting papers which are requifite to render the hiftory complete up to the prefent time; but which can only be procured on the other fide the ocean. We may difcover, however, from the nature of the foregoing articles of capitulation and indemnity, that this commerce muft have been greatly difordered by the intervention of civil wars; and thofe which immediately followed

with

with the French and with the Dutch, cannot, I think, have proved a much lighter interruption to the markets of this early traffic.

I find amongſt the colonial records about this period, various provincial acts for making tobacco a legal tender from individual to individual, as well as in diſcharge of public obligations: ſuch indeed was the ſmoking ſpirit of the times, that he who kept a public houſe was compelled to ſell a dinner or a draught of beer for an equivalent in tobacco leaves; and his tavern rates were regulated by the courts of juſtice in pounds of tobacco, a bill of which was publicly expoſed in his houſe for the information of his gueſts. It is eaſy to trace, from this foundation, the primitive cauſe for rendering tobacco the medium of value in the payment of coſts of ſuit, pariſh and county dues, and many other public demands of a like nature, which continued to be appendages of the regal juriſdiction until the period of the American revolution.

With reſpect to the foundation of impoſts, cuſtoms, exciſe, and ſuch like duties upon tobacco, Mr. Jefferſon recites the title of an act paſſed the 20th of June, 1644*, in the reign of Charles II, charging all tobacco brought

* Jefferſon's Notes, p. 308.

from

from New England with *cuftoms and excife*; and in the records of Virginia I find the following claufe, entered at a general court held at James's City the 28th of March, 1766.

" Whereas his moft facred majefty was gracioufly pleafed by his royal inftructions, dated 12th of September, in the 14th year of his reign, and in the year of our Lord one thoufand fix hundred fixty and two, to confirm to this his majefty's colony of Virginia *an impofition of two fhillings per hogfhead upon all tobacco exported*, with command that the moneys raifed by the faid impofts fhould be imployed for the fupport of the government there, and for the advancement of manufacture and diverfe other good defigns for the advantage of this his majefty's colony; and, whereas, this laft year, feveral fhips, together with their loading, have been taken on their return home from hence by the Dutch men of war, though none went but in fleets according to the command of his majefty and the lords of his moft honourable privy council, except fome few who went contrary to exprefs command : one of which, viz. the Ruffel, of Topham, was taken ; and whereas many of the merchants upon the faid fhip, taken as aforefaid have defired a reimburfement of the faid impoft paid for their goods fo

O   loft,

loft, with fuch limitations as are expreffed in an act of parliament, intituled, "An Act for Tunnage and Poundage," the governour and council taking the premifes into their moft ferious confideration, and withal confidering the prefent great expence of this colony, occafioned by building a fort for the neceffary defence of fhipping, and providing themfelves againft any attempt reafonable to be expected from a foreign enemy, and fuch as are at prefent threatened from our bordering Indians confederated with remoter nations; and having little elfe, by reafon of the prefent extreme low value of tobacco, either to compafs thofe good ends, or defray the charges aforefaid, befides the very fmall revenue raifed of the faid impoft of two fhillings per hogfhead, have thought fit to order, and it is hereby accordingly ordered, that, all fuch repayments to be made upon goods loft as aforefaid, fhall be fufpended until it fhall be declared by his majefty and the lords of his moft honourable privy council, whether the faid impoft being fo fmall, and defigned and imployed for fo many important ends, doth fall within the compafs and equity of the faid act for tunnage and poundage, or not; and if it fhall be judged in the affirmative, that then whether we fhall make fuch repayments according

cording to the faid rules in the faid act pre-
fcribed; or, whether confidering our prefent
great and preffing neceffities, we fhall have a
longer time given us for the fame; to all or
any of which decifions we fhall moft humbly
pay ready obedience, and to all other com-
commands of that moft honourable board."

Mr. Jefferfon fays *, that Virginia exported,
communibus annis, antecedent to the American
war, about fifty-five thoufand hogfheads of tobacco, of one thoufand pounds weight each
hogfhead, and that in the year 1758, they exported feventy thoufand hogfheads; which was
the greateft quantity of tobacco ever produced
in that country in one year.

Mr. John Henry (author of a map of Virginia) tells us in a note affixed to that map,
about the year 1769, or 1770, that the ftaple
trade of Virginia is *tobacco*; but that it does
not yield much to the planter, notwithftanding that above fifty or fixty thoufand hogfheads
are exported, *communibus annis*, to Great Britain.
" Yet," adds he, " as feventeen thoufand tons
of Britifh fhipping are employed, and many
thoufand Britifh inhabitants are fupported
thereby, it is very valuable to the fubjects; and

---

* Jefferfon's Notes, p. 276.

may

may be alfo faid to be a jewel to the crown, *as fo large a fum arifes out of the duties.*"

The country, indeed, is very capable of improvement in every part of it ; and there is no doubt but much more tobacco might be made if the inhabitants were difpofed to extend their powers to this object ; but it remains with time to decide, how far the Virginians will extend the policy of this ftaple : within my day I have no doubt of its *comparative* decline in proportion to the extent of agriculture ; and where-ever this change for a different fpecies of culture fubftitutes the features of content and plenty in the room of poverty and wretched-nefs, it is certainly a change that fhould gladden the heart of man.

Previous to the American war, fome accounts have ftated the exports of Virginia and Maryland at *eighty thoufand hogfheads communibus annis :* the freight of this tobacco in Britifh bottoms, at thirty fhillings per hogfhead, amounting to one hundred and twenty thoufand pounds fterling, per annum, in favour of Britifh navigation.

Between the years 1786 and 1789, the amount of tobacco exported from Virginia, as ftated in the official returns to the folicitor's office, were as follows :

From

Hogſheads.

From October, 1786, to October, 1787, . . . 60,041
From October, 1787, to October, 1788, . . . 58,545
From October, 1788, to October, 1789, . . . 58,673

According to the Level of Europe and America, p. 97, 98, the exportation of tobacco from Virginia * was conſiderable from 1752 to 1755. From 1763 to 1770, it diminiſhed in ſuch a manner that in the interval of thoſe two periods it was reduced to an average of 67,780 hogſheads each year : this, ſays the Level, has been aſcribed by ſome to the cultivation of the ſame production in Holland, Alſace, Palatine, and Ruſſia ; which muſt, as it increaſed, have leſſened the demand upon America.

In the article of tobacco during the foregoing periods, the conſumption in England is ſaid to have advanced to 41,170 hogſheads. According to the account and the balance of imports and exports beween Great Britain and the American Colonies, laid before parliament for eleven years preceding 1774, the advantage annually advanced to about 1,500,000 pounds ſterling. The yearly amount of the payment into the exchequer, according to the account of the duties upon tobacco, from

* Perhaps Maryland was included in this calculation.

1770 to 1774, was 219,117 pounds fterling. One half of this tobacco was imported into Scotland, and four-fifths of that half was exported to France, Holland, Germany, and other countries.

* In 1775, the duties on tobacco arofe to £298,002 fterling. The duties upon this tobacco were fo exceffively high, that in the fame year 131 hogfheads of tobacco, exported on account of a merchant in Charlefton, for Briftol in England, produced to the proprietor but £1307. 4. 1½ fterling. The excife with the nett proceeds amounted to £4912. 8. 0¼ As a better elucidation of this fact the account of fales is hereunto annexed.

Sales of 131 hogfheads of tobacco, fhipped in Charlefton, South Carolina, on the fhip Lively, Captain G. Carter, for Briftol, on account of Mr. L. F. 1775.

Freight at £32. 6. per
   Ton 212 7 6
Premium 10 12 9
Average 9 16 0
                            —————   232 6 9
Duties of entry on 109,280 lb.
   old and new tax, at 3½ per lb. 341 10 0
Additional duty on the new tax
   ⅓, tax 47,59, and impoft at

* Level of Europe.

                                    the

the rate of $7\frac{1}{3}$, deducting 15
per cent. 2838   4   9
Gifts, landing, and carriage   5 17   0
Cooperage, 1s. 6d. per ton ⎫
Addition, 7d.   ⎬   13 12 11
                                     ⎭
Cellarage, 1, weighing, 4 ds.   8 14   8
Premium of infurance on £800
at 40, Policy 13 . . . .   16 13   0
Commiffion and bad debts at 3
per cent.   147   7   6
Nett proceeds . . . . . . 1912 10 $8\frac{1}{2}$

Total £4912 10 $9\frac{1}{2}$

Sold and delivered at different
times to fundry perfons from
the 15th of November, 1775,
to the 16th of January, 1776,
at $8\frac{3}{4}$, $10\frac{1}{2}$, according to the
quality 4762   9   2
For 9 months difcount on
£2834. 4. 9. at 7 per cent.
per annum 149   2   2
Bounty on 573 lb. at $\frac{1}{2}$ per lb.
for average   1   1 $5\frac{1}{2}$

£4912 10 $9\frac{1}{2}$

O 4   According

According to this ftatement, the correfpondent has but 3 per cent. commiffion, that is to fay, £147. 7. 6. fterling; but the charges, taxes, duties, impofts, and additional burdens, deftroy more than 3-4ths of the value of the tobacco, as there remains to the proprietor out of £4912. 10. 8½, but £1912. 10. 8½, and thus the duties have fwallowed up £3448 fterling.

Mr. Morfe tells us (in page 500 of Stockdale's 4to. edition of his Geography), that in the year fucceeding October, 1790, Virginia exported only about 40,000 hogfheads of tobacco : the following abftract from the *official* accounts of the treafury, are, perhaps, the *beft* kind of authority.

Amount of Tobacco exported from the United States of America for the years following, viz.

Hogfheads

From Aug. 1789, to Sep. 1790, the total exports 118,460
From Oct. 1, 1790, to Sep. 30, 1791   .   .   . 101,272

Whereof, from New Hampfhire   7
　　　　　　Maffachufetts   1190
　　　　　　Rhode Ifland   743
　　　　　　Connecticut   499
　　　　　　New York   1290

New

Hogſheads

New Jerſey	7
Pennſylvania	1928
Maryland	25019
Virginia	56288
N. Carolina	4772
S. Carolina	3708
Georgia	5821
Total Hogſheads————101272	

From October 1, 1791, to September 30, 1792.

	Manufactured lbs.	Hogſheads
New Hampſhire		3
Maſſachuſetts . . .	110525 and	1221
Rhode Iſland		1429
Connecticut		105
New York	1600 and	1952
New Jerſey		5
Pennſylvania	2140 and	3203
Delaware		8
Maryland	780 and	28992
Virginia	2025 —	61203
North Carolina		3546
South Carolina . . .	624 and	5290
Georgia	180 —	5471
Total	117874	112428

From October 1, 1792, to September 30, 1793.

Total	137784	59947

From

From October 1, 1793, to September 30, 1794.

	Manufactured lbs.	Hogsheads.
Total	19370	72958

From October 1, 1794, to September 30, 1795.

Total	20263	61050

From October 1, 1795, to September 30, 1796.

Total	29181	69018

From October 1, 1796, to September 30, 1797.

Total	12805	58167

From October 1, 1797, to September 30, 1798.

Total	142268	68567

A Statement exhibiting the Amount of Drawbacks paid on dutiable Tobacco exported from the United States, in the Years 1793, 1794, *and* 1795.

1793.		1794.		1795.	
Duties	Drawback	Duties	Drawback	Duties	Drawback
Dolls. Cents	Dolls. Cents	Dolls. Cents	Dolls. Cents	Dolls. Cents	Dolls. Cents
898 26	444 49	1890 16	272 59	4255 04	18 59

From these different statements, a tolerable approximate information may be obtained touching the progress of the tobacco trade,

8   from

from the earlieft introduction of this ftaple into Europe. If it had been poffible to have procured the neceffary materials from America, without delaying the prefs, I fhould have endeavoured to have made this account more fatisfactory ; and I will not neglect to do it in an appendix, if I fhould be able to find any thing ufeful. As this may, however, be a doubtful point, which may leave the fubject open to others, I beg leave to add, for their affiftance, a fchedule of laws and ftate papers, with which Mr. Jefferfon's notes have furnifhed me.

A Schedule of Proclamations, Laws, and State Papers, touching the Culture and Commerce of the Plant Nicotiana, extracted from Jefferfon's Notes on Virginia.

Commiffio fpecialis concernens le garbling herbæ Nicotianæ.   1620, April 7.   18 Jac. I. —17 Rym. 190.

A Proclamation for the Reftraint of the difordered Trading of Tobacco.   June 29.   18 Jac. I.—17 Rym. 233.

A Proclamation concerning Tobacco.   1624, September 29.   22 Jac. I.—17 Rym 621.

A Proclamation for the utter prohibiting the Importation

Importation and Ufe of all Tobacco which is not of the proper Growth of the Colony of Virginia and the Somer Iflands, or one of them.   1625, Mar. 2.   22 Jac. I.—17 Rym. 668.

Proclamatio de herba Nicotiana.   1625, April 9.   1 Car. I.—18 Rym. 19.

A Proclamation touching Tobacco.   1626, Feb. 17.   2 Car. I.—Rym. 848.

De Proclamatione de Signatione de Tobacco. 1627, Mar. 30.   3 Car. I.—18 Rym. 886.

De Proclamatione pro Ordinatione de To-bacco. 1627, Auguft 9.   3 Car. I.—18 Rym. 920.

A Proclamation concerning Tobacco. 1630, Jan. 6.   5 Car. I.—19 Rym. 235.

A Proclamation to prevent Abufes growing by the unordered retailing of Tobacco.   1633, Aug. 13.   9 Car. I.—Mentioned 3 Rufhworth, 191.

A Proclamation for preventing Abufes grow-ing by the unordered retailing of Tobacco. 1633, October 13.   9 Car. I.—19 Rym. 474.

A Proclamation reftraining the abufive vend-ing of Tobacco.   1633, Mar. 13. Car. I.—19 Rym. 522.

A Proclamation concerning the landing of Tobacco, and alfo forbidding the planting

thereof

thereof in the King's Dominions. 1634, May 19. 10. Car. I.—19 Rym. 553.

A Commiffion concerning Tobacco, MS. 1634, June 19. 10 Car. I.

A Proclamation concerning Tobacco. 1636, Mar. 14. Car. I.—Title in Rufh. 617.

De Commiffione fpeciali Georgio domino Goring et aliis Conceffa concernente venditionem de Tobacco abfque licentia regia.—20 Rym. 116.

A Proclamation concerning Tobacco. 1639. Mar. 25. Car. I.—Title, 4 Rufh. 1060.

A Proclamation declaring his Majefty's pleafure to continue his Commiffion and his Letters Patent for licenfing Retailers of Tobacco. 1639, Auguft 19. 15 Car. I.—20 Rym. 348.

A Proclamation concerning Retailers of Tobacco. 1639. Car. I.—4 Rufh. 966.

An Act for charging of Tobacco brought from New England with Cuftom and Excife. 1644, June 20. Car. II.—Title in American Library, 99, 8.

An Act for advancing and regulating the Trade of Virginia. 1644, Aug. 1. Car. II. Title in American Library, 99, 9.

An Act for prohibiting Trade with Barbadoes, Virginia, Bermudas, and Antego. 1650, October 3. Car. II.—Scobell's Acts, 1027.

An

An Act for increafe of Shipping, and encouragement of the Navigation of America. 1651, Oct. 9.   3 Car. II.—Scobell's Acts, 1449.

Treaty of Weftminfter between France and England.   1655, Nov. 3.—2 Mem. Am. 10. 6 Corps. Diplom. Part II. p. 121.

A Paper concerning the Advancement of Trade.   1656.   Car. II.—5 Thurl. 80.

The Affembly of Virginia to Secretary Thurlow.   1656, Oct. 15.   8 Car. II.—5 Thurl. 497.

The firft Charter granted to the Proprietors of Carolina. 1662-3, Mar. 24.   April 4. —15 Car. II.   4 Mem. Am. 554.—Second Charter, 1665, June 13, 24.   17 Car. II.— 4 Mem. Am. 586.

The following Documents are to be found in Vol. I. of Hazard's State Papers.

Commiffio pro Tobacco.   1604. p. 49.

Commiffio fpecialis concernens le garbling herbæ Nicotiana.   1620. p. 89.

Commiffion to Sir William Ruffel, Knt. and others.   1634. p. 373.

Proclamations

Proclamations concerning ditto.

For Reftraint of diforderly Trading.   1620. p. 93.

Concerning Tobacco.   1624. p. 193.

De Conceffione demiff. Edwardo Dichfeild and Aliis.   1624. p. 198.

Proclamatio de herbæ Nicotianæ.   1625. p. 202.

A Proclamation for the utter prohibiting the Importation and Ufe of all Tobacco which is not of the proper growth of the Collonyes of Virginia and the Sommer Iflands, or one of them.   1625. p. 224.

Act of Parliament impofing Duties of Cuftoms and Excife laid upon Tobacco, the Growth of New England.   June 20, 1650, p. 636.

PART V.

OF THE TOBACCO TRADE OF GREAT BRITAIN.

Of Lighterage by means of River Craft, and of Taking-in, in Virginia.

In the foregoing part of this work we have (fo far as circumftances and materials permit at prefent) taken a view of the culture and commerce of tobacco from the origin of the plant to the act of taking away by the agents of the merchant for the purpofe of exportation. In Part III. we have alfo noticed one of the *water* means of delivery by a fmaller fpecies of lighters, or *fcows*; but this only refpects an occafional method of taking-off from the fhore, where fhoals intervene between the landing-place and fuch veffels as are compelled to ride in the ftream on account of their draught of water.

This is an intermediate operation, which frequently occurs at the *falls* of the principal rivers, which, by their fudden torrents in time

P   of

of the land floods, produces a tendency to fil-
tage and repeated changes of the channel.

This is particularly the cafe at the falls of
James's river in Virginia, where *Richmond*,
the metropolis of that ftate, is fituated. And
on this account, together with the circuitous
windings of the river, the large veffels from
Europe are generally moored at the diftance of
ten or fifteen miles below the town by land;
but which is nearly three times as far by the
water conveyance upon the river.

For the accommodation of this intervening
fpace river craft are employed, which either
take in their freight from the wharfs by the
help of *fkids*, or from the fcows by the help of
tackle; in the fame way by which the cargo is
a fecond time transferred from the river craft
to the fhips which are to bring it to Europe.

Several of the principal rivers in the middle
ftates are fubject to fimilar impediments; and
fuch increafe very much in the rivers fouth-
wardly from the Chefapeak bay, which admits
fea veffels but a very little way up them, yet
have a furprifing extent of interior navigation.
Thefe rivers however are employed very little
for the conveyance of tobacco, their ftaple cul-

8   ture,

ture, admitting a variety of produce *.   Virginia alone is the ftate which furnifhes the greater proportion of this article ; and the warehoufes at the falls of James's river, and upon Appamatox river (which is an arm or branch of the fame water), fhip by far the greater number of the Virginia hogfheads to the markets in Europe : it is on this account that I confine my remarks more particularly to the mart of Richmond, which I would always be underftood to mean when I do not exprefs myfelf to the contrary.

The river craft, which were employed in the tobacco trade antecedent to the American revolution, were, in a great degree, the property of the merchants, or of their factors.   They were generally flats of forty hogfheads burden, managed by negroes, who became very dextrous in their profeffion as frefh water failors ; and many of them made excellent *fkippers* †, and good river pilots.   Since the eftablifhment of the ftate government this employment has experienced fome changes ; and the diftribution of labour feems to obtain ground, in a

---

* For the comparative export of Maryland, fee Part IV. page 201.

† Captains of fmall veffels.

P 2   more

more general introduction of thofe larger floops and fchooners which were formerly but employed occafionally.

The rates of this craftage antecedent to the American revolution were,

In fterling

For a hogfhead of tobacco from Richmond, upon James's river, to the port of Norfolk, upon Elizabeth river, or to Hampton road, the fum of five fhillings Virginia currency . . . . . . fay 3 9

For ditto from ditto to City point, four fhillings . . . . fay 3 0

Of the Stower and his Affiftants, and of flowing the Cargo.

The extent of the Virginia rivers, and the great fcope of country through which the bufinefs of the tobacco trade is neceffarily extended, requires fo much of the captain's attention that he is obliged to be frequently on fhore, and fometimes at a confiderable diftance from his fhip. The important bufinefs of ftowing the cargo advantageoufly, as well as fafely, for the voyage, devolves of courfe upon the chief mate; as, indeed, does every other care of the fhip, infomuch that he may be confidered

fidered the principal executive officer, and is certainly the primary refponfible one for every neglect concerning the fhip and cargo.

This official fituation renders it therefore his ftudy to be conftantly prefent during this part of the operation ; and (as the fafety of the voyage, as well as the confideration of freight, is now dependent on good management) I believe there are few inftances where the chief, or fecond mate as his reprefentative, do not fee every particular hogfhead depofited in its proper birth.

There are, moreover than thefe fuperintendants of the fhip, certain profeffional negroes, and other perfons of great practice and experience in this art, who are to be had on hire for each particular occafion ; and there is certainly a very material faving to the merchant in employing them ; for although the crew of the fhip are always fufficiently employed, and are ufeful in taking in the refpective hogfheads, and in forwarding them to the hands of the ftower, there is a clevernefs and management in his part of the employment which can only be acquired by practice ; and indeed the moft expert failors will find difficulties vanifh before the ftower and the negro labourers who affift him, which might

otherwife

otherwife have impeded very troublefome obftacles. On this ground it is found advantageous to temper the judgment of the feaman
with the advice of the ftower; for by this
condefcenfion many a lee-lurch is provided for
beforehand, when it would be difficult to fecure a fhifting cargo in the time of actual danger : a piece of neglect that perhaps ought to
account for many veffels in the bottom of the
ocean, which, we have to lament, *have never
been heard of**.

The mechanical powers made ufe of in
ftowing tobacco, are, the lever, and the *jack,*
an implement of the fame kind with thofe
which are commonly ufed for raifing up tra-
velling waggons for the purpofe of greafing
their wheels; but the ftowing jack is fomewhat more powerful, although both are fimi-
larly contrived to work upon the *rack* principle †.   By thefe means whole cafks of tobacco
are compreffed into a much fmaller fpace than

---

* This reflection may ferve to remind thofe who have
fuffered fhipwreck, or who have the care of taking in lading,
how much depends, in ordinary cafes, upon duly fecured
fhifting boards.

† The barrel fcrew is an implement of powerful capacity,
which, I think, fhips fhould not be without : it might be
well applied in many cafes for ftowing tobacco.

they

they feem naturally defigned to occupy, and the impreffion that is made upon fo bulky an article can only be properly conceived by thofe who have remarked the powerful impreffion of mechanic aid upon the indented fides of a flat-tened hogfhead. How far this mode of fqueez-ing fuch a fubftance for fake of a few pounds freight may ftrain the ftructure of the fhip, is an inquiry refting, perhaps, in experiment: I fhould in any cafe conceive the end had been completely obtained when a cargo was render-ed fufficiently compact to avoid the danger of its fhifting in heavy weather: but when we find daily inftances in the king's warehoufes of tobacco which had been *fqueezed to death,* as it were, without regard to the proprietor's lofs, it feems to be a proof that there are men who think otherwife.   It is cuftomary to fill up the interftices with ftaves, or lock ftocks; and in fome cafes with loofe bundles of tobacco.

Of the Ship's Officers, and their Privileges.

The privileges of the fhip's officers are, in fome cafes, incommoding to fuch perfons as may happen to become paffengers on board homeward bound *tobacco* fhips; for there are captains, fometimes, in that trade, who prefer

P 4   a little

a little clear gain to their own perfonal com-fort, and are (on this account) in the habit of ftowing their *cabins* with hogfheads of tobacco, as well as the hold and fteerage. How far this may ftrain a fhip's upper works, accumu-late her difburfements, or be ftrictly admiffible, is, I fuppofe, known to the fhip owners where it is cuftomary, and is none of my bufinefs, further than a hint may prove ufeful; but I confefs if I were a fhip owner myfelf, I fhould be difpofed to compenfate for the furrender of fuch privileges by a pecuniary confideration.

I do not pretend to be a *profeffional* judge in matters of this nature, but fo far as equilibri-um is concerned in a rough and rolling fea, I think this feems to be an improper part of the fhip to place fo powerful a leverage; and I am perfuaded I have more than once feen the gulf ftream in a ftate of agitation which muft have put the principle of preponderation to the teft of a dangerous experiment.

In refpect to the nature of thefe privileges, I apprehend them to be different; nor am I certain whether they do not vary on board the particular fhips of the fame port, by fpecific agreement, as they certainly do between one port and another. I have a faint recollection of a cuftomary privilege on board fome of the

Liverpool

Liverpool ſhips, before the American war, amounting, I think, to four hogſheads for the captain, two for the chief mate, and one each for the ſecond mate and carpenter: perhaps this or a ſimilar cuſtom extended to ſhips in the Briſtol trade.

In the Glaſgow trade, I believe, the officers enjoy a privilege with regard to the ſtaves and lockſtocks by which the cargo is ſecured; and perhaps in ſome inſtances the captains have a per centage allowed upon the cargo, and in others ſhare the paſſage money. The objectionable point, in my view of philoſophical gravitation, is that of fixing a heavy weight upon that part of the ſhip where the cabin is ſituated; but, I believe, this is a privilege reſting ſolely with the captain, who is, or ought to be, a profeſſional judge of the balance between his riſk and his intereſt.

Of Freight and Inſurance.

Freight and inſurance are operations of commerce which uſually preponderate in favour of countries which either have ariſen, or are faſt approaching, to their zenith of population and wealth.

America, being yet an infant in the catalogue of

of commercial nations, perhaps may not be
fuppofed to claim any confiderable portion of
thefe advantageous functions.   In her principal
feaports fhe has, neverthelefs, her affluent fhip
owners and underwriters, and has, at leaft, as
much *carrying trade* as comports with her *intereft*.   But, I think, thefe are rather to be
efteemed exotics, or fcions of the old tree,
tranfplanted into a luxuriant foil, than natural
productions, which deferve an eager and extenfive cultivation.   The rates of infurance and
freight muft for a long time be influenced by
the fuperiority of European navies, as well as
by the fluctuations of her exchange and public
fecurities; and that trade would feem moft
likely to promote a mutual profit and good underftanding, which bottoms its commercial
faith upon the forefight of a well fyftemized
correfpondence, tending to multiply the powers of *production* in America, and the *facilities*
of *univerfal intercourfe* on the eaftern fide of the
Atlantic ocean.   The rife and fall of *infurance*
muft neceffarily vary (and particularly in fuch
a war as the prefent) with the caprice of victory, or the fkill of naval tactics; and that of
freight muft experience a fimilar agitation. The
prefent war affords an extraordinary inftance
of variation : previous to the American revolution

tion the freight of *one ton*, containing *four hogf-heads* of tobacco, was fix pounds; it is now (1799) fix guineas per *hogfhead*.

Of the American Clearance.

Since the eftablifhment of the prefent fede-ral government of the United States, the de-partment of the cuftoms is become a branch of the *general government* jurifdiction; and the duties which arife from it form a part of the federal revenue. Its branches are extended into all ports of that extenfive union, where they are deemed neceffary; and their appoint-ments are chiefly filled with officers who evinced particular merits in the contefts of the American revolution.

The branches of this department are ulti-mately refponfible to the revenue department of the treafury; which is ftationary at the feat of Congrefs, and muft, this next year, be re-moved with it to the federal city of Wafhing-ton, from the temporary capital of Philadel-phia.

Each of thefe *branch* offices are affifted by a competent number of revenue cutters and boats; and the bufinefs of the cuftoms is chiefly fhaped to the Britifh pattern.

In

In the James's river (which is the principal) tobacco trade, there are two officers of the cuftoms; one at Norfolk, and the other at City Point. When a veffel has received her cargo and is ready for fea, it is the bufinefs of the captain to have feveral general manifefts of the cargo made out, containing a faithful defcription of all the tobacco which is received on board; and a copy of this manifeft being delivered at the office and fworn to by the captain, before the collector or the cuftoms, together with the manifefts of the infpections (which operate as a check upon the captain's manifeft), a clearance will be granted; and he will be forthwith at liberty to depart, put to fea, and purfue his deftined voyage with the firft favourable wind and weather.

ABSTRACT OF LAWS AND REGULATIONS CONCERNING THE COMMERCE OF TOBACCO IN GREAT BRITAIN.

Of the Duties upon Tobacco.

By an act of parliament paffed in the twenty-ninth year of the reign of his prefent majefty, George the third, entitled, " An Act for repealing

pealing the Duties on Tobacco and Snuff, and for granting new Duties in lieu thereof—" from October the tenth, 1789, the duties impofed on tobacco and fnuff, and the drawbacks allowed on the exportation of tobacco, are to ceafe; and in lieu thereof the following duties of cuftoms and excife are to be paid, viz.

For every pound weight of Portuguefe or Spanifh tobacco imported into Great Britain, the fum of one fhilling and fix pence cuftoms, and two fhillings excife duties.

For every pound weight of tobacco, when delivered from the warehoufe for exportation, the fum of one penny cuftoms, and two pence excife duties.

For every pound weight of Irifh or American tobacco imported, fix pence cuftoms, and nine pence excife duties.

For every pound weight of fnuff imported by the Eaft India company, one fhilling and three pence cuftoms, and two fhillings excife duties.

For every pound weight of fnuff which fhall be imported from Britifh America, or the Spanifh Weft Indies, fix pence cuftoms, and one fhilling excife duties.

For every pound weight of fnuff which fhall be imported into Great Britain from any other place,

place, ten pence cuftoms, and one fhilling and four pence excife duties.

But it is provided, that tobacco of the growth, production, or manufacture, of Spain and Portugal, or of their plantations and dominions, which is imported and warehoufed agreeably to the directions of this act, fhall not pay the duties impofed until it fhall be delivered out of the warehoufe (in which it fhall have been depofited according to the directions of this act), either for home trade, confumption, or manufacture; or for exportation.

The duties in thefe cafes are to be under the management of the commiffioners of the cuftoms and excife in England and Scotland, refpectively.

What Tobacco may be imported into Great Britain.

From and after the tenth of October, 1789, no tobacco whatever is to be imported or brought into Great Britain, other than from the Britifh colonies in America, or from the United States of America; except Spanifh, Portuguefe, and Irifh, tobacco, under the prefent regulations.

From the firft of Auguft, 1790, no tobacco or fnuff is to be imported into Great Britain in any veffel of lefs burden than one hundred and twenty

twenty tons, on pain of forfeiting veſſel and cargo.

No tobacco ſtalks, tobacco ſtalk flour, or ſnuff work, is to be imported, on pain of forfeiture, together with veſſel and cargo.   Nor ſhall any tobacco or ſnuff be imported into Great Britain in caſks leſs than four hundred and fifty pounds nett weight.   But theſe reſtrictions do not extend to make ſeizure of looſe tobacco ſhipped for the uſe of the crew, at the rate of five pounds weight per man : nor ſhall the veſſel be forfeited if proof be made, from the ſmallneſs of the quantity, &c. that any tobacco or ſnuff was on board without knowledge of the owner or maſter.

Hovering on the Coaſt with Tobacco forfeits Ship and Cargo.

Veſſels with more than one hundred pounds of tobacco and ſnuff, or any tobacco ſtalks, manufactured or unmanufactured, tobacco ſtalk flour, or ſnuff work, are forfeited if found at anchor, or hovering within four leagues of the coaſt.

How

How, and into what Ports, Tobacco may be imported.

No tobacco of the growth of any of the British colonies in America can be otherwise imported than from some of the said colonies; nor can any tobacco of the growth or production of the United States be otherwise imported than directly from some port of the United States; nor shall any such tobacco be imported or brought into Great Britain from any part of the said colonies, plantations, islands, or territories, " Unless the ship or vessel in or on board which the same shall be so imported, or brought, shall be British built, registered according to law, and navigated with the master and three-fourths of the mariners *British*; nor shall any such tobacco be imported or brought from any part of the United States, unless the ship or vessel in which the same shall be so imported, or brought, shall be either *British* built, registered, and navigated, as aforesaid, or shall be built in the countries belonging to the United States of America, or any of them, and owned by the subjects of the said United States, or any of them; and navigated with a master

master and three-fourths of the mariners, at least, subjects of the said United States, or any of them," upon pain of forfeiture of ship and cargo.

* Tobacco and snuff is also forfeited if imported or brought into any part of Great Britain, except the ports of *London*, *Bristol*, *Liverpool*, *Lancaster*, *Cowes*, *Falmouth*, *Whitehaven*, *Hull*, *Port Glasgow*, *Greenock*, and *Leith* : By act 31 George III. c. 47. the port of *Newcastle upon Tyne* is added.

American tobacco imported into the *West India* islands in traffic, may be from thence imported into Great Britain, under restriction to *British* built vessels, the names whereof are to be specified in the manifest; and the officers of the customs within his majesty's colonies in America are to deliver to the masters of vessels, at their clearing, a manifest which shall authorize the importation of the tobacco into Great Britain.

Regulations concerning the Manifest.

From October 10, 1790, no tobacco of the growth of the American states shall be imported into Great Britain without a manifest sworn to by the master of the vessel; and mas-

* See also *Appendix*.

Q ters

ters of veſſels importing tobacco from America
without manifeſts are to forfeit two hundred
pounds.   Maſters of ſuch veſſels upon arrival
within four leagues of the coaſt, are to produce
their manifeſts to the proper officers, whenſo-
ever they are by ſuch officers demanded *.
And ſuch officers ſhall certify ſuch production
upon the back of the ſaid manifeſt; and ſuch
captain ſhall give unto ſuch officer, and to
the officer of the exciſe, a copy of ſuch manifeſt; the receipt whereof ſhall be certified by
ſuch officer upon the back of the original,
with the particular day and time when ſuch
officers ſhall have received the ſame reſpectively.

Of ſecuring Hatches on Arrival.

The officer of the cuſtoms who ſhall firſt
come on board is required to batten down the
hatches; in which operation the crew of the
ſhip are to give the neceſſary aſſiſtance; and if
the maſter of the ſhip ſhall refuſe to produce
his manifeſt, or the hatches after being batten-
ed down ſhall be improperly opened, he is to
forfeit the ſum of two hundred pounds.

* 29 George III. c. 68. § xx.

Of

Of breaking Bulk.

If bulk fhall be broken on board any veffel having tobacco on board, within four leagues of the coaft, or in any harbour of Great Britain, or if any part of the tobacco fhall be unladen before the proper officers fhall have duly authorized the fame, fuch veffel and cargo become forfeited ; and the mafter fhall be fined two hundred pounds : cafes of diftrefs and neceffity are excepted on due proof.

If any tobacco or fnuff fhall be landed without a lawful warrant from the proper officer of the cuftoms, the fame fhall be forfeited ; and all perfons aiding and affifting, knowingly, in the fame, fhall forfeit three times the value of fuch article.

Of the Moorings.

The moorings of veffels importing tobacco are to be appointed and regulated by the officers of the cuftoms ; and the veffels when fo moored are to continue until regularly cleared by the proper officer.   Mafters difobeying in this refpect are to forfeit one hundred pounds.

Of

Of the Entry of the Ship.

The mafter of every fhip on board of which any tobacco fhall be imported or brought into any or either of the ports appointed in Great Britain, fhall, immediately at mooring fuch veffel, make true entry, or report, upon oath, before the collector of the cuftoms, of the fhip and cargo under his command, on pain of forfeiting one hundred pounds, together with the tobacco fo imported; and if fuch mafter fhall fail or refufe to deliver a manifeft or paper of contents thereof to the proper officer of the cuftoms, he fhall forfeit the fum of one hundred pounds.

Of Entry by the Importer.

In ten days, *where the major part of the cargo fhall confift of tobacco*; or in fifteen days, *where the major part of the cargo fhall confift of other goods*, after the captain fhall have either reported his fhip, or neglected to have done fo, the importer of tobacco is to make entry with the officers of the cuftoms and excife, of the quantity of tobacco by him imported; and of what particular country the fame is the growth

growth or production.   And the importers of
fnuff fhall make a like entry; and if fuch entry
be not made, the tobacco or fnuff fo neglected
is to be conveyed to the king's warehoufe, and
there depofited at the rate of fix pence per
week ftoreage for each hogfhead, which fhall
be paid before delivery of the fame to the importer; the fnuff within one month after it is
fo warehoufed, and the tobacco within twenty-
four months.   But tobacco or fnuff brought
to any one of the ports enumerated in this act,
may be conveyed in the fame veffel to another
port, if it be fo originally reported.

Of touching for Orders.

Veffels laden wholly with tobacco may come
into *Cowes* and *Falmouth* to wait for orders; *provided* that report and entry is duly made with
the proper officers of the cuftoms, to this end.

Of the Re-exportation of Snuff.

No fnuff imported fhall be entered for exportation, or exported in the fame fhip.

Of the Warehoufe and its lawful Officers.

Commiffioners of the cuftoms are to provide
warehoufes for ftoring tobacco and fnuff.

The

The commiffioners of the cuftoms and ex-cife for England and Scotland, refpectively, are required to appoint one or more officers of the cuftoms and excife for each refpective warehoufe, one or more of whom to be the keeper or keepers thereof.

Of landing the Cargo.

Officers of the cuftoms on board veffels are to mark the hogfheads which are to be landed, with a proper mark, and running numbers; and fuch hogfheads are to be landed and con-veyed in their prefence to the warehoufes, where the tobacco is to be taken out, feparated, and weighed in the proper fcales of the ware-houfe, at the expence of the importer; and if any importer fhall refufe or neglect to comply with fuch regulations, fuch tobacco fhall be fubject to the rate of fix pence per week ware-houfe rent, until all duties fhall be paid, and all requifites of the law fhall be complied with.

Provided that the ftalk fhall not be feparated from the leaf of damaged tobacco, which muft be burnt if the payment of duties for it is re-fufed, and the afhes difpofed of by the com-miffioners of the cuftoms for the moft money which can be obtained.

Of

Of Samples for Sale.

After the tobacco shall have been weighed in the public warehouse, the proprietors, consignees, or other importers, are permitted to take out samples in the presence of the officers of the customs; but these samples must not exceed four pounds weight for each hogshead, which must be returned to such hogshead before the same shall be re-weighed for exportation, or for home trade, consumption, or manufacture. Snuff is in like manner to be taken to the public warehouses, and weighed; after which samples are, in a similar way, allowed, and to be returned before the cask or other package is disposed of.

Of the Exportation of Tobacco.

Tobacco lodged in the public warehouses may be exported from thence on giving twenty-four hours notice, and complying with the rules and regulations prescribed by law; but bond and security is in this case required for the actual exportation of all such tobacco taken out of the warehouse for the avowed purpose of exportation; the penalty of such bond, however, is not to exceed three thousand pounds, or to be charged with ftamp duties ; but no warehoufed tobacco can be delivered for exportation at any other than the place where fuch tobacco was originally imported ; and in the original hogfhead.

After feparation of the damaged tobacco, if the remainder in the hogfhead fhall be under four hundred and fifty pounds weight, it may be repacked in the prefence of the officers of the cuftoms and excife, for exportation.

Tobacco entered outwards may, from time to time, be delivered for exportation, upon producing to the warehoufe-keeper the proper certificates that the requifite bonds are entered into.   But if tobacco fo delivered be concealed and not fhipped within twenty-four hours after fuch delivery, it becomes liable to feizure, together with the cafks or other packages.   And if tobacco fo fhipped for exportation be unfhipped within four leagues of the coaft, or relanded, it becomes forfeited, together with the veffel in which it was fo fhipped.   No tobacco however is to be exported in veffels lefs than feventy tons, except for Ireland ; and if they are fufpected to be lefs, they may be detained until they are properly meafured, and the captain is to forfeit one hundred pounds in cafe of deficiency.

8

Penalty

Penalty for erasing Marks.

Persons erasing marks or brands from the tobacco hogsheads are to forfeit one hundred pounds.

What constitutes a Discharge of Exportation Bonds.

Bonds given for faithful exportation are to be discharged as follows, that is to say, by producing certificates of a bona fide landing of such tobacco in its destined port————if shipped to Ireland, Guernsey, Jersey, Alderney, or Sark, upon production of such certificate to the collector who took such bond, within six months; if entered for any other port in Europe (except the Isle of Man and Island of Faro) in twelve months; the same to any port in the Mediterranean; to America or Africa within eighteen months; and to, or beyond, the Cape of Good Hope within twenty-four months : such certificates to be signed by the consul, or other proper officer *.

---

* In foreign parts where no regular officer can be found, the certificate of two known English merchants, duly authenticated by the constituted authorities of the place, will be the next degree of evidence.

Bonds

Bonds for exporting tobacco to Ireland are not to be deemed forfeited for so small a deficiency as two pounds of tobacco in each hundred pounds.

Prohibited Ports.

From October the 10th, 1789, no tobacco is to be exported to *Jersey*, *Guernsey*, *Aldersey*, or *Sark*, or to the *Isle of Man*, unless permitted by licence of the commissioners of the customs; but this licence has a particular limitation, for each place respectively.

Rules for taking Tobacco from the Warehouse.

All tobacco deposited in the king's warehouse, is to be taken away in twenty-four months; and warehoused snuff in one month. And the duties upon each, respectively, are to be paid and satisfied previous to delivery. Six pence per hogshead warehouse rent per week is to be paid after expiration of eighteen months; and if tobacco be not taken away in twenty-four months, and snuff in one month, they may be sold for payment of duties and storage; and if no more than the amount of duties is offered for such tobacco, it may be burnt, and the ashes sold.

If

If tobacco or fnuff be not taken away in fourteen days from the time it is weighed for exportation, or home confumption, it fhall be fubject to fix pence per week ftorage in like manner as aforefaid *.

Who are to be employed in the King's Warehoufe.

No perfon is to be employed in the king's warehoufe, by importers of tobacco, but fuch as are efpecially licenfed to that end.

Of wrecked Tobacco and Snuff.

All tobacco or fnuff which may be faved from any wreck, or veffel in diftrefs, fhall be lodged in the neareft cuftom-houfe warehoufe, and treated in other refpects as tobacco lawfully depofited, as herein aforefaid.

Thus far the act of parliament begun and holden at Weftminfter, the eighteenth of May, 1784, and continued by feveral prorogations and adjournments to the third day of February, 1789, fo far as the fame concerns the *Englifh commerce* of tobacco ; and which I have endeavoured to abftract faithfully as an outline of ready reference for thofe whom it may concern. As I do not, however, rely on my

* See alfo page 237.

infallibility,

infallibility, where actual contefts may fubfift (and more efpecially as legal diftinctions may arife in a thoufand collateral points), I beg leave to refer thofe who may have property at ftake, to more fkilful counfel. I have endeavoured to fearch the laws fcrupuloufly, neverthelefs, for fuch alterations or amendments as may have occurred fince the paffing of this voluminous act; and I think it proper to add the following abftracts, which have occurred to my notice.

At a parliament begun and holden at Weft-minfter, the 25th of November, 1790, an act was paffed, and publifhed in 1791, intitled, " An Act to prevent other fhips than thofe laden with tobacco from mooring and difcharging their lading at the places appointed by an Act made in the 29th Year of his prefent Majefty, intitled, *An Act for repealing the Duties on Tobacco and Snuff, and for granting new Duties in lieu thereof*, to prohibit the exportation of damaged or mean Tobacco; and for permitting the Importation of Tobacco and Snuff into the Port of Newcaftle upon Tyne."

Limitation of Moorings.

This act recites the act 29 George III. Chap. 68. and enacts, that, none but tobacco fhips fhall be moored, &c. within the limits of the places

places appointed under the above recited act, for mooring such ships, on penalty of twenty pounds.

Damaged Tobacco to be burnt, &c.

That, damaged tobacco shall be burnt, and no allowance shall be made to the importer for the same.——And, that, tobacco and snuff may be imported into Newcastle upon Tyne, under regulation of the acts in force on June the 10th, 1791.

New Regulations of Storage.

By another act of the same session of parliament, continued by prorogation and adjournment, and published in June, 1793, reciting an act passed 29 George III. cap. 68, it is enacted, that in place of six pence, imposed by the said recited act, only three halfpence per week per hogshead shall be paid for warehouse room ; nor shall warehoused tobacco be sold for payment of the duties, unless it should not be cleared in three years. It is further enacted, that, the damaged part may be separated, when warehoused tobacco is brought to be weighed for exportation, or home consumption.

Instance

*Inſtance of a Spaniſh Ship admitted to Entry by
Act of Parliament.*

There is, moreover, in this act a ſingular
inſtance of the admittance of a Spaniſh ſhip,
the *San Juan Baptiſta, from New Orleans*, to
entry. As ſuch examples are exceptions to the
general law, I beg permiſſion to recite this inſtance of Britiſh liberality.

" Whereas a cargo of tobacco, the produce
of Weſt Florida, was, in or about the month
of February, 1793, brought on board a Spaniſh ſhip or veſſel, called the *San Juan Baptiſta*,
from *New Orleans*, into the port of *Plymouth*
in the county of *Devon :* and whereas application was made to the right honourable the
lords commiſſioners of his majeſty's treaſury,
ſetting forth, that the ſaid cargo was originally
intended for *Nantz* in the kingdom of France,
but on account of hoſtilities between Spain
and that country, the ſame was brought into
the port of Plymouth, with a requeſt that
ſaid cargo might be admitted to an entry in
this kingdom as tobacco imported from the
countries belonging to the United States of
America : and whereas in conſideration of the
aforeſaid circumſtance, the right honourable
the

the lords commiffioners of his majefty's treafury, directed that the faid cargo fhould be admitted to entry on payment of the duty of one
fhilling and three pence per pound weight,
being the duty payable upon tobacco the
growth or production of his majefty's colonies,
plantations, iflands, or territories, in America,
or the United States of America, on condition
that fecurity fhould be given to his majefty for
the payment of the duty of three fhillings and
fix pence per pound weight on the faid tobacco,
unlefs provifion fhould be made by parliament
for admitting the fame at a lower duty ; and
fecurity has been given by bond accordingly :
and whereas it is expedient that relief fhould
be given in this cafe ; be it therefore enacted
by the authority aforefaid, that the faid bond
fo given fhall be cancelled ; and that fo much
of the faid cargo as confifts of unmanufactured
tobacco, fhall, upon the delivery thereof for
home trade, confumption, or manufacture,
be admitted to entry, on payment of the fame
duties of cuftoms and excife as are due and
payable on tobacco of the growth or production of the United States of America, or be
delivered for exportation in like manner as tobacco of the growth or production of the
United States may now, by law, be fo delivered ;

vered ; and that the remainder of the faid cargo, being manufactured tobacco, fhall be delivered free of duty, on due entry being made,
for exportation thereof to the port of Hamburgh ; and that all the faid tobacco, upon
the delivery thereof either for home trade,
confumption, or manufacture, or for exportation, as the cafe may be, fhall be fubject and
liable to the rules, regulations, reftrictions, penalties, and forfeitures, to which tobacco of
the growth or production of the United States
of America is now by law fubject and liable."

Tobacco depofited for Exchequer Loans excepted.

Nothing in this act, however, is to affect
any regulation for depofit of tobacco on which
exchequer bills fhall have been lent.

Additional Duties.

By a further act of the fame feffion of parliament paffed and publifhed in October, 1795,
it is enacted, that the following additional
duties of excife upon tobacco and fnuff fhall
be paid, viz.

For Spanifh or Portugal tobacco, imported
on or after the feventh day of December, 1795,
one fhilling per pound.

For

For fuch tobacco, not warehoufed before December 7, 1795, one fhilling per pound.

For fuch tobacco in warehoufe on December 7, 1795, and delivered out for home confumption, one fhilling per pound, and delivered for exportation, one penny per pound.

For Irifh or American tobacco, imported on or after December 7, 1795, four pence per pound.

For fuch tobacco not warehoufed before December 7, 1795, four pence per pound.

For fuch tobacco, in warehoufe on December 7, 1795, and delivered out for home confumption, four pence per pound.

For fnuff imported by the Eaft India company on or after December 7, 1795, one fhilling per pound.

For fuch fnuff, not warehoufed before December 7, 1795, one fhilling per pound.

For fuch fnuff, in warehoufe on December 7, 1795, on delivery thereout one fhilling per pound.

For fnuff imported from Britifh America, or the Spanifh Weft Indies, on or after December 7, 1795, fix pence per pound.

For fuch fnuff, not warehoufed, before December 7, 1795, fix pence per pound.

For fuch fnuff, in warehoufe on December

R   7, 1795,

7, 1795, on delivery thereout, fix pence per pound.

For fnuff imported from any other place, on or after December 7, 1795, feven pence per pound.

For fuch fnuff, not warehoufed before December 7, 1795, feven pence per pound.

For fuch fnuff, in warehoufe on December 7, 1795, feven pence per pound, to be paid on delivery thereout.

Thefe duties are to be under the management of the commiffioners of excife; and to be paid as former duties. On contracts additional duties are to be added to the price agreed for.

On exportation of fhort cut tobacco, fhag tobacco, roll tobacco, or carrot tobacco, refpectively manufactured from tobacco delivered from any warehoufe for home confumption, the following additional drawbacks are to be allowed, viz.

For fhort cut four pence per pound.

For fhag three pence halfpenny per pound.

For roll four pence per pound.

For carrot three pence halfpenny per pound.

The powers of 12 Car. II. Chap. 24, &c. are to extend to this act. The duties are to be carried to the confolidated funds; and are to

7   be

be applied in defraying any increafed charge occafioned by any loan of this feffion, and are for ten years, to be kept with other duties granted for the fame purpofe, feparate from other monies.

American tobaccos imported and ware-houfed, may be removed *duty free* to certain ports for the ufe of land forces on board fhips; but no tobacco fo fhipped can be relanded in Great Britain or Ireland, or in the iflands of Guernfey, Jerfey, Alderney, Sark, or Man, without leave from the proper officers of the cuftoms. Provided that this fupply fhall be limited to fix months, and to two pounds weight per month per man, &c.

Thefe being the principal laws which con-cern the *fair trader*, I fhall omit fome which concern only the *profeffional fmuggler*, and the difpofal of feizures between his majefty and the officers of cuftoms, &c. The laws which regard *manufacturers* will come under that particular head.

*A Summary of the Law concerning the Importa-
tion and warehousing of Tobacco and Snuff,
as certified to, and reported by, the Select
Committee upon the Improvement of the Port of
London, June 28, 1799*.*

Tobacco.

The acts herein reported to govern the importation and warehousing of tobacco are the
29 Geo. III. cap. 68 ; 30 Geo. III. cap. 40 ;
31 Geo. III. cap. 47.

By the operation of the above acts of parliament, the commerce of tobacco is regulated
in the following respects.

It may not be imported into any other than
the ports of London, Bristol, Liverpool, Lancaster, Cowes, Falmouth, Whitehaven, Hull,
Newcastle, Port Glasgow, Greenock, and
Leith, and may be there warehoused duty
free.

It is to be lodged in his majesty's warehouse
at the expense of government. If taken thereout for home consumption to pay duty as follows, viz.

* Appendix (E. 1.), p. 105, 2d Report Select Committee.

The

s.   d.

The produce of Ireland, or the Britifh Plantations in, or United States of,
America . . . . per lb. 0 6$\frac{6}{20}$

Spanifh or Portuguefe tobacco, if ta-
ken out for exportation . . . per lb. 1 6$\frac{13}{20}$

Spanifh or Portuguefe tobacco, per lb. 0 1$\frac{6}{20}$

After remaining three years, the commiffioners of cuftoms or excife may caufe the
fame to be fold.

Snuff.

This article is in like manner regulated by
the operation of the following acts of parliament, viz. 29 Geo. III. cap. 68 ; 30 Geo. III.
cap. 40 ; 31 Geo. III. cap. 47 ; 33 Geo. III.
cap. 57 ; and 37 Geo. III. cap. 97.

By thefe laws fnuff may not be imported
into any other than the ports of London, Briftol, Liverpool, Hull, Lancafter, Cowes, Falmouth, Whitehaven, Newcaftle, Port Glafgow, Greenock, and Leith.

It may there be lodged in his majefty's
warehoufes, without payment of any duty,
and without expence to the proprietor.

If taken out for home confumption or exportation, to pay duty as follows, viz.

R 3   Of

Of the Britiſh plantations in, or the
United States of, America . . per lb. o $6\frac{6}{20}$
Of the Spaniſh Weſt Indies per lb. o $6\frac{6}{20}$
All other . . . . . . per lb. $10\frac{10}{20}$
Subject alſo to the duties of exciſe if taken
out for home conſumption.

After remaining one month, the commiſſioners of cuſtoms and exciſe may cauſe the
ſame to be ſold.

PART VI.

CULTURE AND COMMERCE ACCORDING TO ANDERSON.

A fummary Review of the Culture and Commerce of Tobacco, from the Year 1584 *to the Year* 1748, *inclufive, according to Mr. Anderfon.*

I HAVE lamented much during my progrefs in this work, that I found it fo difficult to procure a copy of Mr. Anderfon's valuable book on commerce, that I began to defpair, even in London, that I fhould be compelled to conclude this undertaking without his af-fiftance. Having at length, however, pro-cured that voluminous book from an inefti-mable friend, I fhall endeavour to collect a fummary from it, as concifely as is confiftent with my defign to diffeminate commercial knowledge, and to multiply the refources of ufeful traffic.

Tobacco

Tobacco brought first to England by Sir W. Raleigh.

Mr. Anderfon recites *, that, Sir Walter (then Mr.) Raleigh, having raifed a confiderable fubfcription in London, for the purpofe of making a fettlement in America, obtained from queen Elizabeth †, on Lady Day, 1584, a charter for that purpofe. And having fent captains *Amidas* and Barlow with two veffels to Virginia, they returned with reports highly favourable to the country, bringing home with them pearls, and *tobacco*.

This attempt was followed by another under fir Richard Grenville in the following year, 1585, who attempted to fettle a colony at the entrance of Roanoke river, now in North Carolina; but thefe fettlers being much haraffed by the Indian natives, and unable to maintain their ground, the remainder of them were taken up by fir Francis Drake, and brought back again to England.

Tobacco brought to England by Mr. Lane.

In 1586, Mr. Lane, one of the Virginia

* Anderfon's Commerce, Vol. II. p. 157.
† See Hazard's State Papers, Vol. I. page 33.

adventurers,

adventurers, is said, by some, to have been the first person who brought tobacoo to England ; and Mr. Anderson here seems to think *, that it might have taken its name from *Tobago* †, one of the Caribbee islands.   When we consider, however, the periods at which this island was discovered, settled, and depopulated, this conjecture does not seem probable.   This year sir Walter Raleigh fitted out two small vessels for America, at Plymouth ; and in the succeeding year, 1587, he fitted out three ships and one hundred and fifty persons of both sexes, who settled at Roanoke, where they found the second colony had been destroyed by the natives : and these, in their turn, being left three years unassisted, removed to *Croatan*, and were supposed to perish wholly, in like manner.

Captain Gosnol's Voyage, 1602.

Captain Gosnol made a voyage in the year 1602, which was the first in sixteen years which had been attempted after sir Walter Raleigh's failure ; and he is said to be the first Englishman who ventured a direct route across

---

* Anderson on Commerce, Vol. II. p. 164.

† See *La Bat's* account on this subject.

the

the Atlantic ocean, making difcoveries upon the coafts commonly called New England; but although he appears to have trafficked with the Indians fuccefsfully, we have no account of his finding tobacco in thofe latitudes.

King James's Proclamation, 1604.

King James I. in the year 1604 *, laid on, of his own accord, and without the confent of parliament (which Mr. Anderfon very naturally thinks unwarranted), a duty of fix fhillings and eight pence per lb. over and above two pence per lb. paid before that period.

His majefty feems, however, to have advanced very fubftantial reafons for this virtual prohibition of tobacco; for if any circumftance can juftify what are termed *ftrong meafures* on the part of a government, certainly the wanton luxury and debauchery of its people muft be amongft the beft apologies for a ftretch of power, which might, in other refpects, have been deemed arbitrary, and unbecoming a Britifh monarch.

* Anderfon's Commerce, Vol. II. p. 223.   Foedra, Vol. XIV. p. 601.

Two

*Two Companies of Adventurers eftablifhed in
1606, by Charter, called the* LONDON, *and
the* PLIMOUTH *Companies.*

From the repeated favourable reports of
captain Gofnold, and all others who had been
in America from the firft difcovery to this period, 1606, king James was induced to grant
two charters to diftinct companies, by the
names of the London adventurers, and the
Plimouth adventurers.   Ships were fitted out
by thefe companies, and the firft *permanent*
fettlements were now made; but we do not,
at this period, find any returns in tobacco.
The company of London adventurers obtained
a confirmation of their charter by the name of
*The Treafurer and Company of Adventurers and
Planters of the City of Lonaon for the firft Colony
of* VIRGINIA, in the year 1610, being the feventh year of king James I*.   In 1618, the
colony of Virginia is found to increafe, and
confiderable quantities of tobacco were cultivated; " which," fays Mr. Anderfon †, " now
began to be well taken off at home."

* See Hazard's State Papers, Vol. I. p. 58.
† Anderfon on Commerce, Vol. II. p. 274.

King

King James's Commiffion for garbling Tobacco.

In 1620, king James, whofe great diflike to tobacco feems to be amply recorded, iffued a proclamation, of which the following is the preamble, &c *.

" Whereas we, out of the diflike we had of the ufe of tobacco, tending to a general and new corruption both of men's bodies and manners; and yet, neverthelefs, holding it, of the two, more tolerable that the fame fhould be imported, amongft many other vanities and fuperfluities which come from beyond feas, than to be permitted to be planted here within this realm, thereby to abufe and mifemploy the foil of this fruitful kingdom : and whereas we have taken into our royal confideration, as well the great wafte and confumption of the wealth of our kingdoms, as the endangering and impairing the health of our fubjects, by the immoderate liberty and abufe of tobacco, being a weed of no neceffary ufe, and but of late years brought into our dominions : We therefore ftrictly charge and command that

* Fœdra, Vol. XVII. p. 233. Anderfon on Commerce, Vol. II. p. 284.

our

our proclamation of December laft, reftraining the planting of tobacco, be obferved, &c."

The fubftance of this proclamation, fays Mr. Anderfon, is given us in the octavo hiftory of Virginia, and is as follows, viz. that the people of Virginia growing numerous, they made fo much tobacco as overftocked the market; wherefore the king *out of pity to the country,* commanded that the planters fhould not make above one hundred weight of tobacco per man ; for the market was fo low that he could not afford to give them above three fhillings per pound for it. The king advifed them rather to turn their fpare time towards providing corn and ftock, and towards making of potafh, or other manufactures : this king had affumed the pre-emption of all tobaccos imported, which he again fold out at much higher prices.

This record * continues, " And that no perfon or perfons other than fuch as fhall be authorifed by our letters patent, do import into England any tobacco from beyond fea, upon pain of forfeiting the faid tobacco, and fuch further penalties as we fhall judge proper to inflict. And to prevent frauds, all tobacco

* Anderfon on Commerce, Vol. II. p. 285.

fhall

fhall be marked or fealed that fhall hencefor-
ward be imported."

Progrefs of the Virginia Plantations from 1621
to 1624.

* The fettlements in Virginia began now
to make rapid progrefs, one thoufand three
hundred perfons being fent thither by the
Virginia company, together with fuitable neceffaries for the ufe of the colony ; but quarrels
with the Indians brought on an unfortunate
maffacre of about four hundred perfons ; yet
this barbarity was repaid in kind ; plantations
were laid out ; a well regulated country began
to make its appearance ; and *religion* flourifhed ; *(the fword preceding the gofpel !) churches
were mounted upon the back bone of victory.*
King James, however, ftill continued his oppofition to the culture of *tobacco* ; and made
great exertions in the next year, 1622, to encourage the culture of mulberry trees, and the
propagation of filk worms. In the year 1623,
(there being many grievous complaints from
the colony of Virginia), king James iffued a
commiffion of inquiry of a very extenfive nature ; for which fee *Fœdra,* p. 490, or that

* Anderfon on Commerce, Vol. II. p. 290.

refpectable

respectable authority, *Anderson on Commerce*, Vol. II. p. 301.

King James's Prohibition of the Importation of foreign Tobacco—1624.

After reciting the various commissions and charters heretofore granted to the several companies of American adventurers, king James now issued a commission, directing a report of certain information concerning the state of affairs in the colony of Virginia, preparatory to granting *a new charter*; and appointed sir Francis Wyatt governor. And in respect to the culture and commerce of tobacco, he thought fit to issue the following proclamation.

* " Whereas our commons, in their last sessions of parliament became humble petitioners to us, that, for many weighty reasons, much concerning the interest of our kingdom, and the trade thereof, we would by our royal power utterly prohibit the use of all foreign tobacco, which is not of the growth of our own dominions : And whereas we have upon all occasions made known our dislike we have ever had of the use of tobacco in general, as

* Anderson on Commerce, Vol. II. p. 309.

tending

tending to the corruption both of the health
and manners of our people. Neverthelefs becaufe we have been often and earneftly impor-
tuned by many of our loving fubjects, planters,
and adventurers in Virginia and the Somer
ifles, that, as thofe colonies are yet but in
their infancy, and cannot be brought to ma-
maturity, unlefs we be pleafed, for a time, to
tolerate unto them the planting and vending of
their *own growth* ; we have *condefcended* to
their defires : and do therefore hereby ftrictly
prohibit the importation of any tobacco from
beyond fea, or from Scotland, into England
or Ireland, other than from our colonies before named : moreover we ftrictly prohibit the
planting of any tobacco either in England or
Ireland." The reft of this proclamation is faid
to relate to fearching for and burning of foreign tobacco, and marking and fealing the
legal tobacco of the colonies.

Death of King James, and Progrefs of Tobacco
under King Charles I.

King James died on the 27th of March,
1625, and was fucceeded by his fon Charles I.
who having ratified his contract of marriage
with France in refpect to the princefs Henri-
6   etta

etta Maria, fifter of Louis XIII. took poffeffion of the ifland of St. Chriftopher's, this
year *, jointly with the crown of France; and
the firft *Englifh* planters employed themfelves
in raifing tobacco.

In this fame year king Charles repeated, in
the fame way of his father, a proclamation
againft the importation of any tobacco not of
the growth of Virginia, or of the Somer
ifles †.

The Virginia company had by this time
raifed a capital of two hundred thoufand
pounds, but difagreeing amongft themfelves,
many felling out their fhares, and others emi-
grating to Virginia with their families and fervants, king Charles thought proper to take the
bufinefs into his own hands, and to eftablifh
a royal government ‡. The primary act of
which was by *proclamation,* in fubftance as
follows, viz. " That whereas, in his royal father's time, the charter of the Virginia company was by a *quo warranto* annulled; and
whereas his faid father was, and he himfelf
alfo is, of opinion, that the government of
that colony by a company incorporated, con-

---

* Anderfon on Commerce, Vol. II. p. 310.
† See Fœdra, Vol. XVIII. p. 19.
‡ Ibid. p. 18.—And. Com. Vol. II. p. 301.

fifting of a multitude of perfons of various difpofitions, amongft whom affairs of the greateft
moment are ruled by a majority of votes, was
not fo proper, for carrying on, profperoufly,
the affairs of the colony : wherefore, to reduce
the government thereof to fuch a courfe as
might beft agree with that form which was
held in his royal monarchy ; and confidering
alfo, that we hold thofe territories of Virginia
and Somer ifles, as alfo that of New England,
lately planted, with the limits thereof, to be
a part of our royal empire ; we ordain that the
government of Virginia fhall immediately depend on ourfelf, and not be committed to any
company or corporation, to whom it may be
proper to truft matters of trade and commerce,
but cannot be fit to commit the ordering of
ftate affairs.   Wherefore our commiffioners
for thofe affairs fhall proceed as directed, till
we eft..blifh a councill here for that colony ;
to be fubordinate to our privy council.   And
that we will alfo eftablifh another council, to
be refident in Virginia ; who fhall be fubordinate to our council here for that colony.   And
at our charge we will maintain thofe public
officers and minifters, and that ftrength of men,
munition, and fortification, which fhall be
neceffary for the defence of that plantation."

6   " And

" And we will alfo fettle and affure the particular rights and interefts of every planter and adventurer.   Laftly, whereas the tobacco of thofe plantations (the only prefent means of their fubfifting) cannot be managed for the good of the plantations, unlefs it be brought into *one hand*, whereby the foreign tobacco may be carefully kept out, and the tobacco of thofe plantations may yield a certain and ready price to the owners thereof: to avoid all differences between the planters and adventurers themfelves, we refolve to take the fame into our own hands, and to give fuch prices for the fame as may give reafonable fatisfaction, whereof we will determine at better leifure."

This meafure feems to have given a tone to the government of Virginia ; and from the encouragement given by this monarch, by granting lands upon the eafy terms of two fhillings per annum quit rent, payable to the crown for each hundred acres, many refpectable families were induced to emigrate to that country, which is now highly cultivated, its jurifprudence rendered more perfect, and its population amazingly increafed.

King Charles, having commenced tobacco merchant and monopolift, as we have already

feen,

feen, he again thought proper, in 1627, to iffue a proclamation, renewing his monopoly more effectually *, by commiffioning certain aldermen, &c. of London, " to feize all foreign tobacco, not of the growth of Virginia or Bermudas, for his benefit, agreeable to a former commiffion : alfo to buy up for his ufe all the tobacco coming from our faid plantations, and to fell the fame again for his benefit." And in the fame month he granted his permiffion to import fifty thoufand pounds weight of Spanifh tobacco ; with provifo, that it was to be all bought by himfelf, and refold to his fubjects. He reftricted the importation of tobacco to the port of London; and, in confideration that great quantities of tobacco were ftill fown in England, contrary to law, he renewed his former prohibition of planting the fame in England.

In the fame year he repeated his prohibitory proclamation concerning tobacco, and for fecuring to himfelf the fole monopoly thereof.

He enjoins the plucking up of all tobacco growing in England and Ireland, and ftrictly prohibits the planting any more †.

* And. Com. Vol. II. p. 321.—Fœdra, Vol. XVIII. p. 831.
† And. Com. Vol. II. p. 326.

He

He prohibits the importation of Spanifh, or other foreign tobacco, without his efpecial commiffion.

And, " becaufe fuch foreign tobacco fhould not be uttered under the pretence of being the tobacco of Virginia and the Somer ifles, and other Englifh colonies; and that the planters in his faid colonies may not give themfelves over to the planting of tobacco only, and neg- lect to apply themfelves to folid commodities, fit for the eftablifhment of colonies, which will utterly deftroy thefe and all other plantations: from henceforth no tobacco, even of our own colonies, fhall be imported without our own fpecial licence: and what fhall be fo import- ed, fhall be delivered to our ufe, upon fuch reafonable price as fhall be agreed on."

" No perfon fhall henceforth buy any to- bacco here but from our commiffioners: which tobacco fhall be fealed or ftamped; and when fold again, a note fhall be made, expreffing the time when bought, and the quantity and quality thereof."

In 1630 *, king Charles publifhed another proclamation for prohibiting the planting of tobacco in England and Ireland, and for li-

* And. Com. Vol. II. p. 343.

S 3   miting

miting the importation of it from Virginia, according to his will, and confining it to the port of London. In the following year, 1631*, he granted a commiffion to feveral great officers of ftate, " to confider of, and report to him, the prefent ftate of Virginia, and of the prod ct, commodities, &c. moft proper to be raifed and advanced in that plantation; and its further fettlement and advancement."

Maryland granted to Lord Baltimore.

In 1632, king Charles granted according to promife to fir George Calvert, who, or his fon, was about that period created *lord Balti-more*, the proprietary territory of Maryland; but, he dying foon after, his fon, Cæcilius lord Baltimore took out the grant in his own name, on the twentieth of June, in the aforefaid year.

In 1633, young lord Baltimore carried two hundred perfons to his new colony, and having the advantage of fupplies from the Virginia fettlements fouth of Potomac, it foon flourifhed.

† " The tobacco of Maryland, called oroo-

* And. Com. Vol. II. p. 345.
† Ibid. p. 352.

noko,

noko, being ftronger than that of Virginia, is not faid to be fo agreeable to the Britifh tafte as the fweet fcented tobacco of the latter colony; but the northern nations of Europe are faid to like it better; and Maryland was thought to raife about as much tobacco, and employ near as many fhips, as Virginia did. Its foil is generally extremely good, being moftly a *level* country.

Thus Mr. Anderfon ftated. I incline to tranfpofe his opinion, in fome degree, concerning the fpecies of the ftaple; and I leave thofe who have travelled through Maryland to decide, whether it is to be called a level country.

Retailers of Tobacco regulated, &c.

In this fame year, 1632, king Charles iffued a proclamation "for regulating the retailers of tobacco in cities and towns; wherein none but reputable and fubftantial traders fhall retail the fame; of whom a catalogue fhall be made for each city and town:" and he exprefsly prohibits "all keepers of taverns, alehoufes, inns, victualling houfes, ftrong-water-fellers, &c. from retailing tobacco."

In 1634, he alfo iffued a proclamation

S 4   againft

againft landing tobacco any where, except at the cuftom-houfe quay at London: " for the better preventing the defrauding his majefty of the duty thereon. Alfo againft planting tobacco in England or Ireland, ftill much practifed; and againft the importation of tobacco feed."

New Regulations of Virginia in 1636.

* In 1636, king Charles undertook to regulate the affairs of Virginia; he " appoints fir John Harvey to be continued governor thereof; and for him and any three of his council to appoint a commiffion for the enlargement of its limits; and for finding out what trades may be moft neceffary to be undertaken for the benefit of the colony. And alfo to fend out forces for fubduing the Indians, and to make war or peace, as may beft fuit the fafety of the colony, and our honour. That in cafe of the governor's death, or his neceffary abfence, *not to be allowed by lefs than four of the council there*, one of the council, to be appointed by the reft, fhall act in his ftead. The governor and council to be fubordinate, fub-

* See Rymer's Fœdera, p. 3.

ject,

jcct, and obedient, to the lords commiſſioners and committees here for our plantations, touching the preſent government of that colony, to whom, as well as to us, the governor ſhall, on the death of any member of the council, give notice thereof, that we may appoint another in his ſtead."

Theſe regulations, being the firſt eſtabliſhment of the kind, and, in general, the outline of colonial juriſdiction under the regal government, it will be unneceſſary to make a further apology for reciting them.

The Origin of Exciſe upon Tobacco, &c.

In 1643, the lords and commons in parliament aſſembled, laid a tax for the enſuing year, on beer and ale, in all counties within the limits of their power, " calling it," ſays **Mr.** Anderſon, " by a new word, *exciſe.*" In this ordinance they alſo laid a duty of four ſhillings per pound on foreign tobacco ; and two ſhillings per pound on Engliſh tobacco : " and the king's parliament at Oxford," ſays **the** ſame author *, " laid a ſimilar tax upon **all** within their power, and never met more at all."

* And. Com. Vol. II. p. 401.

In

In the paragraph immediately preceding this account, the author is fpeaking of the furprife of Antigua by the Englifh in 1745; and he proceeds immediately to a notice of the commerce of *American* tobacco, in a manner which leaves the mind fomewhat unfatisfied whether he refers to the chronological period, 1643, of which he is giving an account, or to the digreffion which he is indulging in regard to the conqueft of Antigua: punctuation (of which I do not pretend to judge) impreffes me with one idea, and the relative account with another; but in either cafe his paffage is as follows.

"By an ordinance of the lords and commons, the duty on our plantation tobacco was now made four pence per pound weight. Yet in the following year they reduced it to three pence per pound, cuftom and excife together; " they finding," (as that ordinance expreffes it) " that the duty of four pence had fomewhat intermitted the trade in that commodity. Which fhews," fays Mr. Anderfon, " that tobacco was by this time become a trade worth the encouragement of parliament." I incline to conclude that he means the year 1643.

The

The Growth of Tobacco in England prohibited by the Rump Parliament in 1652, and from thence, and ultimately, in 1660.

About the middle of this century, tobacco feems to have grown into much greater efteem than formerly in England; confiderable quantities were planted in feveral counties, which throve exceeding well, and proved very good in its kind: " but," fays Mr. Anderfon *, " as this not only leffened the duty on the importation of tobacco, but likewife greatly obftructed the fale of that commodity from our own colonies of Virginia, &c. which had coft fo much expence in planting them; the loud complaints of the planters occafioned an act of the rump parliament, in this year, 1652, abfolutely prohibiting the planting of any in England. Cromwell and his council, in the year 1654, appointed commiffioners for ftrictly putting this act in execution: and that we may not have recourfe again to this fubject, in the twelfth year of king Charles II. chapter 34, in the year 1660, it was legally enacted, that from the firft of January, 1660-1, no perfon

* And. Com. Vol. II. p. 420.

whatever

whatever fhould fow or plant any tobacco in England, under certain penalties. So that an end was effectually put to that practice."

" This act of parliament," continues this author, " takes notice of the great concern and importance of the colonies and plantations of England in America; and that all due and poffible encouragement fhould be given to them; not only as great dominions have there-by been added to the imperial crown of Eng-land, but alfo, that the ftrength and welfare of the kingdom very much depend on them, in regard to the employment of a confiderable part of its fhipping and feamen, and of the vent of very great quantities of its native com-modities and manufactures; as alfo of their fupplying us with many commodities, formerly furnifhed us by foreigners. And forafmuch as tobacco is one of the main products of feve-ral of thofe plantations, it is hereby prohibited to be planted in England or Ireland, as de-priving the king of a confiderable part of his revenue by cuftoms. Befides, that tobacco of our own growth is, by experience, found not to be fo wholefome as our plantation to-bacco.

" The firft earl of Clarendon (lord chancel-lor), in his own defence upon his impeach-
ment

ment in parliament, obferved, that, foon after king Charles's reftoration, he ufed all the endeavours he could for preparing and difpofing his majefty to have a great efteem for his plantations, and to encourage the improvement of them : and that he was confirmed in his faid opinion and defire, as foon as he had a view of the entries at the cuftom-houfe, by which he found what a great revenue accrued to the king from thofe plantations : infomuch, that the receipts from thence had, upon the matter, repaired the decreafe of the cuftoms, which the late troubles have brought upon other parts of the trade."

The firft charter for planting the country, theretofore named *Carolana*, was granted by Charles II. by the more modern name of *Carolina*, on the 24th day of March, 1662-3; and in the year 1663, Cap. XVII. 15 Car. II. it was enacted *, that no merchandize of the growth or manufacture of Europe fhould be imported into America in any other than Englifh bottoms ; and that no tobacco of the growth of the Englifh plantations fhould be carried any where, other than from plantation to plantation, before it had been firft landed in

---

* And. Com. Vol. II. p. 475.

England,

England, under forfeiture of fhip and cargo. There were, however, fome few exceptions to the general principle of European exportation, which it is not material to notice.

Mr. Anderfon further recites again at this period, " And forafmuch as the planting tobacco in England doth continually increafe notwithftanding the act of the twelfth year of this king, Cap. **XXXIV** a further penalty of ten pounds is laid for every rood or pole of land fo planted, either in England, Ireland, Jerfey, or Guernfey : excepting, however, tobacco planted in the phyfic gardens of either Univerfity, or in the private gardens for furgery, fo as the quantity fo planted exceed not half a pole of land in any one garden."

Notwithftanding all former prohibitions, the planting of tobacco in England was found to continue in the year 1670 *, when another act was paffed, whereby the peace officers were required to fearch for and deftroy tobacco wherefoever they found it growing, except in the phyfic gardens, &c. as before mentioned. A claufe was added to this act, whereby it became neceffary to land tobacco folely in England before it was conveyed elfewhere ; and by

* And. Com. Vol. II. p. 502.

this

this law, the kingdom of Ireland became precluded from the commerce of tobacco, through any other means of importation than that of a previous landing in England.

Commerce of Tobacco under King James II.

Hitherto it appears [*], that tobacco had been *taxed* only under the general name of *poundage*; but parliament now ſtepped forward and granted a tax upon *tobacco, nominally*; ſo that, by this law, government drew an increaſe of revenue from this reſource, over and above the former demand of one ſhilling in the pound, or *five per cent. poundage.*

So far the proceedings of the year 1685, which ſeems to be every thing that concerned the commerce of tobacco materially during the reign of this monarch.   But the revocation of the edict of Nantes, by the French king, brought on an emigration, which, under the patronage of the crown, about five years after, proved of material conſequence to Virginia and the tobacco trade.

[*] 1 Jac. II. Cap. IV.—See And. Com. Vol. II. p. 571.

Progreſs

Progreſs under King William.

The revocation of the edict of Nantes oc‑
cafioned a number of French families to take
refuge under the protection of the crown of
England ; and king William having afforded
them his patronage, and granted them lands
in Virginia, in 1690, a fettlement was formed
by them at the Manakin towns, formerly oc‑
cupied by the aborigines of the foil, and which
is one of the moft fertile and eligible tracts of
country in all America. It is fituated on the
fouth bank of James's river, a few miles above
the *falls* ; and muft have proved a ftrong bar‑
rier againft Indian encroachments upon the
Englifh fettlements, as well as the means of
confiderable fupplies ; and the refpectable fa‑
milies who ftill inhabit that tract, moftly by
defcent from the original emigrants, furnifh
an ample teftimony at the prefent period, 1799,
that whatever accumulation the tobacco trade
might have received from the increafe of num‑
bers, which the population of Virginia received
from them, they were not unmindful of thofe
more effential employments which are among
the early requifites of colonization.

In this fame year, 1690, the governor of
New

New York in alliance with the Irroquois Indians, made an attempt upon Quebec.

Commerce of Tobacco under Queen Anne, &c.

In Doctor D'Avenant's Report to the Commiffioners of Accounts, Part I. p. 32, London,
1712 *, the total importation of tobacco from
America into England, is ftated, at a medium
of ten years, ending in 1709, as follows.

	lb.
Imported on a medium, yearly	28,858,666
Exported on a like medium	17,598,007
Confumed in lbs. at home	11,260,659

In a former part of this work I have taken
notice of the progreffive improvements on the
method of rolling tobacco to market, for
which the Virginians have the merit of fome
originality. About the year 1715, we find
pig and *bar iron* manufactured in that country †; a circumftance which muft have been
highly favourable to both the culture and conveyance of this commodity, as it muft have
furnifhed them with means at hand for increaf-

* And. Com. Vol. III. p. 34.
† Ibid. p. 63.

T   ing

ing a quantum of produce which muft have been much reftricted by the delays of importation (not to fpeak of its difappointments), where importation is wholly depended on for a fupply of implements which muft have been continually in demand, and continually varying with the unforefeen cafualties of new adventures.

In, or about the year 1730 *, the Britifh colonifts of Pennfylvania, Virginia, and Maryland, feem to have difcovered mines of iron and lead, and to have built furnaces, forges, and plating mills for drawing out bar iron; the people of New York had alfo difcovered copper before this period; and it would feem reafonable to fuppofe that new adventures in thefe fubjects of fpeculation muft have not only afforded confiderable auxiliaries to agriculture, and to the commerce of the tobacco ftaple, but they muft alfo have had a tendency to quiet popular clamours by engaging the public attention in a greater variety of interefts, which on all hands prefented fubjects of novelty to the fifcal genius of the realm. Add to thefe colonial engagements, we now find New England profperous in the whale fifh-

* And. Com. Vol. III. p. 162.

eries,

eries, Carolina in the culture of rice, and Georgia admitted to the benefits of this latter ſtaple by an act of the 8th of Geo. II. Cap. XIX *.

A pamphlet publiſhed in London in 1731, entitled, *The Importance of the Britiſh Plantations in America to this Kingdom, &c.* which Mr. Anderſon has quoted in his third volume, p. 167, has the following remark, after diſplaying all the advantages of the Weſt India iſlands in detail : " And, to ſay the truth, were it not for the prevention of pirates ſettling there, none of theſe iſles would be worth our while to keep a governor, forts, and garriſon therein," viz. chiefly at Providence, " *conſidering how many finer colonies we have ſtill to improve.*"

" What our author ſays of Carolina," ſays Mr. Anderſon †, " by no means comes up with what we have elſewhere related from very good authority, to which we refer."

" Virginia and Maryland are moſt valuable acquiſitions to Britain, as well for their great ſtaple commodity, tobacco, as for ſome pitch, tar, furs, deer ſkins, walnut tree planks, iron in pigs, and medicinal drugs.

" Maryland is of the ſame nature and pro-

* See And. Com. Vol. III. p. 164.

† And. Com. Vol. III. p. 170.

duce

duce as Virginia ; and both together fend over annually to great Britain fixty thoufand hogf-heads of tobacco, weighing one with another fix hundred pounds weight, which at two pence halfpenny per pound comes to three hundred and feventy-five thoufand pounds." And he thinks that the fhipping employed to bring home their tobacco muft then have been at leaft twenty-four thoufand tons, which, at ten pounds per ton, is two hundred and forty thoufand pounds, the value of the fhipping ; the greateft part thereof, by far, being Englifh built, continually and conftantly fitted and repaired in England. The freight at one pound ten fhillings per hogfhead (the loweft) is ninety thoufand pounds ; and the petty charges and commiffions on each hogfhead, not lefs than one pound, or fixty thoufand pounds. Which two laft named fums jointly, viz. one hundred and fifty thoufand pounds, Britain undoubtedly received from thofe two provinces, upon tobacco only. The nett proceeds of the tobacco will be two hundred and twenty-five thoufand pounds. All which was returned in goods ; only there would further remain with England about five per cent. commiffion and petty charges on the faid goods, being eleven thoufand two hundred and fifty pounds. There muft have been

3   further

further imported in the tobacco fhips from thofe two provinces, lumber to the value of fifteen thoufand pounds; two thirds whereof was clear gain, it not cofting four thoufand pounds in that country, firft coft in goods; and, as it was the mafter's privilege, there was no freight paid for it. Skins and furs about fix thoufand pounds value; four thoufand pounds of which was actual gain to England. So the whole *gain to England* amounted to about one hundred and eighty thoufand pounds annually.

In 1738, fir William Keith, in his hiftory of Virginia, p. 174, in ftating the revenue of Virginia, eftimates the duty of two fhillings per hogfhead upon tobacco at the annual rate of three thoufand two hundred pounds, arifing upon the yearly exportation of thirty-two thoufand hogfheads.

" In the year 1740 *," fays Mr. Anderfon, " it appeared by the information of perfons of worth, concerned in the two Britifh colonies of Virginia and Maryland, that about two hundred Britifh fhips were annually and conftantly employed in that trade, viz. about eighty or ninety fail for Virginia, and about one hundred and ten to one hundred and twenty

---

* And. Com. Vol. III. p. 226.

to Maryland : that the fhips trading thither from the out-ports of Great Britain, were generally of a leffer burden than were thofe from the port of London.   And that of about thirty thoufand hogfheads of tobacco, annually imported from thofe two colonies into Great Britain, eighteen thoufand were brought in the London fhips.   Alfo this computation was exclufive of the veffels employed by thofe two colonies in their trade with the other Britifh, continental, and ifland colonies of America."

The currency of the paper money in circulation in the American continental colonies was regulated in this year, 1740, as follows *.

£. Currency.

New England, containing Maffachufets, Connecticut, Rhode ifland, and New Hampfhire 525	
New York, and the Jerfeys . • . 160	
Pennfylvania . . . . . , . . 170	For £.100 Sterling.
Maryland 200	
North Carolina 1400	
South Carolina . . , . . . 800	

Delaware and Virginia feem not to have needed this regulation.

It only now remains in fumming up the

* See And. Com. Vol. III. p. 227.

hiftory

hiftory of this facred plant for the firft two
centuries (wanting fix years) after the introduction of it into Europe, to take a conclu-
five view of Mr. Anderfon's account of the tobacco trade in the year 1748. It appears from
his ftatements *, that the cuftom-houfe books
for 1744, 1745, and 1746 (omitting the odd
hundred thoufands), recognize a medium importation of forty millions of pounds weight of
tobacco from the American plantations. And
that, by the like medium of three years, there
was exported thirty-three millions : fo that
England annually confumed feven millions of
pounds weight of tobacco.

	£.	s.	d.
If England alone were to pay the duty of four pence three far-things per pound on the faid for-ty millions of pounds, it would amount, in fterling, to . . .	791,666	13	4
But as thirty-three millions of pounds are annually exported, and the whole duty thereof drawn back, the duty is to be deducted	653,125	0	9

So the nett duty of feven millions confumed in England, amounts to . . . . £.138,541 13 4

"Now," fays Mr. Anderfon, "valuing the thirty-three millions of pounds of tobacco at fix pence per pound, that will be 825,000 0 0

"And if Scotland may be allowed to export annually feven millions of pounds, that, at fix pence per pound likewife . .175,000 0 0

"There will then be forty millions annually exported from Great Britain, which, at fix pence per pound, is £.1,000,000 0 0

"Which faid million fterling may be deemed to be all *clear gain to the nation*, over and above this trade's giving employment to about twenty-five thoufand tons of Britifh fhipping."

Some other accounts, which (as Mr. Anderfon obferves) fhould be read with caution in regard to their objects, make the importation of tobacco into Great Britain at this period, 1748, to be about eighty thoufand hogfheads

heads annually, one year with another, weighing nine hundred pounds each, or seventy-two millions of pounds; one fourth part whereof is fuppofed to be confumed at home, and the remaining fifty-four millions annuall, exported for foreign confumption.

Others have made the annual importation about that period, amount to about fixty-two thoufand hogfheads of tobacco, or fifty-five millions eight hundred thoufand pounds weight; and that twelve thoufand hogfheads thereof are confumed in England; which if all paid the duty of four pence three farthings per pound weight, would yield two hundred and thirteen thoufand feven hundred and fifteen pounds to the crown.

*A supplementary Review of the Commerce of To-
bacco, from the Treaty of Aix la Chapelle, in
1748, to the close of the American War in
1783.*

The information that is to be collected
chiefly from Mr. Anderson's voluminous history of commerce, which is suitable for the elucidation of this specific traffick, seems to break
off at this period, 1748 ; and the traces which
I afterwards find upon the subject are less perfectly connected than I had hopes of finding
them.   I am therefore necessitated to leave a
blank in the chronological order, which I
could have wished to have filled, or at most to
rely on an aggregate statement for that approximate data which time and circumstances
compel me to substitute in lieu of the actual
imports, exports, and consumption, of tobacco,
for the period which intervenes between 1748
and 1771.

A comparison of the total imports and exports which composed the materials of trade
at that period, between England on the one
part, and her colonies of Virginia and Maryland on the other, will afford the means of
information by the help of lateral inquiry;

4   and

and when the relative proportion of former periods is afcertained, which difcriminates the quantity of tobacco from the annual aggregate of merchandize, I apprehend a meafure will be obtained to form an average calculation by, which will not vary far from the truth.

Under this perfuafion, I have confulted fir Charles Whitworth's commercial works, and truft the following table will both ferve the occafion, and furnifh a fufficient number of examples to anfwer many other ufeful purpofes.

A Comparifon

A Compariſon of the Imports and Exports made by Great Britain from and to Virginia and Maryland, while under colonial Juriſdiction; with the annual Balances in favour of the reſpective Countries, from 1697 to 1773 incluſive.

Year	Imports.			Exports.			Balance in favour of Imports.			Balance in favour of Exports.		
	£.	s.	d.	£.	s.	d	£.	s.	d.	£.	s.	d.
1697	227756	11	4	58796	10	11	168960	0	5			
1698	174053	4	5	310135	0	0				136081	15	7*
1699	198115	16	10	205078	0	2½				6962	3	4½
1700	317302	12	11¼	173481	10	4	143821	2	7¼			
1701	235738	18	4½	199683	2	3¼	36055	16	1¼			
1702	274782	14	9½	72391	13	11½	202391	0	10			
1703	144928	3	1¼	196713	9	8½				51785	6	7¼
1704	264112	15	9¾	60458	11	1	203654	4	8¾			
1705	116768	17	8¼	174322	17	3¼				57553	19	7
1706	149152	10	1	58015	12	1¾	91136	17	11¼			
1707	207625	8	5	237901	0	3¾				30275	11	10¾
1708	213493	4	1¾	79061	1	1¼	134432	3	0½			
1709	261668	18	7¼	80268	15	9½	181400	2	9¾			
1710	188429	8	6	127639	0	5¾	60790	8	0¼			
1711	273181	4	1½	91535	11	3¾	181645	12	9¾			
1712	297941	9	4	134583	10	2¾	163357	19	1¼			
1713	206263	12	11½	76304	11	3¾	129959	1	7¾			
1714	280470	15	8¼	128873	10	10¾	151597	4	10			
1715	174756	4	6	199[illegible]74	17	1				24518	12	7
1716	281343	4	7	179599	17	7	101743	7	0			
1717	296884	2	7	215962	19	9	80921	2	10			
1718	316576	7	5	191925	0	7	124651	6	10			
1719	332069	14	1	164630	15	4	167438	18	9			
1720	331482	2	5	110717	17	10	220764	4	7			
1721	357812	0	11	127376	15	10	230435	5	1			
1722	283091	13	8	172754	10	5	110337	3	3			
1723	287997	6	8	123853	2	1	164144	4	7			
1724	277344	7	2	161894	6	2	115450	1	0			
1725	214730	2	2	195884	11	6	18845	10	8			
1726	324767	16	4	185981	18	8	138785	17				
1727	421588	2	6	192965	6	10	228622	15	8			
1728	413089	9	9	171092	8	2	241997	1	7			
1729	386174	18	6	108931	0	7	277[illegible]43	17	11			
1730	346823	2	3	150931	6	5	195891	15	10			
1731	408502	14	1	171278	1	5	237224	12	8			
1732	310799	11	6	148289	3	8	162510	7	10			
1733	403198	18	10	186177	13	7	217021	5	3			
1734	373090	16	10	172086	8	9	201004	8	1	* Virginia only.		

Year

Year	Imports.			Exports.			Balance in favour of Imports.			Balance in favour of Exports.		
	£.	s.	d.	£.	s.	d.	£.	s.	d.	£.	s.	d.
1735	394995	12	5	220381	6	9	174614	5	8			
1736	380163	9	9	204794	12	8	175368	17	1			
1737	492246	9	10	211301	12	3	280944	17	7			
1738	391814	15	0	258860	8	0	132954	7	0			
1739	444654	10	2	217200	1	4	227454	8	10			
1740	341997	10	11	281428	10	11	60569	0	0			
1741	577109	1	4	248582	17	1	328526	4	3			
1742	427769	8	4	264186	2	5	163583	5	11			
1743	557821	0	10	328195	0	5	229626	0	5			
1744	402709	15	0	234855	18	4	167853	16	8			
1745	399423	6	3	197799	12	3	201623	14	0			
1746	419371	15	0	282545	8	7	136826	6	5			
1747	492619	6	7	200088	16	10	292530	9	9			
1748	494852	9	5	252624	16	3	242227	13	2			
1749	434618	15	8	323600	6	2	111018	9	6			
1750	508939	1	10	349419	18	3	159519	3	7			
1751	460085	16	9	347027	0	7	113058	16	2			
1752	569453	14	6	325151	13	2	244302	1	4			
1753	632574	4	8	356776	11	3	275797	13	5			
1754	573435	6	1	323513	19	2	249921	6	11			
1755	489668	17	10	285157	4	5	204511	13	5			
1756	337759	18	6	334897	8	6	2862	10	0			
1757	418881	12	3	426687	3	10				7805	11	7
1758	454362	15	4	438471	17	8	15890	17	8			
1759	357228	7	4	459007	0	1				101778	12	9
1760	504451	4	11	605882	19	5				101431	14	6
1761	455083	0	2	545350	14	6				90267	14	4
1762	415709	10	9	417599	15	6				1890	4	9
1763	642294	2	9	555391	12	10	86902	9	11			
1764	559408	15	1	515192	10	6	44216	4	7			
1765	505671	9	9	383224	13	0	122446	16	9			
1766	461693	9	4	372548	16	1	89144	13	3			
1767	437926	15	0	437628	2	6	298	12	6			
1768	406048	13	11	475954	6	2				69905	12	3
1769	361892	12	0	488362	15	1				126470	3	1
1770	435094	9	7	717782	17	3				282688	7	8
1771	577848	16	6	920326	3	8				342477	7	8
1772	5?404	10	6	793910	13	2				265506	7	2
1773	589803	14	5	328904	15	8	260898	18	9			

In the year 1772, being the laſt but one which is comprehended in the foregoing table, (and which leaves a chaſm of twenty-three years before it, which the preſſure of time will not permit me to ſeek the means of fill-

ing

ing up fpecifically) we find that the tobacco*
which was imported from Virginia and Maryland into Great Britain, was 54,915,282 lb.
into England; and 42,883,981 lb. into Scotland; making a total importation for this year,
amounting to 97,799,263 lb. and the exportations for this fame year, were, from England
7458 lb. and none exported from Scotland:
the Britifh confumption, confined to this year,
muft, therefore, have been 97,791,805 lb.
The imports of tobacco into Great Britain in
1773 were 100,472,007 lb. 55,928,957 lb.
were imported by England, and the refidue of
44,543,050 lb. by Scotland.

The exports for this year were 50,386,925
lb. from England, and 46,389,518 lb. from
Scotland, making a total export of 96,776,443
lb. fo that the confumption of Great Britain,
for the year 1773, may be reckoned at
3,695,564 lb. of tobacco, although the exports
from Scotland exceeded her imports.

The importation for the next year, 1774,
was, into England 56,048,957 lb. into Scotland 41,397,252 lb. making a total importation into Great Britain of 97,397,252 lb.

The exportation from Great Britain for this

* Anderfon on Commerce, Vol. IV. p. 447.

fame

fame year, was, from England 44,819,851 lb. and from Scotland 33,857,064 lb. making a total exportation from Great Britain of 78,676,915 lb. fo that the home confumption for this year may be eftimated at 18,698,337 lb. of tobacco.

As this was the laft year of a good underftanding between Great Britain and her colonies, it is not to be wondered at if irregularities fhould be found to follow this period of difquiet until the contending claims of jurifprudence were adjufted by an acknowledged right of jurifdiction in which both parties difcovered their true intereft. The tobacco trade, however, feems to have ftrove hard to avoid a part in the difagreements of policy; for however far thefe contentions might have advanced, or howfoever much the non-remittance of the American trade may have been inveighed againft by popular pretenfions, the public records evince, even in 1775, when hoftilities had commenced, that the importations of tobacco did not diminifh until the following year impeded it by bloodfhed and confufion. But this period affords a new epoch in human events, which demands a diftinct confideration.

State of the Tobacco Trade at the Commencement of the War between Great Britain and America, 1775.

It appears from a fupplementary work, forming a fourth volume of Mr. Anderfon's Hiftory of Commerce, that the tobacco trade directly between Great Britain and her American colonies before the revolution was but little inferior to what it is indirectly at prefent (1799), yet it is not fully returned; "for," fays this author *, " the imports into Great Britain from Virginia and Maryland, before the war, were ninety-fix thoufand hogfheads of tobacco, of which thirteen thoufand five hundred were confumed at home; and the duty on them at twenty-fix pounds one fhilling each, amounted to three hundred and thirty-one thoufand fix hundred and feventy-five pounds : the remaining eighty-two thoufand five hundred were exported by our merchants to different parts of Europe, and brought a great deal of money into this kingdom. This trade alone conftantly employed three hundred and thirty fhips ; and three thoufand nine hundred and fixty failòrs." This year, 1775, a

* Anderfon on Commerce, Vol. IV. p. 187.

I   bill

bill received the royal affent, which went to reftrain and limit the trade of thefe two colonies (in common with the reft) to Great Britain, Ireland, and the Weft India iflands.

A bill was in like manner paffed this year, *to prohibit all Trade with the American Colonies then in actual Rebellion, during the Continuation thereof.*

This act neceffarily operated to interdict the whole commerce of tobacco between Great Britain and America; and after various clamours from thofe concerned, and a partial injury to the Britifh revenue for the fpace of three years, in 1779 it was judged expedient to repeal fo much of feveral acts of parliament as prohibited the growth and produce of tobacco in Ireland, and to permit the importation of tobacco of the growth and produce of that kingdom into Great Britain.

Such were the refults of that interruption to the regular channel of commerce, which is always infeparable from the violent agitations of every momentous revolution in the fyftem of national jurifprudence; but although war or legal reftraint may, for a while, avert the accuftomed courfe of commerce, nature is ever ftruggling to reclaim her pre-eminence when

U   the

the impediments of diforganization fhall be removed. Of this pofition the American revolution affords a very ftriking example ; for although the regular channel of the tobacco
trade was obftructed whenfoever the maxim
dum armes filent leges prevailed, yet we find a
portion of it furmounting this difficulty through
the whole revolutionary period, by fome means
or other ; and the balance returning to Britain among the bleffings of peace.

The two following tables will exhibit this
progrefs more particularly, and fhew, in fome
degree, the relations which fubfifted between
the profpect of conciliation and the profperity
of commerce.

An

*An Account of Tobacco imported into England,
exported from thence, and confumed at Home,
during a period of ten Years, from 1773 to
1783, including the American War by which
this Commerce was greatly interrupted.*

Year.	Pounds weight Imported	Pounds weight Exported.	Pounds weight Confumed.
1773	55928957	50386925	
1774	56048395	44819851	
1775	55965463	43880865	
*1776	7275037	16521412	Exports exceed.
*1777	2146051	2905406	Exports exceed.
1778	9077153	2068175	
1779	14017431	3704436	
1780	12299172	2823005	
1781	11386725	3950815	
1782	7203262	2529146	See detail p.296.
Total	231347644	173590036	57757608

* The years 1776 and 1777 fhew a greater
exportation than importation, by a balance of
10,005,730 lb. confequently it would feem as
if fo much tobacco muft either have been cultivated in England during thofe two years,
fmuggled into that kingdom, or exported out
of old ftock on hand, which might have failed
of the ufual annual confumption through the
turbulency of the times.

The importation into England from 1777

U 2   to

to 1782, inclufive, was 56,129,794 lb. of tobacco.   In 1777 the captures of tobacco commenced; and in the fix years as above, the
prizes in tobacco amounted to 33,974,949 lb.
fo that the balance of 22,154,845 lb. only
(great part whereof appears to have been cultivated elfewhere than in the United States)
may be confidered as fairly imported by the
equitable proprietors.   I leave *captors* to reflect
on the integrity of this traffic at their leifure ;
and to contemplate the miferies which priva-
teering produces, when their cooler moments
afford them time to calculate the product of
honeft induftry upon juftifiable principles.

Account of Tobacco imported into Scotland, exported from thence, and confumed at Home, during a period of ten Years, from 1773 to 1783, including the American War, by which this Commerce was greatly interrupted.

Year.	Imported		Exported.		Confumed.
	Manufact.	Unmanufac.	Manufac	Unmanufact.	
	lb.	lb.	lb.	lb.	lb.
1773	0	44543050	41783	46347735	Exports exceed
1774	30	41348295	62742	33794322	
1775	0	45863154	95352	30228949	
1776	100	7423363	234216	2346716	Exports exceed
1777	267	294896	109009	5400568	Exports exceed
1778	6	2884374	77086	2296622	
1779	12	3138464	12892	2339649	
1780	157	5125638	102304	3024867	
1781	100	1952243	213322	1574735	
1782	175	2624807	233458	700837	See p. 296.
Total	847	155198284	1399095	149181946	
		847		1399095	
		155199131		150581041	4618090

Thus we find the total importation into Scotland, *for the faid ten years*, was . . . . . 155,199,131 lb.

The total exportation for ditto 150,581,041

There would be confumed, of courfe, for ditto 4,610,090

But as the exportations for 1773, 1776, and 1777, very far exceeded the importations for

thofe

thofe years, the prefumption is fuggefted, in like manner as in the cafe of England, that 23,344,897 lb. muft ei her have been home produce for thofe three years, fmuggled in in that time, or remaining of the old ftock through an interruption of the ufual confumption; and that there is a myftery in this bufinefs which is not yet accounted for to government. The facts on which this furmife occurs are as follows.

	lb.	lb.
1773. Unmanufactured	46,347,735	
Manufactured	41,783	
Exported	46,389,518	
Imported	44,543,050	
Excefs of exports	————	1,846,468
1776. Unmanufactured	23,467,162	
Manufactured	234,216	
Exported	23,701,378	
Imported	7,423,463	
Excefs of exports	————	16,277,915
1777. Unmanufactured	5,406,668	
Manufactured	109,009	
Exported	5,515,677	
Imported	295,163	
Excefs of exports	————	5,220,514
Total excefs		23,344,897

Probability,

Probability, therefore, countenances the conclufion, that Great Britain confumes much more tobacco than fhe has been fuppofed to do; and that the means which fupport this extra luxury are unknown to the fifcal department.

In 1781 an act was paffed for laying an additional duty upon tobacco imported into Great Britain; and the following ftatement will fhew the quantities brought into that kingdom from America, and returned again in exports, notwithftanding the interruptions of the then exifting war between the two countries: it will alfo fhew from whence thofe deficiencies were made up which the nature of the war had occafioned.

An Account of Tobacco imported into, and exported from, Great Britain for one year, viz. from Christmas 1781, to Christmas 1782.

Countries from whence Tobacco was, now, imported, &c.	England		Scotland	
	Imported.	Exported.	Imported.	Exported.
	lb.	lb.	lb.	lb.
Africa	......	54447	......	......
Denmark and Norway	......	50497	1408	......
East Country........	......	15443	......	......
East Indies..........	......	24115	......	......
Flanders............	8017	107452	2318	......
France	......	124748	......	......
Germany ,,........	24938	129915	......	......
Holland	......	14907	3212	......
Ireland	......	1048760	......	9428,5
Isle of Man	......	30370	......	......
Ruffia..............	......	1364	......	......
Sweden............	......	3983	11750	......
Canada............	......	64647	......	1304
Carolina............	46810	600	......	......
Florida	105291	......	......	......
Hudson's Bay........	......	1694	......	......
Newfoundland.......	......	32580	......	4905
New York..........	224562	108	102575	120
Nova Scotia.........	61911	365	......	......
Antigua	118169	420	3310	600
Anguilla............	122586	......	......	......
Barbadoes..........	4578	1713	......	233
Jamaica	71130	9302	......	3667
Nevis..............	......	172	......	......
St. Kitts............	1928	......	......	......
St. Lucia	42039	367	......	306
St. Thomas	289402	1268	......	280
Tortola	3274909	343	1505057	......
New Orleans	18570	......	......	......
Bermudas...........	......	......	72170	......
Total	7203562	2529146	2624982	934295

Summary.

Summary.

	lb.
Imported into Great Britain	9,828,244
Exported from ditto	3,463,441
Confumed at home	6,364,803

In 1782 an act was paffed to explain an act made in the 12th year of king Charles II. (entitled *An Act for prohibiting the planting, fetting, or fowing, of Tobacco in England or Ireland),* and to permit the ufe and removal of tobacco, the growth of *Scotland,* into England, for a limited time, under certain reftrictions.

By this law the recited act was extended to Scotland; a report was to be made to the collector and comptroller of his majefty's cuftoms for Scotland, of all tobacco either in poffeffion, being the actual growth of that country, or being then actually growing; and the like duties were impofed which had been theretofore laid upon American tobacco; fuch tobacco was prohibited from a removal into England by land, but was permitted to be conveyed thither by water under certain reftrictions, the hogfheads being marked on the outfide with the words Scots Tobacco.

A penalty was annexed to the crime of altering the legal marks and certificates; and

tobacco

tobacco removed otherwise than duly entered, marked, and certified, according to this act, together with the cattle and carriages which were used for its conveyance, became forfeited.

Duties were also to be paid upon this tobacco without any difcount; the produce of fuch duties was to be fubfituted in lieu of the fufpended duties upon American tobacco; nor was any drawback to be allowed on exportation.

Under this act the people of Scotland were encouraged in the experiment of planting tobacco; but through various caufes (fome of which are perhaps better underftood in Virginia than in England), this project feems to have failed of fuccefs; and the fucceeding parliament thought it advifeable to pafs a law by which four pence per pound was allowed to the planter for all fuch his tobacco as, on account of its inferior quality, or other defect, was infufficient to fupport the payment of duties.

It is faid, alfo, that this bufinefs ultimately terminated in the ufe of the public knife, as an inftrument of difpatch in maturing the crop: I am induced to think another reafon merits a place in the agricultural regifter—*Scotland is farther north than England !*

8   In

In the happy period of 1783, when the war between the two countries terminated, and a pacific difpofition prefented the olive branch of peace to the induftry of commerce and the independence of the American ftates, the ftars of a new people were difplayed in the river Thames; an act of amendment was paffed for the better fecuring of the duties arifing upon the commerce of tobacco; the ferious attention of the Britifh nation became engaged in the nurture of its ancient traffic, and bid fair to repair the damages which an injured revenue had received from an unprofitable fufpenfion of the trade : it will be the office of the following pages to review the profitable refult of this moft favourable accommodation.

A Sketch of the Commerce of Tobacco between England and America, &c. from the Treaty of Peace 1783, *to the prefent Year* 1799.

Thus far we have taken a review of the commerce of tobacco, in refpect to England and America, from the earlieft period to the treaty of Aix la Chapelle in 1748; from that period to the commencement of the American war in 1775; and through that war to the peace of 1783. It remains to examine the ftate of this commerce from the latter period

up

up to the prefent time; which will leave but little of this hiftory to be hereafter unfolded, from the earlieft introduction of tobacco to the end of the eighteenth century.

By comparing the imports and exports of the refpective periods which I have ftated, we may obtain a tolerable eftimate of the quantity of tobacco which has been actually confumed in Great Britain in the courfe of each year fucceffively; and by comparing the three periods of importation which exifted in this kingdom antecedent to the American war, during that war, and fince the return of a happy peace, we may be better able to learn and improve the true reciprocity of intereft which fubfifts between the two countries through the medium of national commerce.

The following ftatement will exhibit the actual importations from 1783, to the prefent year 1799 *.

* The reader in this place will obferve, that although the deficit of importation between the quantity of average imports before and after the American war is confiderable, yet this is not a deficit in the trade of Britain to America; becaufe much Britifh capital is ftationary in America, from whence Englifh remittances are made into Hamburgh and other neutral ports.

*An Account of the Quantity of Tobacco imported
into Great Britain in the following Years.*

	lb.		lb.
1783	19,579,581	1791	52,517,738
1784	43,492,302	1792	44,057,916
1785	43,255,741	1793	24,957,034
1786	45,379,795	1794	33,070,076
1787	39,600,404	1795	22,576,212
1788	48,831,232	1796	23,608,775
1789	59,154,456	1797	26,833,870
1790	57,575,923	1798	40,652,603

The peace between England and the United
States of America took place in the year 1783,
and it will be readily accounted for why the
importation did not return immediately into
its antient channel. In this year it amounted to
the quantity of nineteen millions five hundred
and seventy-nine thousand five hundred and
eighty-one pounds weight only; which left a deficit of 80,319,533 lb. the average importation,
immediately preceding the war, being estimated
at 99,899,114 lb. From thence to the year 1793,
including the nine years immediately following that of pacification, we find the imports
amount to an annual average of 48,207,278 $\frac{5}{9}$
lb. which wants, however, 51,691,835 $\frac{4}{9}$ lb.

pe

per annum to equal the laft three years of colonial commerce with that country.

For five years immediately following the
year 1792, we find that the average annual
importation amounted to no more than
26,409,193⅖ lb. of tobacco; but in the following year, 1798, we find the importation
of this article returning to the amount of
40,652,603 lb.

Now, if, as fome conjecture, the mere caufe
of a fluctuating market had produced this effect, we fhould have difcovered an *excefs* of
importation in fome one year or other; inftead
of which there feems to be grounds to fuf-
pect, that the depredation of French priva-
teering has been more fuccefsful than has been
generally imagined; and that the tobacco
trade partly regained its level in the laft year
the fuccefs of naval victory.

There is another circumftance, however,
which fhould not only account for deficiencies
of American tobacco, but which fhould call
the prudential confiderations of commerce to
anticipate the means of a fuitable fucceda-
neum: the culture of tobacco in America has
greatly given place to wheat and other ftaples;
nor does it, in any part, keep pace with the
progrefs of population.

If

If we may be permitted to notice the *general* state of commerce, in these times of delicate investigation, we may observe that *Mr. Chalmers* * states the *outward* trade of 1783 and 1784 as follows.

	Ships cleared.			*Value of Cargo.*
	Tons Eng.	Tons for.	Total.	£.
1783	795,669	157,969	953,638	13,851,671
1784	846,355	113,064	959,419	14,171,375

I mention this statement because we may happen to have a future occasion to compare the relative proportion of the tobacco trade of these years; and, without commenting warmly upon the author's statement concerning the United States, it gives me pleasure to add his acknowledgment, that the English nation *profited* by the return of peace, in the comparison which he has drawn between the exports and imports of the averaged years 1771, 1772, 1773, and the first year after the conciliatory epoch, 1784.

	Exports to U. S. A.	Imports from U. S. A.
In 1771-2-3	£.3,064,843	£.1,322,532
In 1784	£.3,359,864	£. 701,189†

* Chalmers's Estimate (1794), p. 145, 146, 147.

† As the English merchants *continue* their trade with America, it is fair to presume these balances have been discharged by remittances, unknown to Mr. Chalmers; for commerce does not thrive upon bad debts.

I am,

I am, here, fomewhat puzzled to analyfe the heterogene of this gentleman's argument in ftriking the balance of trade, for in one and the fame paragraph * he flatters himfelf with having removed all caufe for faying, that England has *loft the American commerce* by the independence of the United States; and yet he laments the attempt of the latter to be *great traders without great* CAPITAL : I could wifh this word were lefs indefinite, that I might better underftand him. If he means to imply the idea of a paper circulation bottomed upon imaginary wealth in another perfon's cellar, it is certainly a very crazy foundation for a ftructure of commercial fecurity ; but it has been my *misfortune* to have heretofore fuppofed that a great extent of fertile region, and a rapid increafe of agricultural production, fuch as the United States poffefs, were the moft fubftantial corner-ftones of the edifice called *finance*, which is the afylum of an extenfive trade.

In 1785 the tobacco merchants of London, Briftol, and Glafgow, petitioned parliament concerning the ftate of this traffic; and, as the accuracy of *commercial* calculations affords

* Chalmers's Eftimate, 1784, p. 148.

the

the moſt ſatisfactory kind of information, we may, perhaps, rely on their ſtatements as exact; or, at leaſt, as the neareſt approximate to preciſion : they repreſented to the Houſe of Commons, in ſtrong and explicit terms, that, during the proſperous ſtate of American commerce (in, what the planters uſed to call, *good times*), that the imports of America into Great Britain, at prime coſt, amounted to £.1,500,000 per annum ; of which £.700,000 conſiſted of tobacco. As reaſons for encouraging this trade, they added, that the market of *France* afforded annually a ſale for twenty-five thouſand hogſheads of tobacco ; but that ſhe had not been able to obtain more from America, in the preceding year, than twelve hundred hogſheads, notwithſtanding that ſhe had made great exertions.

That *Holland* (including the market of Germany, which ſhe uſually ſupplied), could vend eighteen thouſand hogſheads per annum ; but that ſhe had only received five thouſand hogſheads from America in the preceding year ; and that, thus, it appeared that both France and Holland were included in a direct export from America within the ſmall amount of ſix thouſand two hundred hogſheads of tobacco for the laſt year, while Great Britain alone

X   imported

imported above thirty thoufand hogfheads from that country in the fame period of time. The fuperiority of Englifh manufactures, the fuperior credit of her merchants, and the predilection of the Americans for the ancient habits of their commerce, were alfo urged; and the chancellor of the exchequer brought in a bill *for the better fecuring of the Duties upon Tobacco*, contemplating to produce the falutary effects which were defired.

He is faid, on introducing this bill, to have declared, that, *the revenue, then arifing from that article, fcarce exceeded one half of what the nett duty would be if it were paid on the whole quantity confumed in the kingdom.*

In 1786, a bill was paffed to prevent the fraudulent removal of tobacco, &c. and, from an inveftigation made in this year by the commiffioners of public accounts, we learn that the eftablifhment for the tobacco bufinefs comprehends the following offices.

Regifter general of
    tobacco
Chief clerk
Second clerk
Third clerk
Fourth clerk

Fifth clerk
Clerks for the inland
    tobacco bufinefs under the collector inwards
Ditto for ditto under the

6

the comptroller in-
wards and outwards
Viewer and examiner
inwards and out-
wards
Inſpector and ſurveyor
of the tobacco burn-
ing ground
Tobacco cooper
Tobacco locker, exa-
miner of manufac-
tured tobacco, and

for attending the
burning ground
Watchmen and la-
labourers at the
burning kiln
Bargemen to convey
tobacco to the kiln
Superintendant of the
tobacco lockers
Seven tobacco lockers
beſides H. ſtone

The total amount of this eſtabliſhment
comprehends the following items; and is as
follows.

	£.	s.	d.
Salaries and allowances from the crown, for ſelves, deputies, and clerks	1892	0	0
Payments by the principal or other officers to the deputies and clerks	24	12	0
Amount of fees, other allow-ances, and gratuities, excluſive of ſhares of ſeizures	209	19	0
Groſs produce of the employ-ments	2126	11	0
Payments for taxes	196	14	4

X 2   Payments

	£.	s.	d.
Payments to the superannuation funds	19	7	10
Payments to deputies and clerks	24	12	0
Nett produce of employments	1885	16	10

In the year 1790, the business of the tobacco manufactures was considerably investigated before parliament, but as these inquiries are only collaterally connected with commerce, I shall, in this place, pass them over.

The importation of tobacco, or, rather the consequent productions of public revenue which arose from the importation of this article, from the fifth of January 1793, to the fifth of January 1797, yielded the following sums, annually, subject to the payment of bounties and management, viz.

	£.	s.	d.
For 1793	213,367	9	3
1794	241,889	13	6
1795	266,360	16	6
1796	252,453	11	0

Produce of condemned tobacco.

	£.	s.	d.
For 1793	2,106	6	3
1794	5,404	15	6¾
1795	1,836	17	3½
1796	5,871	6	1¾
Total	989,290	15	3

The

The nett produce of the duties of excife upon tobacco and fnuff, which was paid into the exchequer (as extracted from the general account), from the fixth of January 1793, to the fifth of January 1797, both days inclufive, was as follows:

£.

For the year ended January 5, 1794   297,128
Ditto 1795   317,105
Ditto 1796   359,202
Ditto 1797   335,048

1,308,483

Duties upon tobacco commencing
December 7, 1795 156,515

Total   1,464,998

The payments into the exchequer, during the fame period, on the part of Scotland, were,

For the year ended January 5, 1794   36,000
Ditto 1795   33,000
Ditto 1796   37,000
Ditto 1797   38,000

Total   144,000

The tax upon tobacco, provided for defraying

X 3   ing

ing the increased charge of the public debt
from January 6, 1793, to January 5, 1797,
amounted to £.164,015.

The duties imposed upon tobacco and snuff
by the 36th George III. commenced December 7, 1795 ; and the first payment into the
exchequer was made January 7, 1797. The
actual receipt at the exchequer from January
5, 1797, to March 7, 1797, (so far as the same
could be made out) was £.27,090 *.

The quantity of tobacco delivered out for
home consumption, at the several ports of
Great Britain, in four years preceding January
5, 1797, with the amount of the gross and nett
duties of *customs* collected thereon, was as follows.

Years	Quantity lb.	Gross Duties £.	s.	d.	Nett Duties £.	s.	d.
1793	10,015,603	250,608	1	0	213,367	9	3
1794	10,848,087	271,201	8	6	241,889	13	6
1795	12,397,910	301,451	13	6	266,360	16	6
1796	11,490,446	287,252	11	0	252,453	11	0
Total	44,752,046	1,110,513	14	0	974,071	10	3

The select committee on finance, in their

* The tax imposed upon tobacco in 1796, paid into the
exchequer, between January 5 and April 5, 1797, the
actual sum of £.39,511.

fourth

fourth report to the houfe of commons in 1797, fanction the practice of warehoufing and bonding goods imported, by the national experience, in refpect to tobacco, in the following terms.

"Your committee cannot conclude their report upon this important branch of the revenue, without fubmitting to the confideration of the houfe, a meafure recommended by the higheft authority in matters of commercial policy *, and fupported by ftrong teftimony, derived from an enlightened and extenfive obfervation of practical details. It is conceived that the produce of the cuftoms might be greatly increafed (and the charges of management diminifhed, if not pofitively, yet comparatively, by the increafe of income), if means could be found for adopting the fyftem of warehoufing goods imported, and bonding the duties, without actually levying them till the goods are taken out for home confumption. That the application of this principle is juftified *by the prefent ufage in the cafe of tobacco*; and that all the moft important advantages of the fame general plan might be obtained by extending the practice to a very few of the

* Wealth of Nations, Vol. III. Book iii. Chap. 2 ; and Appendix (L 3.) of their Report.

　　　　　　　　largeft

largeſt articles of importation. * The policy of ſuch a meaſure, carried even to a wider extent, has been certainly *ſanctioned by the ableſt writings*; and your committee are now warranted by the official opinion of the inſpector general of the commerce of the empire, in recommending its limited execution, as *ſafe for the revenue*, and as *likely to be productive of very great national advantages.*

The tobacco warehouſe eſtabliſhment, for the port of London, in reſpect to *exciſe*, contained, in the year 1797, thirteen officers, whoſe ſalaries amounted to £.1,143, fees £.1. 15. other emoluments £.4. 4 ; total emolument £.1,148. 19. 0; nett emoluments £.1,113. 7. 6 : theſe are eſtimated as an increaſe of thirteen officers, whoſe ſalaries amount to £.1,143 †.

The value of tobacco imported for the half years ending January 5, 1797, July 5, 1797, and January 5, 1798, was as follows.

Half year ending January 5, 1797   £.138,669
    Ditto .   .   . July 5,   1797   151,544
    Ditto .   .   . January 5, 1798   155,695

* The committee cite the authorities herein before referred to.

† See fifth Rep. Com. Fin. 1797, for particulars, inſerted in the Appendix to this work.

The

The nett payment into the exchequer of the produce of duties upon tobacco (fubject to payment of bounties, management, &c.), in the four quarters ending in October 1798, was £.273,165. 5. 0.

The average annual duties arifing from tobacco imported into Ireland *, and collected thereon, for three years preceding March 25, 1798, amounted to £.144,199.

The fame duties upon tobacco of the United States, imported and exported, amounted to the fum of £.38,929. 19. 2.

Under the head of permanent taxes, *for the year* 1796, the produce of duties upon tobacco ending January 5, 1798, amounted to £.168,255.

The fhips laden (or chiefly fo) with tobacco, which (according to the Jerquer's books) arrived in London annually from America, from the year 1792 to 1798, both years inclufive, were as follow, viz.

1792	84 fhips	1796	55 fhips
1793	56 ditto	1797	53 ditto
1794	56 ditto	1798	72 ditto
1795	55 ditto		

* See lord Auckland's fpeech on the union *(Appendix,* No. 6) April 11, 1799.

Mr.

Mr. Irving, infpector general of the exports and imports of Great Britain, on his examination before a committee of the houfe of commons, touching the improvement of the port of London, on the 1ft of July, 1799, gives it as his opinion, that it would be eligible to warehoufe tobacco (as an article which he enumerates among others), at Wapping, or the Ifle of Dogs; leaving the proprietors their choice. He ftates objections to the king's warehoufes upon Tower-hill; becaufe, inftead of being landed directly from the veffel on the quays or wharfs, and rolled from thence into the adjacent warehoufes, as the cafe would be if it were difcharged in the docks, it is brought up from fhips moored about a quarter of a mile below the Tower in lighters, landed on the legal quays, and from thence conveyed in carts, at the expence of one fhilling and fourpence per hogfhead, to the king's warehoufes on Tower-hill.

The fame trouble, and nearly the fame expence, is faid to attach to exportation; and this is confidered to be, chiefly, a depot article: the quantity ufed for home confumption being fmall in proportion to what is re-exported.

Tobacco and rice are allowed to form two confiderable

confiderable articles of the imports of Great Britain; both thefe are efteemed proper fubjects for the warehoufing fyftem; and as the proportion of rice from Virginia, or Maryland, or of tobacco from Carolina, or Georgia, is likely to be very inconfiderable in comparifon, there does not appear to be any material reafon to feparate them far apart.

From what has been faid, and the foregoing details, it will be readily feen that it is of great importance to the Britifh nation to ftand well with the *tobacco* ftates of America. I hope hereafter to have a better opportunity of enlarging upon thefe fubjects. I fhall only, at prefent, add a few points which have been paffed over, from the higheft authority of the Britifh government.

The quantity of tobacco imported from America in 1791, was 14,119,636 lb. of the value of £.588,318. In the year 1792 the quantity of tobacco imported into great Britain, from America, was 22,427,124 lb. of the value of £.934,463. For the year 1798, the importation of tobacco *is ftated* at the fame quantity with the year 1791*, viz. 14,119,636 lb. which feems to be fomewhat extraordinary.

* See fecond Report of the Committee on the improvement of the Port of London, 1799, p. 119.

Under

Under the *exiſting* laws*, tobacco is ware-houſed on importation without payment of any exciſe duty; and may be taken out again for exportation free of any exciſe duty, or with a drawback thereof. But it is com-plained of, that *tobacco* is among the articles which are permitted to remain longer in the warehouſe than is conſiſtent with the ſafety of the revenue.

---

* See ſecond Report of the Committee on the Improve-ment of the Port of London, 1799, p. 121,

APPENDIX.

APPENDIX.

An Account of what Increase or Diminution has taken place since 1782, *in the Number, or in the Amount of the Salaries, concerning Tobacco, in the Office of* CUSTOMS *for London and the out Ports, extracted from Appendix (G* 1.*) VI. Rep. Sel. Com. on Finance, July* 1797.

For the Port of London.

SIX of the landing waiters and deputy king's waiters are appointed by rotation to the tobacco department, for a certain time, during which they have an additional £.100 per annum each, amounting to six hundred pounds per annum, by an order of the board, May 5, 1786.

The office of register general of tobacco is abolished, and one of the clerks thereof is allowed £.55 per annum for life. The reduction of officers, and saving of salaries, which result from this measure are as follow.

Register

	Officers.	Salaries.
Regifter general of tobacco	1	£.380
Clerks to ditto	5	360
Bargeman for conveying damaged tobacco from the quays to the kiln	1	40
Clerks for the inland tobacco bufinefs under the collector . .	2	120
Clerks for the inland tobacco bufinefs under the comptroller	2	120
Superintendant of the tobacco lockers	1	5
Tobacco cooper	1	40
Viewer and examiner of tobacco	1	

The annual faving is   14   £.1065

The increafe of officers, of falary, the time, authority, and tenure of appointments, introduced, are as follow.

	Officers.	Salary.	Date of appointment.	Authority.	Tenure.
Principal furveyor in the tobacco department . . .	1	£.400	March 28, 1787	Treafury	dur. plea.
Comptrolling furveyor, ditto	1	350	Ditto	Ditto	Ditto
Warehoufe keeper of the tobacco department	1	200	Ditto	Ditto	Ditto
Firft clerk of the tobacco department	1	60	Aug. 29, 1787	Board'sMin.	Ditto

Second

	Officers.	Salary.	Date of appointment.	Authority.	Tenure.
Second department	1	50	May 5, 1786	Boards Ord.	Ditto
Two gate keepers at the tobacco ware-houſes, each £.50	2	100			
Three lockers Three landing officers Four ſtationed guard at the tobacco ware-houſes			Theſe are allowed each one ſhilling per day when employed, in addition to their pay as preferable weighers.		
A tide waiter for acting as inſpector of the tobacco water guard		61	July 14, 1786 Jan. 22, 1792	Board's Ord. Board's Min.	Ditto Ditto
Three additional tide ſurveyors, for acting in the tobacco department . . .		63 10	July 14, 1786	Board's Ord.	Ditto
Meſſenger in the tobacco department	1	40	July 29, 1789	Board's Min.	Ditto
The annual increaſe is	8	£.1324 10 *			

An officer for taking care of the damaged tobacco, &c. diſcontinued, by which reduction there is a ſaving of one officer, and £.40 ſalary †.

Appointer of tobacco weighers for the port of London, his ſalary increaſed £.15 ‡.

* Extracted as above from the fourth Rep. Select Com. on Finance, 1797, Appendix (G 1.).

† See fourth Rep. Com. Fin. p. 94.—Appendix, (G 1.) March 13, and April 9, 1795.

‡ See fourth Rep. Com. Fin. 1797, p. 94, Appendix (G 1.)

Aſſiſtant

Affiftant to the fearchers for detecting frauds in manufacturing tobacco, &c. difcontinued, by which there is faved one officer, and £.80 falary *.

Allowance to the collector at Whitehaven for a tobacco clerk, increafed one officer, £.40, March 27, 1787, by order of the board †.

At Liverpool.

Affiftant warehoufe keeper for tobacco, one officer and £.100 falary, November 3, 1786, board's order.

Two landing waiters employed in the tobacco warehoufes in lieu of fees, each £.80, two officers, and £.160 falary, November 3, 1786, September 7, 1790, board's order.

Two weighing porters employed in the fame department, in lieu of fees fix pence per day, two officers and £.15. 12. falary, June 27, 1788, board's order ‡.

The poundage upon feizures is *now* (though not formerly) extended to *tobacco* ; upon which it is allowed to the officers of the cuftoms §.

* See fourth Rep. Com. Fin. 1797, p. 94, Appendix (G 1.)
† Ibid p. 104.   ‡ Ibid. p. 106.
§ See examination of John Dally, Efq. taken May 24, 1797.—Fourth Rep. Com. Fin, 1797, p. 111.
N. B. See examination of William Cooper, Efq. touch-
ing

ing the moſt complete collection of the cuſtom laws. Fourth Rep. Com. Fin. 1797, Appendix, (L 2.) p. 138.

It does not appear that there is any collection of the exciſe laws printed and ſold for public uſe ; but there is a collection of all the ſtatutes paſſed previous to the 33d of George III. printed for the uſe of the office, with a complete analyſis of their contents. The committee ſee no reaſon why this ſhould not be *publiſhed* unreſervedly.

Q. Would the ſyſtem of warehouſing goods in general, imported upon principles ſimilar to that of tobacco, be productive of any eſſential benefit to the trade and revenues of the country ?

See Mr. Irving's anſwer to this queſtion, fourth Rep. Com. Fin. 1797, Appendix (L 3.) p. 140.

Excise

EXCISE ESTABLISHMENTS of the *Tobacco Warehouse* for the Port of *London*, taken from the fifth Report from the Select Committee on Finance, 1797, Appendix, (C 1.) p. 52.

No. of Off.	Employments	Gross Emoluments: Sall. & fixed Allow.	Fees	Other Emolum.	Total of Emoluments	Deductions: Taxes	Other Deduc. tions	Total Deduc. tions	Nett Emoluments	Appointm	Dur. of Int.	Increa. since 1782.	OBSERVATIONS.
	Tobacco warehouses	£.	£. s.	£. s.	£. s.	£. s. d.		£. s. d.	£. s. d.			£.	
1	Surveyor. Richard Jones	150	1 15 2		153 17 2	11 5 0		11 5 0	142 12 0			150	—Thefe fees are a payment of fix pence per lot for all feizures of tobacco and fnuff fold and delivered; and thefe emoluments of £.2 2 are an allowance of two guineas on each writ of appraifement of fuch feizures for condemnation in the exchequer, as the appraifer.
1	Chief warehoufe keeper.												
1	John Bilton.,........	95		2 2	97	2 7 6		2 7 6	94 14 6			*9	* This emolument is £.1 1 on each writ above mentioned, as the other appraifer.
1	Ditto. Samuel Smith....	95			95	2 7 6		2 7 6	92 12 6			95	
1	Ditto. George Avins....	95			95	2 7 6		2 7 6	92 12 6			95	
6	Warehoufe keepers. Each £.92 0 0 Taxes 2 6 Nett 89 14	552			552	13 16 0		13 16 0	538 0 0	By the Commiffioners.	During pleafure.	552	
2	Lockers, Each 58 0 0 Taxes 1 9 Nett £.56 11	116			116	2 18 0		2 18 0	113 2 0			116	
1	Porter and fire lighter.....	40			40				40 0 0			40	
13	Total	1143	1 15 4	2 2	1148 19 4	35 1 6		35 1 6	1117 17 6			1143	

The

The duty of the furveyor is to fuperintend the officers of this department; to compare the accounts of excife duties paid for tobacco and fnuff, and take charge of feizures thereof. The chief warehoufe keepers keep account of goods brought in and fent out, and of duties paid to the collector at the port; and they grant permits, and make out a weekly voucher of fuch duties. The warehoufe keepers attend the weighing of tobacco and fnuff inwards and outwards, and take account of the weights. The lockers attend the ftowing away, and the delivery of the goods. And the porter watches the gate, lights the fires, and cleans the rooms in which the officers of this revenue perform their bufinefs.

Since 1782, this eftablifhment has been made, in confequence of the placing tobacco and fnuff under furvey of the officers of the *excife*. It having been lately reported to the board, that from a change of the mode in which the American merchants conduct their bufinefs, a much lefs quantity of tobacco is imported for exportation than formerly. It is now in contemplation to drop two warehoufe keepers, by which there will be a faving to the revenue of £.184 a year.

Duties

Duties payable upon Tobacco in Great Britain,
     1799.   Referred to in p. 225.

" Tobacco * may be imported on paying the
fame duties of cuftoms and excife, as when
imported by Britifh fubjects from Britifh plantations in America; and fnuff, upon payment
of the fame duties as fnuff, the manufacture
of Europe, when imported from Europe; tobacco and fnuff paying alfo the *countervailing*
duties †, when imported in American fhips."

According to *Mafcall's* Tables, p. 112, *Tobacco*, now (1799), *if regularly imported, entered, landed, and warehoufed,* is to pafs free
from duty.

It is neverthelefs to be underftood that tobacco and fnuff cannot be imported in lefs
cafks than 450 lb. nett weight, except it be
in fmall quantities for fhips' ufe, not exceeding
five pounds per man, and in veffels of one
hundred and twenty tons burden or upwards.
Thefe are limited to the ports of London, Briftol, Liverpool, Lancafter, Cowes, Falmouth,
Whitehaven, Hull, Glafgow, Greenock, Leith,

---

* Steel's Tables, p. 2.

† *Countervailing* duties are certain *additional* duties impofed upon importations from the United States in *American*
fhips.

ʃ   **and**

and Newcaftle upon Tyne ; but fuch fhips, laden wholly with tobacco, may go into Cowes or Falmouth, and wait fourteen days, in thofe ports, for orders.

Tobacco, which is cleared from the king's warehoufes for home confumption, muft pay the following duties, viz.

Tobacco of the growth, production, or manufacture of Spain or Portugal, or their dominions, muft pay one fhilling and fix pence per pound weight for confolidated cuftoms, and eighteen twentieths of a penny per pound weight for duties of 1796. For convoy duty two fhillings and fix pence per hundred pounds ; and for excife three fhillings.

Tobacco of the growth or production of the United States of America, when imported in an American fhip, muft pay fix pence per pound weight confolidated cuftoms, and is allowed fix pence per pound weight drawback ; it alfo pays fix-twentieth parts of a penny per pound weight duty of 1796. For every hundred pounds weight it pays alfo one fhilling and fix pence countervailing duties ; convoy duty two fhillings and fix pence ; and one fhilling and one penny excife.

Tobacco of the United States, or Britifh plantations, when imported in a Britifh built
fhip,

ſhip, muſt pay ſix pence per pound weight conſolidated cuſtoms, ſix-twentieth part of a penny per pound weight duty of 1796 ; two ſhillings and ſix pence per hundred pounds weight convoy ; and one ſhilling and one penny exciſe.

Tobacco of Ireland pays ſix pence per pound weight conſolidated cuſtoms ; ſix-twentieth parts of a penny per pound weight duty of 1796 ; and one ſhilling and one penny exciſe.

An Account of the Value of all Imports into, and all Exports from, Great Britain, for twelve Years preceding January 5, 1799.

Imports.

Years	Value of Imports excluſive of the Eaſt Indies and China.			Value of Imports from the Eaſt Indies and China.			Total Value imported.		
1787	14373156	15	7	3430806	0	6	17804024	16	1
1788	14573290	17	9	3453897	3	5	18027188	1	2
1789	14461954	9	2	3359148	1	5	17821102	10	7
1790	15981015	11	0	3149870	14	3	19130886	5	3
1791	15971069	0	7	3698713	13	0	19669782	13	7
1792	16957810	17	3	2701547	9	4	19659358	6	7
1793	15757693	16	10	3499023	12	10	19256717	9	8
1794	17830418	19		4458475	1	5	22288894	0	5
1795	16976179	1	8	5760710	8	3	22736889	9	11
1796	19800957	0	5	3386362	18	0	23187319	18	5
1797	17063794	8	5	3950162	9	0	21013956	17	5
1798	20236285	19	11						

Exports.

Exports.

Years.	Value of British Manufactures exported.			Value of foreign Merchandize exported.			Total Value of Exports.		
1787	12054224	3	2	4815890	2	5	16870114	5	7
1788	12724612	7	1	4747 96	0 .	6	17472408	7	7
1789	13779506	2	6	5561042	14	5	19340548	16	11
1790	14921084	9	7	5199037	7	11	20120121	17	6
1791	16810018	16	4	5921976	10	11	22731995	7	3
1792	18336851	6	11	6568348	16	6	24905200	3	5
1793	13992268	17	7	6497911	9	3	20390180	6	10
1794	16725 02	16	2	10023564	19	3	26748967	15	5
1795	6527213	2	2	10785125	15	2	27312338	17	4
1796	19106444	17	5	11317740	0	8	30424184	18	1
1797	16903103	6	1	12013907	2	0	28917010	8	1
1798	19771510	11	4	13883885	18	11	33655396	10	3

N. B. The declared value is fuppofed to exceed the rate of value in the infpector general's books about 71 per cent.

The account of the imports from China for the laft year (1798) could not be obtained in time for infertion.

In the fummer of 1796, the infpectors of tobacco at certain warehoufes in the town of Peterfburgh in Virginia, are faid to have been fufpected of making ufe of tobacco, depofited in thefe public warehoufes, to anfwer their own occafions. This fufpicion brought about an inveftigation, in the month of November

of

of the fame year, whereby the deficiency was afcertained to be about *two hundred hogfheads*. It is fuppofed that there was a deficiency of this nature as early as 1794; but the infpectors had it in their power to fubftitute tobacco fraudulently, in order to cover their fcheme, by felling returned notes, and iffuing them a *fecond time* * into the world as the medium of circulation in this extraordinary fpecies of peculation. They not only thus re-iffued the notes which fhould have been officially *cancelled*, but are faid to have iffued *falfe* notes upon a fimilar bafis, and to have been detected in both inftances.

The infpectors endeavoured (as I am informed) to charge the merchants with this malfeafance ; and the merchants, on the other hand, combined to detect a mifdemeanour fo injurious to the reputation of commerce, and tending to implicate themfelves in the iffue of this weak and impracticable fubterfuge. Finally, the guilt was afcertained ; the infpectors are faid to have either connived at, or acted in the premifes both perfonally and by the help of others ; and the deficiency was faddled upon one or more of thefe agents of

* See page 86.

the

the public trade, who appeared to have re-fold the notes after the fubject matter of their re-ponfibility had been fhipped.

The legiflature were now petitioned, unfuc-cefsfully, by the parties who had been de-ceived ; and the latter were ultimately driven to an action at law againft the ftate, which I underftand to be yet undetermined *.

Immediately after this petition of the fuf-ferers was rejected, an act of the legiflature was paffed for the amendment of the tobacco laws; and commiffioners were appointed to examine the infpectors' books from time to time, to take inventories of the tobacco in the warehoufes, to adjuft the weights, &c. Thefe commiffioners have now a confiderable controul over the infpectors in all neceffary inftances ; but they have no power to reftrain or direct them in regard to paffing or refufing the crop. There are fix commiffioners, now in office, who officiate for the infpections at Peterf-burgh : and they are faid to have been already of very great fervice to the trade.

I am happy to learn, and think it my duty to add to this recital, the exculpation of the fenior infpector, who, I am informed, ap-

* See page 72.

peared

peared to be innocent as to the *crime,* and no farther blameable as to the *permiſſion* of it than what might be aſcribable to an overſight; or, perhaps, to an unſuſpecting confidence in his fellows in office.

THE END.

Printed by T. BENSLEY, Bolt Court, Fleet Street, London.

2.

William Tatham and
the Culture of Tobacco

By G. MELVIN HERNDON

CHAPTER 1

The Book

FEW people were better qualified to write a detailed descriptive account of American tobacco culture at the end of the eighteenth century than William Tatham. Following his arrival in Virginia in 1769, he spent the next quarter of a century in Virginia, North Carolina, and the Tennessee settlements. Tobacco was produced in all three of these areas, emerging in the backcountry about the time Tatham became associated with the Watauga Settlements. While Tatham was successful neither as a farmer nor as a merchant, his experiences in both of these ventures served to strengthen his firsthand knowledge of every detailed facet of the culture of the "golden weed," from the preparation of the plant bed until the staple was prized into the hogshead, marketed, and exported. Not only did he possess knowledge gained from his own practical experiences, he also made ample use of available historical material, both American and English. Tatham was an avid collector of books and manuscript material and had written and published several pamphlets and at least one book prior to 1800.

Despite his many and varied interests and occupations, Tatham confessed that his greatest interests lay in the areas of agriculture and civil engineering. Many of his writings dealt with problems and topics involving considerable knowledge of civil engineering, yet except for his *An Historical and Practical Essay on the Culture and Commerce of Tobacco* (London, 1800) few people have ever heard of William Tatham. It is as an agricultural historian that he has earned some recognition.

His *Essay on Tobacco* is frequently referred to and cited, but seldom read. It is one of the most complete and extensive contemporary essays on the history of tobacco culture in eighteenth century America. And, most important, the many unique practices involved from planting to marketing the staple are described simply and clearly, enabling those unfamiliar with early American agriculture to understand this aspect of it with little or no difficulty. Since the book deals with the staple commodity so important to the total existence of several colonies, it also has historical value beyond the singular topic of tobacco.

Tatham seems to have had definite objectives in mind when he wrote the book: (1) to emphasize the nature of the decline of the Anglo-American tobacco trade following the American Revolution, (2) to point out the economic value of this trade to both parties, and (3) to suggest what might be done to strengthen this branch of commerce. He was writing primarily for British consumption and hoped it would influence trade relations with the United States.

The book is divided into six parts. In parts I, II, and III the author was at his best, and it is these three sections that make the work a classic on the culture of tobacco. Here he clearly describes in one hundred pages the numerous tasks involved in growing, harvesting, curing, and marketing tobacco. No one surpassed Tatham's contribution in describing the tobacco culture of his era. These three sections were written largely from his twenty-five years of observation and experiences in those areas of North America where tobacco was an important staple. His detailed drawings—showing the typical tobacco barn, the curing process, the operation of prizing tobacco into hogsheads, the process of inspection at public warehouses, and those illustrating the methods of transporting tobacco to market—are picturesque and often have been reproduced by historians working with this period.

In the latter portion of Part III, Tatham provides an excellent summary of the labor force used on tobacco plantations, including comments on what was no doubt the general attitude towards slavery in the southern region of post-Revolutionary America, especially Virginia. "It is true, indeed that the policy of the law has invested the master with an absolute authority to tyrannize; but this is rarely exercised, and especially since the American revolution" (p. 105). He described the slave master as kind and paternalistic and the slave as happy with his lot; ". . . prudence often elevates their circumstances above the industrious labourer of Europe; . . . the mitigated condition of their present shackles, renders the name of the thing more horrible than the restraint, . . ." (p. 105). Concluding his commentary on slavery, Tatham wrote: "Happily for myself, I neither am, nor ever shall be, a slave-holder" (p. 106).

Part III, *Supplementary,* consists largely of excerpts and summaries of three published works that dealt with the culture of tobacco in Virginia and Maryland. This section provides little additional significant material on the subject, but a comparison of these commentaries with Tatham's own descriptions illustrates two significant points. First, the section taken from Hugh Jones, *The Present State of Virginia* (London, 1724), indicates that no major changes had taken place in the general method of growing tobacco in Virginia during the eighteenth century. Second, the summary account, "Method of Raising and Curing Tobacco in Maryland," written in 1786, suggests the universality of the general methods and practices of growing tobacco in all of the various tobacco-producing areas. The careful observer will note, however, in the brief essay on tobacco by a Judge Richard Parker, that in northern Virginia cultural methods were somewhat different as to details. In regard to the description of tobacco culture in Maryland, there was one development worthy of observation. Many growers had learned to cure a particular type known as Kite-foot, which was somewhat lighter in color and had a smoked taste, by using active hickory fires until the curing process was completed.

This type commanded superior prices at the end of the eighteenth century. Thus Maryland produced a "bright" tobacco before the real Bright-tobacco type emerged in Virginia and North Carolina in the antebellum period.

Parts IV, V, and VI deal almost exclusively with the commerce of tobacco. These sections are for the most part less readable and contain little information not already in print at that time. By the time Tatham reached this portion of his project he seems to have been compelled to hurriedly complete the work. This was one of his peculiar traits. On virtually every project he undertook he seemed to lose interest before its completion and could hardly wait to embark on a new one. These sections consist largely of paragraphs, whole sections, and numerous charts taken from various sources. This made organization and a readable style most difficult, and these parts lack the care and deliberation with which the first parts were written. The statistics of these sections, however, provide an excellent source of reference material on the commerce of tobacco between America and Great Britain.

Part IV was an overambitious attempt to summarize the culture and commerce of tobacco from its sixteenth century origins in the New World to the end of the eighteenth century. This proved to be a task far beyond the scope of Tatham's knowledge of the material at his command. The summary turned out to be sporadic and somewhat disjoined, a fact which Tatham himself had come to realize by the time he had completed the section, and for which he offered an apology and provided

some additional material in an Appendix. Despite
its shortcomings, this section points out the importance of tobacco in Virginia as an item of barter
and its status as legal tender and as an item of
taxation to support local government. Part IV also
contains a lengthy summary of the legislation designed to regulate the quantity and quality of tobacco in an effort to improve its status in the domestic and foreign markets. Thus the problems of
quantity and quality controls in the American tobacco industry have their origins in the Colonial
period rather than in relatively recent years.

Part V contains an excellent account of the commerce of tobacco in terms of tasks, problems, and
regulations involved from the time the hogsheads
were taken from the inspection warehouses in
America until properly disposed of at storage facilities in England. This section is superior to parts
IV or VI. Here as in the first three parts Tatham
writes largely from first-hand knowledge based
upon previous experiences in mercantile pursuits.
He explains how tobacco hogsheads were loaded
aboard seagoing vessels anchored at various points
along navigable inland waterways. He then dis-
cusses such matters as insurance, freight rates, and
procedures for clearing American waters. Then
such matters as duties, ports of entry for tobacco
cargoes, and the numerous regulations involved in
getting ships docked and unloaded are dealt with.
One is impressed by the amount of red tape and the
rigid regulations involved in the process of exporting tobacco to British ports, especially after the
Revolution. Such conditions reveal the high value

placed upon the tobacco trade by the British as a source of customs revenue and the great desire of Britons for the commodity. The majority of the regulations were designed to prevent tobacco from being smuggled into the country, a practice that increased considerably during and after the Revolution and grew progressively worse in the decades before the Civil War. It has been estimated that by 1860 nearly half of the tobacco consumed in Great Britain was smuggled in.[1] Characteristically, Tatham had advice to offer. He suggested how the British might modify their customs procedure and pointed out the advantages of adopting a more favorable policy towards the American tobacco trade.

In Part VI Tatham attempted to strengthen and justify his plea for better commercial relations with the tobacco-producing states of the United States. Relying heavily on Adam Anderson's four volume edition of *An Historical and Chronological Deduction of the Origin of Commerce from the Earliest Accounts to the Present Time* (London, 1787–1789) and George Chalmers' *An Estimate of the Comparative Strength of Britain during the Present and Four Preceding Reigns* (London, 1794), Tatham summarized the tobacco trade between America and Great Britain for two centuries: ". . . my design," wrote Tatham, [is] "to disseminate commercial knowledge, and to multiply the resources of useful traffic" (p. 247); ". . . by comparing the three periods of importation which existed in this kingdom antecedent to the American war, during the war, and since the return of a happy peace, we may be better able to learn and improve the true reciprocity of interest which subsists between the two countries through the medium of national commerce" (p. 300).

In summarizing the British-American tobacco trade prior to the Revolution, Tatham chose the most impressive statistics to use as illustrations. Selecting the years 1744, 1745, and 1746 to get a good medium figure to work with, he pointed out that Great Britain imported forty-seven million pounds of tobacco annually, and the Crown netted for the above three-year period an annual medium revenue duty of £138,541/13/4 on the seven million pounds of tobacco consumed at home. In view of the fact that Great Britain exported about eighty percent of her imported tobacco, forty million pounds of tobacco at six pence per pound amounted to £1,000,000, "Which said million sterling may be deemed to be *clear gain to the nation,* over and above this trade's giving employment to about twenty-five thousand tons of British shipping" (p. 280). In the last several years before the opening of hostilities the annual importation of American tobacco into Great Britain rose to about 100,000,000 pounds.

By the close of the Revolution the tobacco trade had reached a very low ebb. In 1782 tobacco imports into Great Britain from all sources had dropped to about 10,000 pounds annually. The termination of hostilities and the restoration of the prewar draw-back policy by the British orders in council in 1783 and 1785 brought about a sizable revival of the American tobacco trade. Official British tobacco imports were still less than half that of the immediate prewar period. In 1798 Great Britain imported 40,652,603 pounds. Within a few years after the close of the war American tobacco exports to Europe surpassed the prewar average. "From what has been said, and the foregoing details," Tatham wrote, "it will be readily seen that it is of great importance to the British nation to stand well with the *tobacco* states of America" (p. 315).

Tatham pointed out two major reasons as to why the British-American tobacco trade did not return to the prewar level following the war. Tobacco for consumption in Great Britain was subjected to excise duties in addition to heavy customs duties. These heavy duties encouraged a very extensive practice of smuggling. In addition to this, political independence encouraged prewar notions of direct trade with other nations. Thus it was important that the British nation "stand well" with the tobacco states. Tatham had reason to anticipate the expansion of tobacco culture in the backcountry and believed that Britain should not only encourage a return to the prewar level in the tobacco trade, but that she and the tobacco-producing states would be mutually rewarded by the expansion of American tobacco culture.

Tatham's ". . . confident hopes that the public approbation will call for a supplementary part" (p. iv) to his *Essay on Tobacco* that would include a general history of tobacco in Europe were not realized. Few Englishmen were interested in a detailed description of how tobacco was grown in former British colonies. As to the sections on the commerce of tobacco, an Englishman might very easily have raised the question as to which of the two parties Tatham was most concerned about, the British or the "tobacco states" in America. The British apparently received his essay on tobacco as they did his *Communication Concerning the Agriculture and Commerce of the United States of America,* also published in 1800, of which one reviewer wrote: "The general impression we felt on reading this pamphlet was singular; it bears such constant internal proofs of American habits in the author, that we felt a sensation as if in a new world." [2]

Lyon G. Tyler, in his *History of Virginia: The Federal Period, 1763–1861,* assigned Tatham's *Essay on Tobacco* an important place as an agricultural treatise in early nineteenth century Virginia. Following the Revolution the culture of tobacco was soon abandoned in Tidewater Virginia as planters and farmers turned largely to the growing of wheat and other small grains. However, the culture of tobacco expanded into the western and southwestern counties as rapidly as it was abandoned in the old tobacco-producing areas. In regard to this agricultural transformation in Virginia, Tyler wrote: "But tobacco still remained a favorite staple, and its intelligent production was much encouraged by a book written by William Tatham. . . ." [3] Lewis C. Gray, the great agricultural historian, listed Tatham's *Essay on Tobacco* as one of "a number of contemporary treatises on agriculture [that] deserve to rank as sources.

. . ." [4] Joseph C. Robert, one of the foremost authorities on the history of tobacco in the United States, called Tatham's book "A classic account of early tobacco culture . . ." [5] Perhaps the greatest tribute to Tatham's book is the frequency with which distinguished scholars have used it as a major source on the subject.

CHAPTER 2

William Tatham

WILLIAM TATHAM, age seventeen, arrived in Virginia from his native England April 13, 1769 "with no more than one single family guinea in his pocket" and "without profession, trade or employment." [1] He became a clerk, merchant, soldier, surveyor, engineer, lawyer, and legislator. He was also an agriculturalist, inventor, adventurer, author, and book-collector, as well as a friend of many great men of his day both in America and in England. He called at Monticello and frequently corresponded with Thomas Jefferson. He was also one of the two Americans holding membership in the Royal Society of Arts in the early nineteenth century. [2] A prominent London magazine wrote: "He was a man of great information, of great genius, and of great resource of mind." [3]

He was truly one of the most remarkable men of his time, yet despite his great intellect and many talents, he was a failure in most of his endeavors, in part a victim of his own versatility. In several instances his ideas and projects were too far ahead of his time. He was eccentric, incapable of managing his finances, and in later years became addicted to alcohol and lived in poverty. He died, apparently by suicide, in Richmond, Virginia, February 22, 1819,[4] as poor as he was the day he first arrived in America fifty years earlier.

William Tatham was born at Hutton-in-the-Forest in the County of Cumberland, England, in 1752, the eldest son of Reverend Sanford Tatham, rector of the parish of Hutton. The rector's salary was inadequate to maintain a household containing five children; consequently, William was sent to live with his maternal grandmother, the widow of Henry Marsden, Esquire of Gisborne Hall, at Lancaster until her death in 1760. Following her death, he was removed from the Friends' School at Lancaster and placed for a time under the tutelage of the Reverend Mr. Lee, Curate of Lancaster Church. The remainder of the scanty education his parents and relatives were able to provide was administered by a Reverend Watson and a Mr. Pooler at Over Kellet.[5] According to Tatham, "In the autumn of 1768, my father sent me from school in Liverpool, thence to be sent to Messrs. Carter and Trent, native American merchants on the James River, to be brought up in the commercial pursuits of the tobacco trade. On my birth day [April 13] in 1769 I arrived in Virginia, and was immediately received into their employ, serving them faithfully several years. . . ."[6] Carter and Trent maintained a branch on the James River in Amherst County, Virginia, and it was apparently there that Tatham was first employed by the firm as a clerk. He stayed with this mercantile concern until the partnership of Carter and Trent was dissolved in February, 1774.[7] Tatham then attempted to operate a trading business of his own. His commercial speculations soon ended in failure, which he was quick to blame on recent British policies and the impact of the American "Non-importation Associations."[8]

Undaunted by his business failure, Tatham then hastened to enter military service to fight against the British, despite pressure to the contrary from his family in England. When the Revolution erupted he was forbidden by his family to join the American cause, ". . . but my own opinion of national rights preponderating, I joined Gatlands Volunteers, in Lunenburg, Virginia, but was not with them at the battle of the Great Bridge (Norfolk) [December 9, 1775] on account of my return from Petersburg to Lunenburg on important business, under orders verbally."[9] Tatham's failure to find excitement at Great Bridge probably caused him to remove to the western frontier in search of adventure and fortune; in addition, John Carter, a good friend and a relative of his former employer, was already well established in the Tennessee country. In April, 1776, Tatham headed for the Watauga-Holston settlements.[10]

On this first venture into the backcountry, Tatham remained for a little more than a year. His varied activities during this period indicate that he found much adventure but little fortune. His knowledge and experience in the use of the pen and his former association with the Carters were his most important assets. John Carter was already deeply involved in public affairs, trade, farming, and land speculation, and was in need of Tatham's services as clerk, bookkeeper, and apprentice surveyor. Tatham also served as temporary clerk of the Watauga Court in the spring of 1776 and drafted the "Petition of Inhabitants" to the North Carolina legislature (July 5, 1776) that requested recognition of Washington District. Following the creation of the new district, Tatham was appointed adjutant of the military force for the district and served in this capacity under Colonel John Carter during the attack by the Cherokees and Creeks on Fort Caswell on the Watauga River. He served in the same capacity under Major William Russell, who was based at Long Island on the Holston River, and participated in the erection of Fort Patrick Henry opposite Long Island. In the summer of 1777 the Indians sued for peace. When the peace commissioners from Virginia and North Carolina met with the Indian chiefs at Fort Patrick Henry, Tatham was selected as one of the clerks to record the proceedings of the meeting and later composed the official communications sent to the Governor of North Carolina. Soon thereafter he was commissioned quartermaster at Fort Williams, on the Nolachucky River, under Colonel John Sevier. The acquisition of a tract of land on the Nolachucky River did not prevent his wanderlust from urging him to move on. He left the Nolachucky country and returned to Virginia in the early fall of 1777.[11]

Tatham again entered the mercantile business in 1778, with no more success than his first such efforts in 1774–1775. He then re-entered the military service, joining a dashing voluntary cavalry unit made up of young gentlemen of Virginia who had equipped themselves at their own expense to serve under the command of General Thomas Nelson. The one active campaign of this special unit was assistance in quelling the riots at South Quay in 1778. During the year 1779 Tatham joined a military force under General Charles Scott, who commanded at Williamsburg. His knowledge of the countryside and his English background caused General Scott to use him largely as a scout to reconnoiter enemy troop movements and positions.[12]

While serving with General Scott, Tatham became acquainted with Samuel Hardy, a forceful member of the Virginia Bar and later a member of both the Virginia Legislature and the Continental Congress.[13] Hardy, a William and Mary College Phi Beta Kappa, seems to have recognized Tatham's intellectual potential and persuaded him to work toward entering the legal profession. During part of the winter of 1779–1780 Tatham attended sessions of the court and began to study law under the direction of his friend.[14] After being cooped up in Hardy's law office for several months, Tatham had had enough, at least for the moment. The call of the wild, the urgent need to see after his property, or the call of his benefactor, John Carter—or perhaps all of these—caused him to give up his studies and again head for the western frontier of North Carolina. Either by accident or by request, Tatham arrived in Washington County in the spring of 1780 at a time when his newly acquired legal knowledge and past clerical experience were

badly needed by the Carter family. John Carter
had recently resigned the office of entrytaker of
western lands and was succeeded by his son Lan-
don. Tatham assisted the son in straightening out
the office and spent several months attending to
legal matters for the Carter family.[15] During this
time he became intimately acquainted with two emi-
nent lawyers of North Carolina, Spruce Macay,
soon to become one of the judges of the Superior
Court in North Carolina, and William R. Davie,
both of whom were attending the courts in Washington County. Tatham later completed his law
studies under Davie and was first admitted to the
bar in North Carolina.

Warm friends in the backcountry could not compete with the thoughts of the cold hard winter
months ahead in an open log cabin, so Tatham
hastened back to Richmond, Virginia, before the
end of 1780. Upon his return to Richmond, he
became acquainted with Colonel John Todd, a del-
egate from the Kentucky country to the Virginia
General Assembly. The two of them combined
their knowledge and talents to compose "one of the
first manuscript sketches of the history of the western Country." [16] It was probably never printed, and
the manuscript has never been found; however, it
was this joint historical project that brought
Tatham into contact with Governor Thomas Jefferson and marked the beginning of their long and
warm friendship. Apparently Tatham and Todd
took their manuscript to the Governor's office, and
Jefferson seems to have been impressed with both
Tatham and the manuscript. In a letter to General

Nathanael Greene in December, 1780, Jefferson wrote of Tatham: "He is particularly acquainted with the Western Country of Virginia and Carolina beyond the mountains of which he has made a pretty good map; he is versed in writing and accounts and possesses understanding." [17]

Still in his twenties, Tatham's wanderlust, curiosity, and intelligence created in him an intense interest in various frontier regions of his adopted country. No doubt more interested in seeking knowledge of the more remote states of South Carolina and Georgia than in military service, Tatham used his newly acquired friendship with Governor Jefferson to get an assignment with General Greene. In a letter of introduction to Greene in the latter part of December, 1780, Jefferson wrote: "Being very anxious to take some station in or about the Southern army I thought it not amiss to make him [Tatham] known to you. He is represented to me as possessing in the fullest degree that spirit which is of the essence of a soldier. He has skill in draughts, of which you may form your own judgment on the samples he can shew you. . . ." [18]

Tatham was preparing to leave Richmond to join General Greene when he received the news of General Benedict Arnold's arrival within the Virginia capes. "I had my horses Portmanteau &c. ready fixed at the door, (& perhaps my foot actually in the stirrupp). . . ." [19] Instead of riding south, he rode over to Governor Jefferson's residence to discuss the situation and to offer his services. Jefferson suggested that he go to Baron von Steuben's camp "at Wilton . . . & receive his orders if needful." Steuben dispatched him to General Nelson at Williamsburg. Tatham found General Nelson at Kings Mills with about fifty-five men waiting to engage the enemy as they landed. "I delivered Baron Steubens orders to General Nelson & was invited to join his suite." [20] Due to his considerable knowledge of the country and possession of a good mount, Tatham was given the task of scouting the enemy: "I was alternately in view of the Enemy & in personal communication with the commanding officer, many miles apart, sometimes repeatedly in twenty four hours; so that I had speedily ridden down several very fine horses." [21] When the enemy reached the Charles City Court House, General Nelson became concerned about conflicting reports as to the safety of Governor Jefferson. He ordered Tatham to "find him be he wheresoever he might. . . ." [22] Tatham successfully avoided all enemy troop movements and "Enemy Picquets," entered Richmond, and learned that Governor Jefferson was across the James River in Manchester. With assistance from several "affected Citizens," Tatham finally located Jefferson and there ". . . delivered my dispatches & spent part of the evening." [23]

Tatham continued to serve as a major source of communication between Jefferson, General Nelson, and von Steuben until "I received a hurt in Amelia County, by falling in with about three hundred of the present Major Genl. Tarleton['s] Mounted legion alone; though by ten days hard struggle I had good fortune to get clear of them. This circumstance rendered me unfit for service, till I joined the army at Williamsburg, before Genl. Washington took command on our way to the siege of York[town]." Tatham was among those who stormed the redoubts at Yorktown.[24]

After several months of military inactivity following Yorktown Tatham accepted the position of Assistant Clerk to the Board of the Privy Council of Virginia. This appointment was probably due to the influence of his friend Samuel Hardy, a member of the Board. Tatham's adventuresome spirit found little excitement in his clerical tasks, and he resigned in August, 1782, after serving a little less than a month.[25] According to an English sketch of Tatham: "having engaged in an enterprize confident solely to his friend Mr. Hardy . . . , [he] went to sea in a broken vessel which depended greatly on her pumps for safety." [26] Tatham later wrote of the mysterious voyage: "In October, 1782, I was shipwrecked on the Jersey Coast and landed on a desert Island about five miles from the main land. On my reaching the main land in a canoe, I landed at the house of one Ludlam, on Cape May. . . ." [27] From there he made his way to Philadelphia and "entered again into commercial pursuits."

Tatham abandoned his "commercial pursuits" in Philadelphia in the spring of 1783, and armed with "a useful introductory" from Jefferson, he left Philadelphia on April 19 for Havana "in order to combine a knowledge of the Spanish interests in the West Indies with that he had acquired in those Western Countries of the United States which border on the Mississippi territories of his Catholic

Majesty. After spending some weeks at Havannah, and satisfying himself concerning the importance of that place in respect to the settlements just alluded to," [28] he returned briefly to Virginia and then made his way to North Carolina to the plantation of his friend, the prominent North Carolinian, William R. Davie.

The purpose of his journey to the Davie plantation was to complete the law studies he had begun under Samuel Hardy in 1779. He completed his "studies in the law" under Davie and became a member of the bar in North Carolina in March, 1784,[29] "with a practice worth $8000 per ann. . . ." [30] For the next several years Tatham appears to have been more interested in surveying, exploring, gathering geographical information of the backcountry, and working on projects to develop inland navigation than in the legal profession. He explored the rivers of North Carolina with a special interest in possible communications to the west toward the Mississippi River and South Carolina.

In 1786 John Willis, Tatham, and four others laid out and established the town of Lumberton in Robeson County, North Carolina. An act of the legislature in November, 1788, officially established the town, and the court named Henry Lightfoot, Elias Barnes, Jacob Rhodes, Sampson Bridgers, and William Tatham, Esquires as the original trustees. Although John Willis did convey "a certain quantity of land" to these trustees,[31] and no doubt they were in search of monetary gains, Tatham's primary interest and influence can be seen in the location of Lumberton and the engineering project he had in mind. Lumberton was founded on Drowning Creek about thirty miles below Fayetteville. With his engineering talents and experience, Tatham hoped to make Drowning Creek a major highway of communication. Regarding earlier experience with the improvement of navigation on inland waters, Tatham wrote: "I was an inhabitant of the County of Amherst in the year 1769; and, so far as an active Boy in a store could go, had from that period a share in preparing the way to the improved navigation of the James river and the general promotion of commercial transportation." [32]

As a resident of Robeson County, Tatham established himself as a respectable and substantial citizen. The title "Esquire" was soon attached to his name in the county records; in August, 1787 he was elected to the state legislature, and in December he was commissioned Lieutenant Colonel of the Fayetteville militia district. From this time on, he was frequently referred to as Colonel Tatham. In December, 1787, Tatham was selected as one of twelve nominees of the state legislature, from which six were to be chosen by ballot to serve in the Congress of the Confederation. He was not among the six chosen, however, [33] and the seat in the North Carolina legislature was to remain the only elective office he ever held.

Tatham seems to have taken his membership in the legislature seriously. He served on several committees, usually those concerned with questions in which his legal knowledge was helpful; he introduced several bills; and he frequently helped constituents with petitions to be presented to the legislature. His activities reveal a real interest in, and concern for, the people in the backcountry when issues such as land taxation and land speculation were involved. That his actions were based upon principle as well as upon concern for the geographical area is seen in his reaction to a question involving property rights in New Bern. In 1768 the Assembly deeded certain lots in the town to the "Governor and his Successors." Richard Dobbs Spaight later claimed that he had not been compensated for several of the lots that had belonged to him, and petitioned the legislature for correction of this injustice. In December, 1787, the legislature was asked to give its opinion. The House resolved that the lots in question constituted public property. Tatham voted against the resolution.

A week later Tatham displayed his disapproval of the former Loyalist element when he presented a committee report on "the Conduct of several Justices of the Peace in New Hanover County." The five justices of the peace involved had served the enemy during the Revolution. They previously had been suspended by a resolution of the Assembly, but had refused to give up their offices on the grounds that "the Resolution suspending them was contrary to the act of the Assembly under which they came into Court and took their seats. . . ." [34] The committee recommended "that their suspension be continued, that the Court be directed not to admit them on the Bench for the future, and the Clerk was not to record any of their transactions as the Acts of the Courts" until the General Assembly lifted the suspension at some future date.

Tatham felt as strongly about suffrage as he did about protection of property rights. He presented a bill to "enforce the attendance, of such Free-holders and Freemen as are entitled to vote for representatives for the Senate or House of Commons of the State of North Carolina, to give them suffrage at the annual Elections hereafter in this State, under a penalty. . . ." His bill found little support and was rejected after the first reading.[35] Another Tatham proposal that failed to win acceptance was his bill "to encourage the Citizens of this State and others, to promote and improve the several Arts, Sciences & Manufactures within the limits of the same. . . ." [36] His activities represent a respectable performance in the legislature in view of the fact that he actually served only a few months.

Tatham was a resident of Robeson County for about three years, and it appeared that he might finally be ready to settle down permanently. He seemed to have had every intention of remaining, until important family business caused him to return to England for the first time in twenty years. On March 8, 1788, he wrote John Gray Blount, prominent North Carolina planter and merchant, and brother of the well known William Blount:

> The arrival of my Brother [37] who came to me a few days ago gives me great hopes from my affairs in Europe, and determines me to go immediately to England, where I find my Personell presence will be absolutely necessary as speedily as possible. —The Ship *Irish Volunteer* sails in a few days from Wilmington to Liverpool and I shall endeavor to en-

counter every difficulty to gain passage in Her, which
I hope leave it in my power to be [back] in time for
the Hillsberough [Hillsborough] Convention of the
Assembly at Fayetteville at fartherest if I find affairs in Europe in proper train, shou'd I be obliged
to continue there any time do myself the honor to
open a regular correspondence. It is probable that I
shall be gone in The *Volunteer* before (my express)
the bearer returns, in which case my Brother will
attend to my Business and receive my Letters. —I
have however, for fear of disappointments taken the
liberty to accept Mr. Blounts [William?] friendly
offer "to endorse my Bills" and have for that purpose
inclosed the Sum of Two hundred and Fifty Pounds
Sterling in Five setts of Fifty Pounds each, to use in
case of emergency which will put me independent of
my prospects here and leave me a sufficiency to answer the purpose of the Voyage. —Mr Blount will
enclose these, and the power and Grants he spoke
of to care of Mr. William B. Grove [38] of Fayetteville with whom I shall leave instructions.

Shou'd I be disappointed of a passage on the *Vol-
unteer,* information from Mr. Blount of any prospect
He can carve out may be serviceable to me as my
Rout may be changed on missing the present chance.[39]

Tatham failed to sail on the *Irish Volunteer* as
planned, but he was able to secure passage on the
ship *America,* which reached England in the latter
part of September, 1788.[40] He apparently expected
to come into some money or property, or both.
Concerning his voyage to England, Tatham later
wrote: "Family concerns, (wherein I found a trick
concerning the statute of limitations) induced me
to go to England," [41] but he seems to have returned
empty-handed and without final settlement of
"family concerns." In 1810, Tatham stated that

hereditary rights were decided in his favor "when I was last in Engl[and] . . ." [1796 to 1805].[42] Tatham returned to the United States in July, 1789, arriving at Norfolk, Virginia, with the intention of returning to North Carolina, but the condition of his health caused him to go to Richmond by water to take care of some old business.[43] While recovering from his illness at the home of Robert Goode, a good friend of Revolutionary War days, in nearby Manchester, Thomas Jefferson arrived in Richmond from his diplomatic post in France. Tatham immediately wrote to Jefferson to welcome him home, and in the course of a rather lengthy letter referred to some difficulty he was having getting an appointment. General Henry Knox, Secretary of War, had instructed Governor Beverley Randolph and his advisors to select someone capable of supplying the War Department with topographical information on portions of the southern and western frontiers. Randolph was in favor of giving the position to Tatham. Benjamin Harrison, ex-Governor of Virginia, had some reason to distrust Tatham, an Anglo-American, for a task relative to military defenses and vigorously opposed his appointment. Despite the fact that Governor Randolph and others came to his defense, Tatham was not given the post until after Jefferson's return. Jefferson apparently interceded on his behalf.

Early in 1790 Tatham was busy at his newly assigned task in Richmond. Governor Randolph gave him free access to public records, papers, and the data in the archives. In February Tatham wrote Jefferson: "I have taken a slight view of what is there depicted, but find the appearance of information far short of what it was in your administration, perhaps they have been destroyed by Arnold, but I will flatter myself and will suppose they were preserved as your private property, since I recollect some of them were." [44] In April he received from Governor Randolph a sizable bundle of papers concerning the western parts of Virginia. After acknowledging receipt of this material, he wrote the Governor: "These Authorities, with the surveys of the Potowmack, and maps in my own possession, will enable me to come as near your Excellency's request as any individual, but I am clearly of opinion it will at present be impractical to answer the Secretarie's [Knox's] expectations. . . ." [45] By August he had almost completed a large map of the southern part of the United States below the Pennsylvania line. The astute Tatham then sought the Governor's advice on an interesting matter:

This morning's work on my map brings me to a very serious subject which (tho' it may escape common observation, as it appears trifling at first view) I conceive my duty to consult your Excellency on, as a confidential business. It is simply the coloring of the Islands in the Mississippi; for if We ever mean to contest the sole Exclusive navigation with the Spaniards (which one day must be the case,) we ought to neglect no step to propogate the earliest evidence of perpetual claim, and as Maps have a tendency to beget prejudice, which often times the Scale of Fact on intricate and distance matter, there can be nothing amiss, I suppose, in such a peaceable assertion of our future expectations, for, if I am right in my general observations, such is the disposition of the People and common course of nature, whatever present policy may dictate officially.

I would not, however, have it understood that I apply to your Excellency for anything more than your opinion and advice Founded on ample information, for if you think it well to consult the supreme authority, perhaps the Communication would come thro' your Excellencie's hands with the greatest propriety. At all events I am persuaded the People of Carolina, Georgia, and the Western Settlements abstractedly considered, will avail themselves when they have the power to seize the whole to their use independent of Eastern consequence.[46]

Tatham knew the sentiment of the backcountry and probably had wind of some talk of intrigue. In addition to the map, Tatham completed *An Analysis of the State of Virginia,* was first published in Richmond in 1791. It was later printed again in Philadelphia. During the course of his work as geographer of Virginia, Tatham came to think in terms of a similar general survey of America. In February, 1790, Tatham wrote Jefferson:

I have suggested to his excellency [the Governor of Virginia] a hint towards a public office similar to one in England. . . . I mean the Surveyor General of Roads to which in this extensive Country other duties might be annexed such as the Superintendancy of Ferrys, inland navigation, Bridges &c. Thro this Channell each County Suveyor might with a very few days labour furnish the Government with full information. The legislature would be enabled to remedy public inconveniences the conveyances of Commerce and Locomotion would be made more easy and comfortable, distances would be shortened   system

and beauty would be added to the face of the Country, and an uninformed and emigrateing World
would see their way clearly to temporal conveniency
and happiness. I would readily engage in this branch
without regard to individual involvement. The objection that occurs to his excellency is the Infancy of
the Country. I should with due submission suppose
that circumstance a strong arguement to enforce immediate establishment for the removal of obstacles
will be in proportion a far less difficulty (if roads
were properly classed) than a future and uncertain
cutting thro farms, Houses, and improvements to
regulate errors which we should conceive ought to
have been forseen by our Ancestors.[47]

Toward the end of 1791, Tatham was making
plans to submit his proposal to Congress and to the
Virginia Assembly. He again wrote Jefferson for
assistance: "I have persevered this far without
help, but the meeting of the Assembly is again
approaching and it will most likely be out of my
power to be in Philadelphia before that time. I
know of no better way than to solicit your attention
toward recommending the several works to the
Public. Notice and aid of either Congress or the
individual State. Your private opinion on this subject (if an official step is improper) may generally
influence the tone of the legislature." [48] Tatham's
plan for a general topographical survey of America
was too far ahead of its time for it to be accepted
by Congress, even with Jefferson's backing. In December, 1791, however, the Virginia Assembly authorized a lottery to raise a maximum of £4,000 to
enable Tatham to complete the geographic surveys
he had begun.[49] In the meantime Tatham became

involved in a more immediate project and the lottery was never held.

In July, 1791, Jefferson authorized Augustine Davis, editor of the Virginia *Gazette* and postmaster at Richmond, to attempt to establish a post road from Richmond to the southwest. At the same time Jefferson consulted with the Postmaster General about the possibility of establishing cross-post routes in Virginia and the southwest. The Postmaster General informed Jefferson that the cross-post must support itself so as to be of no public expense; mail contracts must be given for one year only, and the contractor was to receive the "whole postage and nothing more." [50] Since Tatham was familiar with the routes into the backcountry and still had friends there, Jefferson may have solicited his assistance on the project. In August, 1791, Tatham wrote Jefferson: "I catch a moment to mention, that Mr. [David] Ross [51] and myself in pursuance and aid of your proposals for a Western Post Dispatch[ed] my Brother (who is well Acquainted) in order to favor the Contracts and Arrangements to the North Fork of Holston agreeable to yr. Plan—I have also set a Subscription on foot among the merchants, as a certain inducement to some men of enterprise who may be dispos'd to engage in pushing the matter as far as possible." [52] Both Jefferson and Tatham proceeded to lay out post routes. Jefferson contemplated two routes, the first from Richmond to Staunton via Charlottesville, and a second from Richmond to New London and the Peaks of Otter (both in Bedford County), through Montgomery, Wythe, and Washington

counties, and along the Holston "toward the seat
of the South Western government." [53] In the meantime Tatham was hard at work on the project:

I have sent my Brother to Governor [William]
Blount, on the Western Post, & other business . . . .
He is authorized by Mr. Davis to make contracts
agreeable to your directions, but I think he will not
succeed on this Journey, I have made some estimates
from my knowledge of both Routes, and their de-
pendencies. I think a Capital of 1000£ will be necessary. The proposition of this that will be sunk in
the annual expenditures will risque too much for one
years contract only, and the two posts at best as far as
Columbia will interfere because the routes will then
come within 4 miles & Generally ten at most—would
it not be better that the post should continue in one
to Columbia running two horse stage as far as Staunton & Lynchburg, the last of which I understand has
14 Stores & some of the merchants are anxious to
encourage this . . . . If Government would give up
those posts for three years, I think I could bring
about the following Establishment.

From Richmond to Columbia [on the James
River, Fluvanna County].
A Two horse stage once a week.
The same from Columbia to Lynchburg & Staunton.
From Lynchburg to Bottetourt Court House.
A single Horse and Mail, one in four weeks.
From Bottetourt to Abington at Washington Court
House, a horse and mail once a month.
From Abington to Ross's Iron Works and thence a
tour through Govr. Blounts territory, a single Horse
and Mail Monthly.
The Kentuckie Post being subject to Contingencies
must pass the Wilderness
Thro' difficult roads, Consequently Ross's Iron

Works near long Island, will be the Western Office of this Rout.

The Rout from Staunton by Bath & Lewis built towards the mouth of the Kanhawa, may be established on a similar footing and during the fall Season a Stage may pass to the springs.[54]

The Davis-Jefferson-Tatham plan for mail routes into the recently created Southwest Territory failed to materialize in 1791 due to the inability to get contracts for service beyond Staunton. The two conditions, one year contracts and postage rates as the sole source of revenue for the contractors, imposed by the Postmaster General were largely to blame. The initial cost and risk made the one year contract restriction unattractive, despite the possibility of renewal. The refusal to subsidize the route beyond Staunton was also a factor. Since the postage rates were to provide the sole source of revenue for the contractors, the cost of the service to those using it would be too high. But this effort was not a total failure. The great need for improved communication caused Congress to pass an act to establish post offices and post roads in the United States with a provision that new contracts were to be made for two years.[55]

For the next several years Tatham worked at gathering historical and geographical material for his own collection and for a general topographical survey of America, which he still hoped to undertake. In 1792 he went with Governor Henry Lee on his tour of the southwestern counties of the state. From there he continued on to the Southwest

Territory. To support himself and to provide a collection center, Tatham established a law office in Jonesborough in September, 1792; two weeks later he was licensed to practice law in the courts of Virginia and opened an office in Abingdon. He then placed a notice in the Knoxville *Gazette* of his desire to obtain information on the early history of that region. By March, 1793, Tatham had moved from Jonesborough to Knoxville. There for a brief period he practiced law, bought himself 300 acres of land, did small favors for Governor William Blount, and collected geographical and historical data. Charles Tatham, his brother, was in Knoxville assisting him and also serving as express letter carrier to and from the Richmond postoffice for Governor Blount.[56]

After "surveying, and collecting surveys and other information, and completing the Tennessee, Kentucky and Georgia frontiers . . ." Tatham "left an office fitted up at Knoxville, a similar one at Abingdon . . ." [57] and returned to Richmond in October, 1793, after being "solicited by the Marshall of the United States for the federal district of Virginia, to subdivide that district into ridings, for the accommodation of the public by the help of a dozen of deputies." [58] Settling down momentarily in Richmond, he completed this task and a manuscript on canal construction, published in 1794 as a pamphlet entitled "Address to the Shareholders and others Interested in Canals in Virginia."

He then "fitted out" an office "on the eastern side of Shockoe Creek" to collect and compile data, and acquired letters of introduction for a visit to

Georgetown and Washington from his old revolutionary friend and compatriot, Colonel Edward Carrington. In August, 1794, he set out for Georgetown, "the only populated part of Columbia; I fixed an office in the house of Messrs. Bowman & Co. of Baltimore, made all possible progress in collecting materials and doing public good. . . ." From Georgetown, Tatham went to Baltimore to make arrangements with an engraver for his maps, but a raging epidemic of yellow fever there caused him to hasten to Philadelphia. There he established an office in the house of Charles Young on Chestnut Street and began negotiations with Messrs. Thackora and Vallance, "the only competent engravers then in that place." The engravers were at that time at work on Griffith's map of Maryland and were unable to begin work on Tatham's maps until some future date. Tatham then proceeded to New York, where he "found no engravers in the map line." In November, 1795, he sailed from New York on board a Swedish ship bound for Cadiz, Spain, and reached his destination on Christmas Day.

Tatham never revealed the true purpose of his visit to Spain to friends in the United States. In his old age Tatham gave a rather simple explanation. He said that while in Philadelphia collecting topographical material and attempting to find an engraver, he became acquainted with Don Josef Jaudenes, Spanish Minister to the United States. Jaudenes suggested that a Senor Lopez, an excellent engraver in Madrid, might be able to accommodate him, and that "he [Jaudenes] had a strong desire that my maps should be engraved in the capital of his native country, and the two nations become intimately known to each other, and bound in the reciprocal interests of Commerce." Jaudenes then furnished Tatham with "letters of introduction and credit to his family in Madrid, about Court, his private purse, and passports. . . ." Upon his arrival in Madrid, Tatham apparently found Lopez and all of his assistants engaged on an important and extensive work for the King.[59]

Another version, published in *Public Characters* (London, 1801), tells a much more complex and intriguing story. Tatham's well known collection of geographical material, combined with his great knowledge of the "interests and public economy of North America," caused many individuals and interests to cultivate his acquaintance, "both from policy and speculation." As a result, Tatham was supposedly well informed about several intrigues and designs of the times. Caught between his private knowledge of a serious plot involving the western country and his allegiance to the United States and to some of the individuals involved in the plot, he conferred with Jaudenes in Philadelphia. With purse and patronage furnished by the Spanish Minister, Tatham left New York in November, 1795, bound for the Court of Spain. Upon his arrival, the Prime Minister issued Tatham "a *prontamente,* or appointment to come to the palace at eight o'clock the next evening." At that very moment France was trying to persuade Spain to enter the war against England. "On this occasion Colonel T.[atham] made use of what little influ-

ence he possessed to continue the kingdom in a
state of peace and neutrality, and strengthen her
good understanding with the United States of
America. . . ." According to this account, Tatham's frequent visits to see the Marquis of Bute,
the British Ambassador to Spain, aroused suspicion
and led to his notice of eviction from Spain on July
8, 1796. He left Madrid July 20 and made his way
to London.[60]

In July, 1795, England's former ally, Spain,
signed a treaty of alliance with France. It was
generally believed that the treaty contained a se-
cret clause providing for the retrocession of Louisiana. In October, 1795, the English government
instructed Lieutenant Governor John G. Simcoe of
Canada to cultivate the interest of the leading men
in the western settlements of the United States so
as to enable England to acquire the services of the
frontiersmen against the Spanish settlements
should war break out between England and Spain.
In March, 1796, Pierre Adet, the French Minister
to the United States, commissioned General Victor
Collot to travel in the West for the purpose of
making a military survey of the defenses and lines
of communication west of the Alleghenies. Many of
the great land speculators, including William
Blount, expressed fear at the possible transfer of
Louisiana from Spain to France. Also, a strong
nation like France might in the future seize the
Mississippi Valley and even Canada. In Blount's
opinion this situation made western lands virtually
worthless and threatened him and others with finan-

cial ruin, which they naturally attempted to prevent happening.

The details for carrying out the "Blount Conspiracy" were probably never really settled upon but in general outline the scheme involved a three-pronged attack. One force, consisting of a group of frontiersmen collected on the frontiers of New York and Pennsylvania and led by John Mitchell and a Major Craig, was to be joined at some point on the Ohio River by the famous or infamous Joseph Brandt and a band of Indians, and possibly by an additional force from Canada. This combined force was to capture New Madrid and then proceed to the head of the Red River and take possession of the silver mines there. A second attack was to be made against New Orleans by a force of southwesterners and Indian allies led by William Blount. The third was to be made against Pensacola. The British were to retain possession of Louisiana or the Floridas, or both. New Orleans was to be made a free port, and the Mississippi was to be open to both Americans and British.[61]

The intrigues referred to in the account in *Public Characters* no doubt concerned what was then known as the "Blount Conspiracy." Tatham probably did not know all the details, but he certainly must have known a plot was being hatched. Tatham was in Tennessee and associated with William Blount from time to time during the years of 1792–1794. He even helped prepare detailed maps and prospectuses of western lands that Blount planned to sell to speculators and possible investors. While in Philadelphia in 1795, Tatham knew enough about what might happen to advise Robert Morris and his associates not to go through with a speculative deal which Blount had outlined.[62] Letters from Tatham to William Henry Cavendish Bentenck, Duke of Portland and Home Secretary, and to Rufus King, American Minister to London, following his arrival in England from Spain clearly show that Tatham had knowledge of some foreign intrigue or conspiracy.[63]

According to an explanation either written by or dictated in part by Tatham, he was "animated by the purest motives." The case had already developed "beyond the control of any department which could have been consulted. To have conferred with General Washington, (not to speak of the intrusion) would have subjected that excellent man to almost unavoidable censure, and involved the United States in a war in which they might have been vanquished." The one remedy for the impending crisis, in Tatham's opinion, was "to confer with the Spanish Minister, on certain ill-timed measures, grounded on recently propagated errors in Spain, which (probably) none but their two selves had attained a thorough knowledge of; and the result of which no men in America had sufficient power and authority to parry in due time." Tatham "preferred the risk of his own person to that of involving the nation in a torrent of bloodshed; but the prospect of rescuing the country and its innocent western inhabitants from misery, was an event accompanied with inexpressible satisfaction." It was under these circumstances, according to Tatham,

that the Spanish Minister gave him purse and patronage to enable him "to attempt at the Court of
Spain, that which could not be done in America.
Under these auspices, and without the privity of
any one of the material points of his mission
. . ." [64] Tatham went to Spain.

Tatham's approach to the Spanish Court was to
emphasize the growth of the backcountry, its
emerging affluence, the importance of the use of the
Mississippi River, and the present contentment of
the backcountry yeomanry. He suggested that
there were no grounds to suspect that these people
would actually take part in the rumored conspiracy.
In June, 1796, Tatham completed a sixty-page
manuscript entitled, "A Few Hints and Remarks
for the Use of the Officers, Physicians, and Students of his M. C. Majesty's Botanic Garden at
Madrid." Following flowery praise of his Majesty's Botanic Garden and noting the vast accumulation of items gathered together from all over the
globe at great expense, Tatham apologized for perceiving "very few from a country which may be
considered in toto, to be one of the most abundant
of nature's Gardens. . . ." He then described
briefly a few of the prominent people who lived in
various parts of the backcountry, and the many
plants and herbs growing in abundance there. He
suggested that Spain send botanists into this area
via the principal rivers of Pennsylvania, Virginia,
and North Carolina. "And, as all these Routes lead
them into the Western Country upon Waters of
the Mississippi which become navigable for Canoes
in a short distance from their receptive sources,

they would readily engage the assistance of woods-men to accompany them to New Orleans and experience the same Friendly reception on the route." Such pointed references to the backcountry, the people there, the accessibility of the Mississippi River and New Orleans, and the fact that the document was addressed "To His Excellency The Principe de la Paz, &c. &c. &c.," [65] indicates that it was meant to convey something more than merely a list and description of the flowers and shrubs of that area of North America.

Tatham's letters to Don Diego de Gardoqui, Minister of Finance, reiterated the same message. He admitted that a few individuals interested in speculative ventures were busy attempting to organize foreign intrigue, and he offered his services to deal with them. The use of force by the Spanish would spell ultimate defeat, even if successful in regard to her colonial possessions. Such action would arouse fierce animosity among Americans and prevent peaceful relations for years to come, and at the same time give the French the opportunity to recapture Canada. "Is it not well," asked Tatham, "to examine the ground on which France would *retake Canada?* Does not the Act at once extend itself to an implication of the same thing in the Spanish Colonies, and ought not Spain to dread the inroad thro the United States which becomes thus favorably improved for designs (which *I know* to be allready form'd) against her American Dominions in either Case?" [66]

The egotistical William Tatham came to believe that he was on a vital mission and that his advice, for which he would also be rewarded, would be readily sought by the Spanish Court. He apparently convinced Jaudenes that he did possess a valuable collection of books, documents, and maps and that he possessed intimate knowledge of the back-country and of the intrigues being hatched there. Jaudenes sent Tatham and his collection of material to Spain believing that the Spanish government might find them valuable enough to purchase. Jaudenes also intimated to Tatham that his government might see fit to find employment for him in the service of Spain.[67] By the time Tatham reached Spain he was full of vague schemes designed to prevent the immediate danger of bloodshed between the two countries on the Spanish-American frontier.[68] The Spanish officials tolerated him and paid his room and board until they could examine the trunks of books, documents, and maps he had brought with him.[69]

Finally, after examining Tatham's material and determining them to be of no value to the Spanish government, Spanish officials ordered Tatham to leave Spain. They were afraid that the American government might discover that Tatham was being sustained there by the Spanish government and that he had been attempting to make some kind of proposals to that government. Spain did not want to give the United States any reason to distrust her or the recently signed Pinckney Treaty. Tatham was asked to leave Spain on July 8, 1796.[70] On July 20, he departed from Madrid for England. He reached Plymouth on August 16 and hurried to London.[71]

It would perhaps be difficult to prove that Tatham deliberately went to England to get more "mileage" out of his knowledge that some kind of backcountry conspiracy was being hatched. Nevertheless, in London he indicated he had such information and advised Rufus King, the American Minister. King seems to have been rather confused, or under several delusions, regarding the conspiracy. He attempted to create the notion of one great conspiracy and to push John D. Chisholm, one of its ringleaders, into a pro-Spanish position, while mildly rebuking Lord William Grenville in regard to Robert Liston (British Minister to the United States) and his connection with the intrigue. Secretary of State Timothy Pickering and other Federalists at home also seemed bent on demonstrating to the world the innocence of the British government. Pickering, like King, attempted to make the whole matter a Blount-Spanish or a French plot. King was spurred on in part by Tatham's correspondence. At the same time Tatham was corresponding with British officials, insinuating that he possessed considerable knowledge that had not yet been revealed.[72] At war with France and Spain, England was interested in maintaining good relations with the United States and willing to compensate Tatham for his information.

Tatham may have had some other legitimate sources of income, but it is extremely doubtful that he was self-supporting despite his several utterances about his industry as an author and civil engineer."[73] He lived most of his life, directly or indirectly, on favors, offices, and rewards given him for his "public services." He lived nine years (1796–1805) in London partly at the expense of the British and American governments, receiving financial assistance from Rufus King as well as the British for his diplomatic services.[73] When these sources of subsistence dried up in 1805, Tatham returned to the United States where his good friend Thomas Jefferson, then President, was in the position to give him some kind of acceptable employment.

The nine years Tatham spent in London were in many ways his "best" years. There he was able to live like a gentleman, more successfully than at any other time in his life; he was allowed to continue to "dabble and meddle" in political and diplomatic affairs; he had the opportunity to apply his engineering skills; and, finally, he was able to pursue with better results than ever before his efforts to write and publish.[74]

It is extremely doubtful that Tatham was able to exert any real influence in political and diplomatic circles in London despite his strenuous efforts. Of these efforts Tatham wrote: "I exerted myself in London till Autumn, 1804, trying the whole time . . . to effect our purpose against Mr. Pitt's violent opposition to our countrys prosperity. . . . I continually conferred with our ministers, King and Monroe." [75] Judging from the results, he must have spent most of his time and effort in gathering historical, geographical, and topographical material, in writing, and in publishing.

When Tatham arrived in London in 1796 he became acquainted with Robert Fulton, and appar-

ently they freely discussed subjects of mutual interests, inland coastwise canals and boats. According
to Tatham, the two of them jointly worked out
plans for an inland coastal canal from Fayetteville,
North Carolina to Georgetown, South Carolina,
using the waters of Cape Fear, Drowning Creek,
and the Waggamaw and Pee Dee rivers. The project included the purchase of the harbor at Little
River in South Carolina for the purpose of establishing a new seaport to tap the West Indian trade.
Their joint engineering skills were also responsible
for the plans for a steamboat. In December, 1796,
Tatham and Fulton supposedly drew up a contract
to the effect that these projects were to be pursued
only by their joint effort. In a letter printed in the
National Intelligencer, January 12, 1814, Tatham
wrote of their supposedly joint plans for a seaport
at Little River: "This place he [Fulton] now calls
Fultonville"; as to the "their" steamboat, Tatham
wrote: "Whether Mr. Fulton, or myself, should
have the *credit* and *profits* of the steam boat, (or
our moities of the latter) will be better determined
on comparing our rights and contracts in court."
Quite frankly, Tatham asserted: "He [Fulton] is
. . . fully indebted for the claim he sets up to
navigate what are called *Fulton's* steam boats, on
principles confided to him by me in faith of contracts. . . ." Tatham's own specifications were a
matter of record, he insisted, properly registered
and certified in London in June, 1797, and later
deposited in the Patent Office in Washington.[76]

Tatham had given much thought and effort to
the subject of inland canals. Just before leaving

Virginia in 1794, he had published a pamphlet on canal construction entitled, "Address to the Share-holders and others interested in Canals in Virginia." His first publication after his arrival in London in 1796 was a pamphlet on the same sub-ject, "Plan for Insulating the Metropolis by a Canal." The following year he wrote "Remarks on Inland Canals." In 1799 he published a 500 page work entitled, *Political Economy of Inland Navigation, Irrigation and Drainage.*[77] While one might question Tatham's claims regarding the steamboat, his knowledge and interests on the subject of inland canals cannot be denied.

In 1800 Tatham temporarily abandoned the sub-ject of canals and navigation for one in which he was even better versed. For twenty-five years he had seen tobacco planted, cultivated, harvested, and marketed in Virginia, North Carolina, and in the backcountry. He had even tried growing it him-self. Having served as a clerk for a mercantile firm during his first years in Virginia, and having been engaged in the mercantile business on several occa-sions himself, he was thoroughly familiar with the commercial aspects of the product. Before the end of the year he had completed and published *An Historical and Practical Essay on the Culture and Commerce of Tobacco* and *Communications Con-cerning the Agriculture and Commerce of America.* The latter book was an attempt to refute an unfa-vorable report on the subject to the British Board of Agriculture.[78]

Early in 1801 Tatham was appointed superin-tendent of the Office of Works at the London docks at Wapping, which employed about 500 workmen. While his several recent publications on inland canals and navigation may have "brought him into notice and repute as a scientist and engineer," this appointment was more likely the product of "friendly intervention," perhaps the final reward for his role during the excitement created by the Blount conspiracy. Those responsible for Tatham's appointment were certainly aware of the fact that the Office of Works at Wapping was soon to be abolished. At the time of Tatham's appointment the Court of Directors had already dismissed the board of engineers, and Tatham was given the responsibility of executing their plans. Obviously the decision by the Court of Directors "to complete what remains to be done by contract" had already been made. On July 11, 1801, Tatham passed out of this service, and most of the 500 workmen under him were discharged.[79]

Tatham probably also hastened the end of his own employment. He accepted the office with great enthusiasm and envisioned it as an opportunity to apply his "superb engineering knowledge and theories." He was somewhat mortified to discover that the plans of the board of engineers were to be "executed without opposition," even though his own might be "superior on the score of method, expedition and expense." He was occasionally allowed to indulge in his own plans, and he felt that "he hath left a lasting memorial in the first piling of the foundation for the *drainage pipe,* which was executed under his superintendance and driven in *interpiled quincunx,* according to his own suggestion. . . ." [80]

Upon leaving the dockyards Tatham returned to his literary pursuits, and before the year ended he had written and published another essay concerned with his two favorite subjects, engineering and agriculture, entitled, "National Irrigation, or the various Methods of watering Meadows." He had no sooner completed it than he received a letter from a member of the Royal Society of Arts that offered him another opportunity to improve his prestige and reputation. After the American Revolution the British government began to think of Canada as a possible source of hemp fiber. The French royal government had encouraged the cultivation of the fiber before the fall of Quebec, and there was reason to believe that its cultivation might succeed. In the 1790's the Committee of the Privy Council for Trade and Plantations joined the Agricultural Society of Quebec and the Provincial Government in their efforts to establish the staple there. The three groups agreed that the bounty system should be extended to Canadian-produced hemp. By the end of the century the demand for naval stores at home had increased considerably, and in 1801 the Royal Society of Arts joined in encouraging Canadian hemp production by offering an annual reward, the Gold Medal or Fifty Guineas, "To the person who shall sow hemp (in drills at least 18 inches asunder) the greatest quantity of land in the province of Upper Canada, not less than ten acres statue measure. . . ." [81]

Full information concerning the Society's reward was sent to Canada in April, 1801, but the year ended without any claims having been received. It was generally agreed that something was wrong with the conditions imposed for claiming the reward. Joseph Colen, a member of the Society's Committee on Colonies and Trade and former Governor of York Fort, Hudson Bay, asked Tatham for his advice. This simple request by Colen sparked an intense interest, which lasted about two years before it began to wane, in the Society on the part of Tatham. Before the end of the year 1802 Tatham had accomplished what was probably his primary objective—membership in the Royal Society of Arts.

Instead of replying to Colen, Tatham took the matter up directly with Charles Taylor, Secretary of the Society.[82] In his first letter to the Secretary, Tatham emphasized his own great experience regarding the agriculture of North America (without mentioning the fact that he had never been to Canada). He was, however, familiar with hemp culture since the fiber had been rather widely produced in Virginia during the Revolution. As usual, Tatham had much advice to offer. He recommended that the Society offer rewards of varying amounts instead of one single large one, and that rewards be given for the shipment of hemp from Canada to Great Britain as well as for its actual cultivation.[83] In January, 1802, Tatham wrote two more letters to the Secretary, one of which contained historical evidence of the growth of hemp culture in New England and Canada.[84] Several other letters contained the results of his further research on hemp production. In addition to the subject of hemp, Tatham wrote on "Silk Grass" of North America and on the subject of dyeing.[85] He hoped that these efforts would aid him in his bid for a position supervising hemp culture in Canada. His suggestions regarding rewards were incorporated by the Society into the premium list for 1802, and additional premiums were paid in 1804, 1806, and 1809. However, the unfavorable climate and the War of 1812 prevented hemp from becoming an established staple there.

Tatham made a very favorable impression in the Society. On March 10, 1802, he was elected to membership and appointed to the Committee of Colonies and Trade. A week later Tatham presented the Society with a bust of George Washington, with an accompanying note which read: "No temptations of popular power, or selfish emolument had sufficient charms to bias his mind from the walks of piety, private retirement, and domestic benevolence." [86] The Society thanked him for the gift, but had difficulty finding accommodations for it. He also presented copies of his book on irrigation and his three works on the subjects of agriculture and commerce. Within three weeks following his election to the Society, he presented it with a manuscript essay entitled, "On the Extension of Commerce and the Culture of Latent Resources in America." The essay was apparently intended largely as an address to the Society itself. "The ordinary attention paid by the Society to the Department of *Colonies and Trade*," wrote Tatham, "has by no means kept pace with the progress of human changes, but is restricted by a constitution varying wide from the essential intendment of this honourable establishment, which evidently contemplated to benefit the nation by the results of a traffic connecting itself as an *extrinsic advantage,* whether colonial or, more expressly, foreign." [87] He then strongly urged the Society to do all in its power to promote the exchange of knowledge between the United States and Great Britain. According to Tatham, the best way to attain this end was to appoint several American citizens as Corresponding Members of the Society.

Tatham soon followed through on his recommendation for American Corresponding Members by proposing eight names: Benjamin Smith Benton, Arthur Campbell, William Allen Dangerfield, Robert Fulton, Samuel Latham, Henry Lee, William Thornton, and St. George Tucker. The proposal slips for the eight Americans were signed by Tatham and two other members of the Society, William Lumley and John Robinson. Lumley was chairman of the Society's Committee of Accounts, and Robinson was one of the more influential members of Parliament. Despite the signatures of its two prominent members, the Society in general was strongly opposed to the eight names submitted, as well as to the idea of American membership. During a lively discussion from the floor, Tatham was accused of getting the names he proposed from a newspaper. The group also expressed fear of foreign domination. [88] The following morning (April 1, 1802) Tatham wrote to the President of the

Society, the Duke of Norfolk, withdrawing his nominations but suggesting that the names "remain in your archives . . . [as an] index of honour and virtue till the mouldering of time shall destroy them." [89]

Despite his "awkward predicament" with the Society of Royal Arts, Tatham continued to make "occasional attendance" at meetings until May, 1804. He continued to write on some of his favorite topics and projects and seems to have attended meetings of the Society whenever he had a particular plan or scheme to promote. He was successful in getting the Society to increase the award that had been voted to a tree-planting candidate and to modify the premiums offered to encourage the art of engraving. In 1803 he wrote two essays, "Report on an Examination of Certain Impediments and Obstructions in the Navigation of the Thames River" and "The Navigation and Conservancy of the River Thames." Neither these two essays nor his previous writings on canal development influenced the Society on the subject. In the spring of 1804 he ended his active participation in the Society with a note calling attention to the manufactures produced by the students of a school for the indigent blind in Lambert; for this he received a vote of appreciation. [90]

Tatham began to think of returning to the United States. His position at Wapping Docks had been eliminated; he felt rebuked by the Royal Society of Arts; he had failed in his efforts to secure a job in Canada promoting the culture of hemp; and his "diplomatic services" were no longer sought

with the restoration of more favorable relations
between Great Britain and the United States. At
the same time he was somewhat concerned about
whether his reputation back in Virginia was
tainted. Several rumors at home had connected
Tatham with foreign intrigue, and in some circles
his integrity was seriously questioned. In 1802
Tatham started paving the way for his return to
the United States by renewing old acquaintances.
He began by writing to Thomas Jefferson, President of the United States. He began his letter with
a description of an improved lifeboat that recently
had been put to use very successfully in saving
crews of vessels wrecked amidst the great breakers
off the English Coast. He suggested that such a
boat might be appropriate for use in such areas as
the New Jersey coast, the Hatteras shoals, and on
the Great Lakes. Tatham then got down to the real
purpose of the letter: "Knowing, sir, as you do for
many years, the nature of my objects and perser-
verance, I beg leave to refer you to Doctr. [William
A.] Dangerfield: from whom, I trust, you will
learn that my integrity is yet unshaken by the con-
temptible smiles or frowns of foreign intrigue; and
that I shall, ultimately, prove to you something
more than an unprofitable servant of society." [91]

The arrival of his friend and fellow Virginian,
James Monroe, as American Minister to London
in 1804 provided Tatham with the opportunity to
make the proper return to the United States.
Tatham visited Monroe frequently and was soon
ready to leave England for America, armed with a
passport and letter of introduction and recommen-

dation by Monroe to James Madison, Secretary of State.[92] Tatham left London in October, 1804 and reached the United States in April, 1805.[93] From 1805 until late 1817, Tatham was periodically employed, a variety of his talents being utilized in various military departments by Presidents Jefferson, Madison, and Monroe. During this same period Tatham was seldom without a project or scheme of his own, usually one concerning inland canals and military fortifications, which he tried to sell to the federal government.

Upon his return to the United States, Tatham was at first somewhat reluctant to contact his old friend Thomas Jefferson. There had been little correspondence between them since Tatham's departure from the United States for Spain in 1795; indeed, Tatham's letter of July, 1802, may have been the only contact. But his dire need for employment or his sincere desire to renew their friendship, or both, persuaded Tatham to write to Jefferson in May, 1805. In his letter, Tatham explained why their previous cordial relationship had suffered an elapse. In 1794 a letter that Tatham had written Jefferson had been returned to the sender with no explanation. Soon thereafter, Governor Henry Lee had deepened the wound by telling Tatham that he had so intruded upon Jefferson's time during his last visit to Richmond that Jefferson had returned to Monticello without completing the business at hand. Tatham asked Jefferson for a frank and honest reply.[94] Two days later Jefferson replied and denied ever having returned a letter to him unanswered.[95] He also invited him to dinner. Jefferson's response renewed the warmth that Tatham had previously felt towards him. For the next four years Tatham was ready at a moment's notice to come to the aid of the President. Once, while seated at the dinner table, Jefferson expressed the wish that someone would invent a means of facilitating the passage of decanters around the table. The next day Tatham wrote the President:

> I will engage to furnish you one, in a few days, which shall afford a useful lesson in the public economy of our country, and it can be no where else so happily introduced. It shall be cheap, simple, powerful, ornamental, and accommodating to yourself and Guests; and he must be a dull brain, indeed, who does not carry home more instruction than wine.
>
> If you like my proposition, Sir, you will be so good as to permit my moddeler (who brings this note) to take the dimensions of your tables; and obtain a loan of one of your three Bottle Coasters.[96]

Before the year was over Tatham came to Jefferson's aid on a more important matter. In 1805 Jefferson not only had to face Federalist opposition, but dissension, led by John Randolph, within his own party. William A. Burwell, Jefferson's private secretary, spent a great deal of time in search of men and material with which to answer the critics. More than once Jefferson had been criticized for "fleeing" Richmond, while Governor of Virginia, when the British forces threatened the Capitol in 1781. Several weeks after Tatham's dinner with the President, Burwell wrote Tatham for some information concerning Jefferson's behavior in 1781. Tatham replied: "I frequently heard of Mr. Jefferson's exertions individually, when the militia left him to shift for himself,—and I am persuaded that if it had been too [as?] easy to raise recruits at that day as it was stock jobbers, speculators, and land mongers afterwards, Mr Jefferson (though left alone by many coajutors who should be ashamed of themselves) would never have had occasion to retreat far from the falls of James River, I have been thus particular to refresh the recollection of others." [97]

Tatham was soon rewarded for his loyal support, as well as for his talents, by being commissioned by the President to make a topographical survey from Norfolk, Virginia, southward along the North Carolina coast. Throughout Jefferson's second administration Tatham was busy surveying and serving as Jefferson's eyes and ears regarding British activities off the coast of Virginia and North Carolina. Tatham also found time to give advice and to formulate his own schemes designed to promote the defense of the coasts. Despite interruptions by the British fleet just off the coast and at times within the North Carolina inlets, Tatham completed his map of North Carolina in 1807. In that same year, upon Jefferson's recommendation for the establishment of a permanent coastal survey, Congress passed a bill appropriating $50,000 for carrying on the work on a larger scale.

In 1807, when a British squadron under the command of Commodore Douglas anchored in the Chesapeake Bay near Norfolk, Jefferson ordered Tatham to make use of the coast-surveying cutter, the *Governor Williams,* in keeping watch over the activities of British ships. During the period of the most activity by British ships (June to August, 1807) Tatham operated between Norfolk, Virginia, and New Bern, North Carolina, keeping Jefferson informed as to ship movements, the number and names of ships, landings of shore parties, and the general state of the coastal defenses in and around the Norfolk area.[98] Tatham continued these activities until the *Governor Williams* hit a reef and sank.

The years following Tatham's return to the United States in 1805 were not happy ones, especially those following Jefferson's presidency. Tatham's greatest ambition and his major goal in life was to achieve greatness as a public servant. He failed to do so in four efforts in three different countries: in post-Revolutionary America, in Spain, in England, and again in the United States in the early nineteenth century. He was a failure for several reasons: he was a victim of his own versatility, he lacked discipline and perseverance, and his ideas and schemes were too grandiose and frequently too far ahead of his time.

During the presidencies of Jefferson and Madison, Tatham was full of ideas and great schemes that he felt sure would enhance their administrations and the welfare of the nation as a whole. Two of his proposals stood far above all others or, perhaps more properly, incorporated most of his previous schemes. In July, 1805, Tatham sent President Jefferson an outline plan of a Department of Works and Public Economy to be administered by the President and the secretaries of State, Treasury, War, and Navy. It would serve as a central depository and reference source for such areas as civil engineering, topographical material, agriculture, commerce, military, and American history in general. It would function, in part, as a national educational institution to train public servants for work as draftsmen, engineers, and military personnel. He even suggested that West Point be moved to Washington. The department would also be responsible for promoting agriculture and commerce.[99] The following February Tatham offered to sell the government his collection of books, maps, manuscripts, etc. to form the basis for this new department. Congress rejected his offer.[100]

The impact of the Jeffersonian commercial policy and the War of 1812 caused Tatham to piece together into one grand scheme several ideas and projects, old and new. He insisted that without great difficulty and expense the United States could put into operation an internal communication system running from Boston to Beaufort, North Carolina, that could later be extended to the St. Lawrence and south to the Gulf of Mexico.[101] He would use canals and rivers to connect the numerous inlets and coastal waters unfit for oceangoing vessels from Massachusetts to North Carolina. By fortifying such areas as the Chesapeake with cannon, floating batteries, torpedoes (of his own superior design), gunboats, a telegraph system (which he also devised), and a few large ships of war the entire coast could be easily defended. He pointed out that engineering principles would allow all ships and gunboats to be constructed of "very superior metal." The establishment of a "Maritime Infantry" would provide a mobile military force that could move from one area to another without wear and tear and fatigue. Such a communication system would not only provide adequate defense, but would promote internal commerce and "general Union." [102]

Much to his disappointment, Tatham was unable to get adequate support at the national level for any portion of his projects. Such massive schemes or even portions of them were out of tune with the economic policy of the period; sectional jealousy regarding location of his "gun-boat canals" hampered his efforts; and the secretaries of War and Navy would have no part of Tatham's assistance or ideas. Both secretaries looked upon Tatham as a meddler. General Henry Dearborn, Secretary of War from 1801 to 1809, once told Tatham that unless he had a degree as a student of the Military Academy he could not be permitted to construct model military works even at his own expense. [103] According to Tatham, in 1814 Monroe recommended that Congress appropriate $100,000 to complete the inland waterway from Long Island to Florida, [104] but the country was not ready for such expansion of governmental authority and expenditure even during wartime.

In his last years Tatham became more and more disillusioned and disappointed, and he finally became an alcoholic and died in poverty. He was never able to manage his financial affairs, but always seemed to be able to live above his means.

Beginning about 1807 he began to make frequent
references to his dire financial status. Before leaving England in 1805, Tatham had been hired by an
English mercantile firm, Learmonth and Berry, to
act as agent in the United States. His services and
salary were discontinued by the firm following the
British attack on the American frigate, the *Chesapeake*, a few miles out of Norfolk, Virginia in
June, 1807. Some time later he wrote of being
disinherited by his family in England, intimating
the loss of a considerable amount of wealth. He
was careful to inform Jefferson about all of this
and to point out that he had spent considerable
amounts of his own money from time to time "in
support of our common cause." [105] Tatham then
took the opportunity to renew his offer to sell the
government his "vast" collection of material,[106]
which was again rejected.

As the year 1808 drew to a close, Tatham was
aware that with his friend Jefferson out of office his
own services might no longer be needed or desired.
As early as October, 1808, he attempted to get
Madison to personally submit his inland canal project to President Jefferson and to use his influence
for its support among other department heads and
legislators.[107] Tatham's appeal to Madison brought
no immediate results, and in February, 1809,
Tatham sent a letter by his friend Commodore
Stephen Decatur to Wilson Cary Nicholas, a member of Congress from Virginia, requesting intervention in his behalf for "some late employments in
the Naval Department . . . within the knowledge
of my friend the bearer. . . ." [108] In August, 1809,

he wrote President Madison again. The letter was in essence a plea for some kind of indoor job, including a list of various positions that he felt qualified to fill.

President Madison was not as sympathetic and kind as Jefferson to Tatham, though this did not discourage him from seeking his patronage. He repeatedly informed Madison of his dire financial condition, due largely to his personal expenditures for the "common cause." Tatham also continued to renew his offer to sell portions or all of his collection, and he had friends in Congress attempt to intercede on his behalf. In 1812 Madison finally saw to it that Tatham was given employment. He seems to have been shifted around in various military departments, working as a draftsman and geographer throughout the war period with an "annual allowance" of $1200,[109] less than a subsistence wage for Tatham.

In 1817, three months before President Monroe gave him a more comfortable position, Tatham made another effort to sell his material to the government. Representative Hugh Nelson of Virginia interceded on his behalf and recommended that Congress appropriate $5,000 for the purchase,[110] but to no avail.

Several months after the inauguration of Monroe as President, Tatham was given a commission in the regular army as storekeeper at the new United States Arsenal on the James River, a few miles above Richmond.[111] Tatham resigned his position at the Arsenal on December 31, 1817, perhaps aware that he was no longer physically or mentally capable of such duties. He moved to Richmond (where he resided until his death in 1819 [112]), and turned to the General Assembly of Virginia for assistance. On February, 9, 1819, the Assembly revived the unused lottery scheme of 1791, which had authorized the raising of a sum, not to exceed £4,000, to be used by Tatham to complete the geographical work he was then engaged in. Additional trustees were added to administer the lottery.[113]

For a destitute, lonely, and broken-hearted old man who had believed that success was always just around the corner, this gesture was too little and too late. On February 22, 1819, the Public Guards assembled in front of the Armory at the southwest corner of Richmond's Capital Square to fire the sundown salute in honor of Washington's birthday. Tatham, who with a young friend had come to observe the firing of the salute, committed suicide by stepping in front of the muzzle of the second cannon after the order of "fire" had been given. The following day the *Daily Compiler* described the event:

A most melancholy catastrophe closed the day [February 22]. Col. William Tatham, so well known in England and in this country, for his acquaintance with civil engineering, who has been residing in the city for two or three years, but whose utility was considerably arrested by an unfortunate habit to which he had become addicted, was destined on this day to breathe his last. In a moment of intemperance, as he stood by the piece of artillery which was firing the evening salute, he exclaimed that he wished to die. As the second was about to fire, and immediately after the commanding officer had given the word "fire" Col. Tatham presented himself in front of the muzzle of the piece, and by its discharge his abdomen was almost literally blown to pieces. His body was raised a few feet in the air by the violence of the explosion, and he fell upon his face without uttering one word that was heard by the bye-standers. When he was taken up, he was found perfectly lifeless.

Col. T. died without any family: circumstances had stript life of much of its attractions in his eyes. . . .

This was a man of great information; of great genius; of great resource of mind—But to this melancholy end he arrived.[114]

It seems apropos here to note that the wad from the cannon which ended Tatham's life was composed of tobacco stems packed tight against the powder to produce a louder report.[115]

Intellectually Tatham belonged with the intelligentsia with whom he associated. He was a talented, versatile, and energetic individual until his last years. He was a product of the Age of Enlightenment, living proof of what rational man could do. Yet Tatham was a failure in terms of concrete achievements; he lacked, most of all, the self-discipline and direction necessary to become more than a white-collar "jack-of-all trades and master of none." Philosophically he was never able to achieve a proper balance between rationalism and romanticism. He allowed the rational Tatham to become an excessive romanticist; he was overly optimistic and highly egotistical. For Tatham, fame and fortune were always almost within reach, or would

come with a new profession, or with his next grand
scheme.

Tatham and several of his contemporaries made
many references to an extensive collection of books,
maps, surveys, and manuscript material he supposedly had amassed over the years. The day after his
death the Richmond *Enquirer* wrote: "He has left
behind him a valuable stock of maps, plats, charts
and explanatory manuscripts, which it is hoped,
will be carefully preserved." [116] This "vast collection" has never been located. Samuel Cole Williams, in his *William Tatham, Wataugan,* suggests
that after being rebuffed or repulsed time and time
again in his efforts to sell his collection to Congress, "grimly determined that his treasure should
die with him. If that be a fact, one of the high
tragedies in American history was enacted when
each document or map was torn to pieces and given
to the flame in a humble lodging place in
Richmond." [117]

I suggest that Tatham never had in his possession
at any one time a "vast collection." He undoubtedly possessed at various times throughout his wan-
dering career what collectively would have
amounted to a mountain of material. Tatham was
too unorganized and undisciplined and wandered
about too freely to maintain a sizable collection. He
did leave a great number of letters, maps, documents, and books, but he left them scattered from
New York to North Carolina and across the mountains into Tennessee and Kentucky. Some were no
doubt lost in the ocean off the coasts of New Jersey
and North Carolina when he was shipwrecked on

two different occasions. According to his own count, he left 283 books, pamphlets, and documents in Spain in 1796.[118] These were probably later sent to England. The British Public Records Office and other depositories in London contain numerous Tatham letters. Many collections of prominent Americans of his period contain at least one Tatham letter. Tatham probably did not destroy his collection, but scattered it wherever he went. If and when it is brought together it would indeed be a vast and valuable collection, and William Tatham might then achieve the recognition he sought so desperately a century and a half ago.

CHAPTER 3

The Culture of Tobacco Since 1800

THE culture of tobacco as described by Tatham was basically the same as it had been since the establishment of the staple as a commercial commodity by John Rolfe in early seventeenth century Virginia. At the end of the Colonial period, tobacco was still an important commercial staple in three colonies: Virginia, Maryland, and North Carolina. In the many decades since the publication of Tatham's work, a number of major changes have taken place. Tatham pointed out two significant trends following the American Revolution: the expansion of the culture of tobacco into several new areas and the decrease in the amount of American export tobacco being carried in English bottoms and handled by English merchants. Tatham had traveled extensively in the backcountry before and after the Revolution and had seen emigrants from Virginia and North Carolina moving into the early Tennessee and Kentucky settlements. The "western country" was soon to become a major tobacco-producing area. While surveying the inland waterways in North and South Carolina he had seen a similar movement by tobacco farmers and planters into South Carolina and upper Georgia. He foresaw that the expansion of tobacco production into these new areas would soon create the need for a greater export market.

The exportation of tobacco reached its approximate pre-Revolutionary War level in less than a decade after the cessation of hostilities. In 1791 the United States exported 101,272 hogsheads of tobacco.[1] Assuming that the average net weight per hogshead was still 1,000 pounds, tobacco production and exportation then approximated the prewar annual average (1771–1775) of 102,000,000 pounds.[2] Of the amount exported in 1791, Virginia and Maryland contributed about 80 percent, the remainder being distributed mainly among Georgia, North Carolina, South Carolina, New York, and Massachusetts (in the order named), with smaller amounts from Rhode Island, Connecticut, New Jersey, and New Hampshire.[3] After the Revolution approximately 75 percent of American export tobacco was carried directly to Europe, no longer primarily in English ships or in the hands of English merchants, but by the Dutch and French as well. England lost none of the revenue on tobacco consumed at home, which had returned to prewar levels, but she did lose considerable social wealth by the shifting of trade profits from British to continental and American merchants. Glasgow, which had been the leading tobacco center of the world, suffered considerably from this shift in the tobacco trade.[4]

Some authorities contend that although a temporary revival in the export tobacco trade occurred about 1790, recovery did not come until about 1840. A more recent study disagrees with the above conclusion and insists that exports of leaf tobacco by the late 1820's probably exceeded that of the 1790 period, and that production of tobacco by the late 1830's was as great as it had been at any time during the eighteenth century, before or after the Revolution. The export statistics of the early nineteenth century have misled some historians who did not detect the fact that a hogshead of tobacco in the 1820's weighed several hundred pounds more than in the 1790's. At the same time it must be noted that in terms of the proportion of population at home and abroad, the period 1790–1840 was a period of retrogression for the American tobacco industry.[5] England's commercial policies and revenue system as well as those of Europe in general were among the factors that checked the rate of expansion of tobacco production in this country prior to about 1840. High duties on tobacco in England and elsewhere in Europe checked per capita consumption and promoted the production of the staple in Europe.

While exportation of tobacco was an important factor in the expansion of tobacco culture in the United States, another factor became even more important. In 1790 about 78 percent of our total production was exported, the remaining 22 percent being consumed at home. By 1839 domestic consumption was up to 41 percent; it jumped to 55 percent in 1859, climbed to 60 percent in 1900,[6] and in 1965 reached 73 percent of our total production.[7] It has been estimated that the average per capita consumption of tobacco by fifteen year olds and over was about three pounds during the antebellum period;[8] in 1881 it was up to 4.3 pounds; 5.5 pounds in 1900;[9] a little less than seven pounds by the end of World War I; 9.3 pounds in 1947;[10] and in 1960 was 11.3 pounds.[11] Since 1790, domestic consumption of the total United States tobacco crop has risen from approximately 22 to 73 percent, while exports have declined from 78 to 27 percent of the total crop.[12] Thus population growth and per capita consumption have been the primary factors in expansion of tobacco culture in the United States.

One of the most conspicuous developments in the tobacco industry in the century and a half following the Revolutionary era was its geographical expansion as a commercial staple. The decline and later the end of tobacco production in Tidewater Virginia was accompanied by a comparable expansion into the Piedmont district. A notable extension of tobacco culture occurred in North Carolina, and tobacco became an important export staple in South Carolina and upper Georgia. In 1791 and 1792 Georgia ranked third among the southern states producing tobacco, but what promised to be a new and important staple in South Carolina and Georgia was soon displaced by cotton. Tobacco returned to both of these states about a century later, and today they constitute a part of the Bright-tobacco Belt, the largest and most productive of all the tobacco-producing areas in the United States.

Tobacco was first cultivated for market in Florida in 1829 in Gadsden County, where a Virginia gentleman supposedly made it profitable. The depression in the cotton industry in the 1840's resulted in a sizable expansion in the production of the Cuban cigar type of tobacco. Production jumped from 75,274 pounds in 1840 to almost a million pounds in 1850 as its culture was extended to include Calhoun, Leon, Jefferson, and Marion counties. A limited market and overextension in the industry in Florida resulted in a drastic decline; production dropped in 1870 to 157,405 pounds, most of which was grown in Gadsden County. Toward the end of the century there was a revival of interest in Cuban and Sumatran varieties in the Gadsden district as well as in Decatur County, Georgia.[13] The tobacco industry was strengthened in Florida following World War I by the introduction of Bright-tobacco in the upper part of the state.

Tobacco had been grown in Louisiana since the early eighteenth century. At the beginning of the nineteenth century around 2,000 hogsheads of this tobacco was being exported annually from New Orleans, and it appeared that Louisiana might become an important tobacco-producing area. Growing competition from a better quality of the product coming down the river from Tennessee and Kentucky soon caused a gradual decline in production until it was of little significance by the mid-1820's. Complete abandonment of tobacco during this period was prevented when Pierre Chenet introduced a new method of curing that resulted in the development of a dark and aromatic tobacco known as Perique. Due to its limited use and market it became established only in the St. James Parish,[14] Louisiana, where it is still produced in small quantities.

"Western tobacco" proved to be the greatest competitor to the old established tobacco-producing states as emigrants with the knowledge of its culture moved into such areas as Tennessee, Kentucky, Ohio, and Missouri. By 1810 tobacco had become an important staple in Tennessee and Kentucky, and within another decade thousands of hogsheads were sent annually to New Orleans on flatboats.[15] According to the 1840 census returns, Kentucky was second only to Virginia in tobacco production and Tennessee ranked third.[16] The production in Virginia for the same year was but little greater than in the pre-Revolutionary period, while tobacco production in Maryland was actually less.

By the end of the first quarter of the nineteenth century tobacco had become a staple crop in Missouri and Ohio. Former Virginians and Marylanders were among those producing tobacco commercially in Pike and adjoining counties in the 1820's, helping elevate Missouri to fifth rank by 1850. After the Civil War the tobacco industry there gradually declined and never returned to the prewar level. By 1825, yellow-leaf tobacco of the Maryland type was being grown as a cash crop in the hilly regions of Ohio around Licking, Fairfield, Perry, and Muskingum counties. High prices for this type produced a tobacco fever in Ohio similar to that seen in Missouri, and Marylanders poured into eastern Ohio. Within a few years the European market was glutted and prices fell sharply, resulting in a decline in the production of this type. In the meantime another type of tobacco was introduced into the state. In 1832, Thomas Pomeroy of Suffield, Connecticut, introduced a cigar variety in the Miami Valley that soon became the leading type grown in Ohio.[17]

The culture of tobacco continued to move west with the tide of emigrants. Just prior to 1820 several reports told of the successful experiments in growing tobacco in Indiana. The crop was soon well established in the southwestern counties between the Ohio and White rivers and in southern Illinois. By 1850 both states were producing approximately 1,000,000 pounds of tobacco annually. In 1863, A. Simmons of Stephens County began experimenting with a cigar type variety, which resulted in the establishment of the industry in northern Illinois.[18]

By 1840 the culture of tobacco had reached the Black River area in the northwest corner of Arkansas. Although Arkansas produced only about 200,000 pounds in 1850, by 1860 production had increased five-fold. In 1879 the state ranked sixteenth among the tobacco-producing states, and J. B. Killebrew, the noted tobacco expert, wrote: "The quality is very similar to that produced in Virginia." This proved to be false, and Arkansas virtually disappeared from the tobacco-producing ranks after the turn of the century.[19]

Although attempts were made to grow tobacco commercially in the northern states in the Colonial period, the development of the tobacco industry there did not really begin until about 1825. As late as 1801 the entire tobacco crop of New England was only 20,000 pounds, the amount exported by Virginia in 1620. Beginning around 1800 tobacco production in the Connecticut Valley increased gradually as local shops began to manufacture plug and twist tobacco. In 1810 a cigar factory was established in East Windsor and another at Suffield, Connecticut, using mostly imported Cuban leaf. Connecticut-grown tobacco was soon being used to make cheap cigars, and a new era emerged in the Connecticut Valley as its tobacco gained a good reputation, especially on the New York market. In 1833, broadleaf tobacco from Maryland was introduced by B. P. Barber of East Windsor; by 1840 tobacco was a general crop in the Valley, with production up to a half million pounds. In 1860 the combined crop produced by Massachusetts and Connecticut was almost 10,000,000 pounds, with production in Connecticut double that of Massachusetts.[20]

Attempts to establish tobacco commercially in Pennsylvania failed until about 1828 when some Lancaster County farmers began to roll their leaf tobacco into cigars for their own use, selling any surplus ones to local merchants. These became known as "stogies," the term supposedly a contraction of the Conestoga River in that region. Another story has it that the name resulted from the fact that these cigars were among the items being peddled about the countryside in Conestoga wagons. In 1837 Benjamin Thomas of York County experimented successfully with some Havana tobacco; three years later York and Lancaster counties combined produced a quarter of a million pounds.[21] On the eve of the Civil War, Lancaster County was producing 2,000,000 pounds annually and York County 700,000 pounds. Tobacco culture spread to other counties after the war, but on a very small scale.[22]

Tobacco culture began in New York in Onondaga County, where it was introduced by Nathan Grimes and others in 1845. In the following decade it became established in several adjoining counties. Soon after the Civil War, New York was producing several million pounds annually.[23]

The first attempt to grow tobacco for market in Wisconsin was made in the southern part of the state near Madison by Ralph Pomeroy and J. J. Heistand several years before the Civil War, but little progress was made until after the end of the hostilities. Production increased from a mere 1,200 pounds in 1850 to about 1,000,000 pounds in the southern district in 1869. The northern Wisconsin tobacco district did not emerge until near the end of the century.[24] In the twentieth century this district expanded across the border into Minnesota.

During the half-century following the publication of Tatham's *Essay on Tobacco* some tobacco was grown in virtually every state and territory in the Union. The twenty states touched upon briefly in the preceding pages represent (with a few periodic exceptions) the states that produced tobacco as a cash crop with the greatest degree of success. The general geographical outline of the present-day tobacco-producing states had thus emerged by the Civil War era. While several factors resulted in fluctuations in tobacco production in many of these states, with a few exceptions those that grew tobacco commercially during part or all of the period 1800–1860 still constituted the major tobacco-producing states in 1960. The vast expansion of tobacco production in the century after the Civil War was primarily the result of expansion of the industry within these same states.

After the Civil War several notable developments occurred in the culture of tobacco. While some of these changes had their origin in the antebellum period, the full impact was not felt in most cases until the half century following the war. In addition to continued expansion, one of the most significant developments was the gradual differentiation of the tobacco crop into several distinctive types; this largely explains why tobacco became a staple commodity only in certain states and in limited areas within these states. The development of distinct types of tobacco was due largely to three factors: (1) the spread of the culture to new soil types, (2) the inevitable hybridization, and (3) the development of three distinct curing methods. Foreign and domestic consumer demands also came to play an important role.

During the Colonial period, Europe recognized only two general classes or types of tobacco, Virginia and Spanish. Tobacco produced west of the mountains in the post-Revolutionary period was first known as "western tobacco." Burley, the most common type of tobacco in early Tennessee and Kentucky, was no doubt derived from seed that some settler had brought from Virginia. Several strains or sorts of Burley came to be recognized by 1860, such as Red Burley, Twist Bud, and Standup Burley, indicating particular characteristics of the plant. White Burley (now simply called Burley) was the result of a rare biological development known as a sport, a sudden deviation from a standard type. This peculiar variation was discovered in 1864 by George Webb of Brown County, Ohio, a product of seed said to have come from Bracken County, Kentucky. It was called White Burley because of its remarkable color (soft brown, not white) and its supposed origin from the old Burley. Due to certain qualities, it became quite popular with the manufacturers of chewing tobacco. Its culture spread rapidly over a large part of Kentucky and into adjoining states that possessed similar soil types: silt loams of limestone origin that contained liberal amounts of plant food elements. The rapid spread of White Burley along with the devastating effects of the Civil War on tobacco production in Virginia caused Kentucky to replace Virginia as the major tobacco-producing state by 1870.[25]

The tobacco of Colonial Virginia was a rather dark, air-cured type, though by the end of the Colonial period small open wood fires on the earthen floors of tobacco barns, to drive out excessive moisture or to hasten the curing process, were in use. When tobacco culture was carried into Tennessee and Kentucky some farmers air-cured their tobacco, some cured with open fires, and others used a combination of the two methods. At about the

time of the outbreak of the War of 1812 the European export market began to show a preference for
the smoky flavored leaf produced by curing with
open wood fires. This came at the time of the
expansion of tobacco culture in Tennessee and Kentucky and caused a larger number of farmers there
and elsewhere to fire-cure their tobacco. It was
soon discovered that certain areas produced a type
of fire-cured tobacco more desirable on the European market than tobacco fire-cured in other areas.
Fire-curing became a distinct method of curing the
tobacco grown in such sections of Tennessee and
Kentucky as the Hopkinsville, Clarksville, and
Paducah-Mayfield areas. These sections still produce most of the fire-cured tobacco. By the time
White Burley emerged, domestic demand, which
objected to the smoky flavor, had caused a rever-
sion to air-curing in certain areas. Thus in the ex-
panding White Burley Belt air-curing became the
distinctive method of curing.

During the same period in which these changes
were taking place in the "western country," certain
developments were taking place in Virginia and
North Carolina that would eventually cause North
Carolina to surpass Kentucky in tobacco production. Two distinct developments in the antebellum
period produced a new type of tobacco in Virginia
and North Carolina known as Bright-tobacco: (1)
the expansion of tobacco culture into the light,
gray, poor soils in the Piedmont district of Virginia
and North Carolina in and around Pittsylvania and
Caswell counties respectively, and (2) a new curing method.[26]

Bright- or "yellow" tobacco had been produced in something of a hit-or-miss fashion in Virginia and North Carolina from time to time following the European demand for the smoky flavored leaf and the frequent use of open wood fires in this area as well as west of the mountains. When the domestic market objected to the smoky flavor produced by wood fires, farmers in some areas switched to charcoal fuel. A serious quest to perfect a formula that would insure a "yellow" cure, using open charcoal fires, began immediately following the accidental curing of a whole barn of yellow or Bright-tobacco by a young slave on the Slade farm in Caswell County, North Carolina in 1839. By 1860 knowledge of the "Slade method" of curing was in great demand, and instructions for its use were printed in several farm magazines. The use of flues to carry the heat into the barn from outside furnaces had been attempted as early as the 1820's, but abandoned. Open fires of charcoal continued to be the most common method of curing Bright-tobacco until after the Civil War, when better and more effective flue-curing systems were perfected.[27] The Bright or Flue-cured Tobacco Belt eventually came to include portions of six states: Virginia, North Carolina, South Carolina, Georgia, Florida, and Alabama. Variations in the type of soil essential for the production of this type of tobacco resulted in the development of five types of Bright-tobacco as its culture expanded southward.

An important factor in the rapid growth of the cigar industry in the latter half of the nineteenth century was the recognition of the fact that soil requirements differed for the production of good cigar wrapper, binder, and filler types of leaf, and that certain areas and soil types were especially adapted to produce particular types. The Connecticut Valley and the Florida districts grew the best wrapper leaf type, Wisconsin and New York the best binder, and Lancaster County, Pennsylvania and the Miami Valley of Ohio the best filler type. All three types of cigar leaf were (and still are) air-cured. The importance of soil types, curing methods, and hybridization in the development of distinct types of tobacco can also be readily seen in other examples: tobacco grown on soils outside of the Bright Belt will not produce a marketable Bright-tobacco even if flue-cured, nor will a Bright-tobacco strain produce good Burley leaf even if grown in Kentucky and air-cured. The Maryland Broadleaf, originally a very popular smoking type, later became an important cigar type in Connecticut.

Changes in the popular methods of consuming tobacco and the increase in per capita domestic consumption had a profound effect on the development and growth of various tobacco types. At the end of the Colonial period, all American tobacco tended to be classified as Oronoko by warehouse inspectors, and tobacco was consumed at home and abroad primarily in two ways: it was smoked in clay pipes or ground up and used as snuff. Chewing during the Colonial period was restricted largely to a negligible number of workingmen and sailors. After the Revolution there was a general switch to chewing, and Americans smoked less and took less snuff, a custom which had been popular since the French and Indian War. Chewing became the chief method of consuming tobacco during the first half of the nineteenth century and held this position until near the end of the century. The switch to chewing represented, in part, "a rejection, final and complete, of Europeans in general and the British in particular, with their inlaid snuff-boxes, formal airs and silk handkerchiefs." [28] The American habit of chewing tobacco was adopted to some extent by the British, but never became popular on the Continent. For busy Americans on the move, chewing was also more practical and convenient. Chewing did not necessitate a cessation of one's activities to fill and light a pipe, and one's spittoon was the whole outdoors. The improved quality and mildness that came with the expansion of tobacco culture to virgin soils in the western country, and the emergence of "yellow tobacco" from the depleted gray soils in the old growing areas were also factors. This suggests that the change in tobacco fashion was "based on the development of a better way of bringing out the best in *Nicotiana tabacum*." [29]

The chewing custom was especially important in the rapid expansion of the cultivation of Burley in Kentucky and adjoining states. The darker tobaccos of this general area were popular for making the chewing plug and twist as well as for export. Burley leaf contained far less sugar content than the tobacco grown east of the mountains and was thus capable of absorbing more of the additives, such as licorice, rum, sugar, or honey,[30] that were used to produce variety in taste. Air-cured tobacco was also more absorptive than fire-cured, as the smoky open fires tended to close the pores of the tobacco leaf.[31] In 1839, American tobacco growers produced a record crop of 219,163,000 pounds, with the states east of the mountains producing slightly more than those west. While the total 1849 crop was 10 percent less than that of 1839, production in the Virginia–North Carolina district showed a 34 percent decline. The center of production was shifting to the west, even though Virginia was still the leading producer in 1859 with 28.4 percent of the total crop; Kentucky was close on her heels with 27.8 percent.[32] The popularity of the Burley leaf for chewing and the impact of the war in Virginia enabled Kentucky to replace Virginia as the leading tobacco-producing state soon after the Civil War.

It was also the chewing era that breathed some new life into the declining tobacco culture in Virginia and North Carolina. The chewing public came to demand that the "quid" be pleasing to the eye as well as to the taste. Manufacturers began searching for hogsheads of light-colored or "yellow" tobacco to use as wrappers for the dark licorice-ladened plugs. Bright-tobacco leaf did not turn black when subjected to the juices and pressure necessary in the manufacture of the chewing plug. The superior prices paid for yellow tobacco resulted in increased efforts by growers in Virginia and North Carolina to produce such a leaf. This was also the period when the spangled tobacco of the Maryland type spread rapidly into Missouri and Ohio. The demand for a bright or yellow leaf, plus the growing objection to wood-smoked tobacco by Americans, led to the widespread use of charcoal and, later, flues in the Virginia–North Carolina district. Bright-tobacco was emerging as a distinct type before it became popular as a smoking leaf.[33]

The American cigar leaf industry originated in Connecticut in the early nineteenth century and grew very slowly until the Civil War period. By the 1830's cigar consumption was apparently large enough to cause a small handful of New Englanders to attempt to grow cigar leaf there that would compete with the imported Cuban tobacco used in the small cigar factories in Connecticut. New England tobacco was used to make cheap cigars. In 1833 the Maryland Broadleaf was introduced into Connecticut and proved to be an excellent wrapper type for the imported Cuban filler. In 1845 Cuban tobacco was introduced into the Housatonic Valley to produce the filler type. The acclimation of this tobacco in Connecticut is probably the beginning of what is known as Havana seed.

Americans were now producing much of their own cigar leaf.[34] The infant cigar leaf industry was stimulated by the growth of the popularity of cigars following the Mexican War. In the decade 1849–1859 cigar leaf production increased 3,000 percent in Massachusetts, 400 percent in Connecticut, 7,000 percent in New York, and 245 percent in Pennsylvania. Despite the tremendous percent of increase in production in this period, cigar leaf production in the United States constituted less than 10 percent of the total crop; [36] however, better days lay ahead.

The tobacco industry in general had fully recovered from the Civil War era by 1879, as total production for that year exceeded the record 1859 crop of 434,000,000 pounds. Total annual production by 1900 was double that of 1860 and by 1910 had passed the one billion pound mark. [37] Domestic consumption reached 60 percent of the total production by 1900, and it continued to climb as per capita consumption increased steadily. It was not until 1890 that chewing tobacco consumption per capita reached its peak and then began its decline. By 1880 cigar consumption accounted for about 30 percent of the tobacco used in the manufacture of all tobacco products. [38] The production of the cigar leaf became more specialized as the cigar industry attempted to satisfy the tastes of cigar smokers. For the aristocratic cigar user the old stogie or common cigar was inadequate. His cigar had to possess a good flavor and aroma, and had to burn properly, be well-shaped, and be wrapped in a pleasing cover. Thus a good cigar consisted of three types of tobacco: (1) filler, to give it the proper taste, (2) a tough binder to maintain the proper shape, and (3) an attractive wrapper. As already noted, certain geographical areas specialized in the production of a distinct cigar type, though the same plant produced all three types of leaf. For example, the wrapper type of tobacco was expected to produce more wrappers than the filler or binder, just as the filler type produced mostly filler leaf, but also some binder and wrapper leaves. The cigar managed to maintain its popularity throughout the remainder of the nineteenth century, and this caused northern Wisconsin, Georgia, and Florida to enter the commercial production of the cigar leaf. In 1904 the percent of the total tobacco crop used in the manufacture of the cigar dropped to 27 percent, and per capita cigar consumption reached its peak in 1907.[39]

Long before chewing tobacco and cigar consumption reached their peak of per capita consumption, Americans began to return to pipe smoking in larger numbers and to add the cigarette habit, which was introduced to Europeans during the Crimean War as a result of their contact with the Turks. John R. Green, tobacco manufacturer of Durham Station, North Carolina, believing that a trend toward smoking and away from chewing was in the making, shredded his tobacco rather than making it into the traditional plug or twist. The story of the consumption of Green's entire stock by some 80,000 Confederate and Yankee troops being mustered out nearby following the surrender in 1865 and the impact of the demand for the mild bright shredded leaf is a classic tale.[40] Post-Civil War days saw a rapid growth of the demand for and consumption of "smoking tobacco," i.e., tobacco shredded for consumption in pipes and for roll-your-own cigarettes. The peak of "smoking tobacco" consumption per capita came in 1910.

Burley and Bright-tobacco (in that order) were by far the most important smoking tobaccos. The increase in the consumption of smoking tobacco benefitted the already popular Burley and started Bright-tobacco and Tatham's southern states on the road to eventual supremacy in tobacco production. Bright-tobacco expanded into eastern North Carolina soon after the Civil War and by 1890 had crossed over into South Carolina. Following the invention of the cigarette machine in 1872 the "tailor-made" American cigarette was added as a new category. The first cigarettes were "straights," for example, all Burley or all Bright-tobacco. The blended American cigarette introduced in 1913 was more than half Bright-tobacco, from one- to two-fifths Burley, and the remainder Turkish and Maryland tobaccos.[41] The rapid growth of the popularity of blended cigarettes and the proportional makeup of the blend was soon reflected in the production of the various types, especially Bright-tobacco. Production was stimulated not only in the older areas but following World War I the Bright Belt came to include Georgia, Florida, and a small portion of Alabama.

By the end of World War I chewing tobacco, smoking tobacco, and snuff accounted for about 50 percent of the tobacco consumption in the United States, cigars 25 percent, and cigarettes 25 percent.[42] In 1921 the cigarette became the leading form of tobacco consumed in the United States, and in the following year authorities pronounced Bright-tobacco the world's leading tobacco crop. Although Kentucky remained for the moment the top tobacco producer, Burley—the most feared competitor of the Bright-tobacco industry—fell about 33 percent below the yield of Bright-tobacco.

In 1920 Bright-tobacco constituted one-third of the total tobacco production; in 1929 it had climbed to 49 percent, and North Carolina became the leading tobacco-producing state. Surpassing Kentucky by a 20 percent margin, North Carolina alone produced 65 percent of the total volume of Bright-tobacco.[43] In 1965 Burley constituted about 29 percent of the total production and Bright-tobacco about 49 percent, two-thirds of which was grown in North Carolina. Since 1960 Bright-tobacco production has declined about 2 percent, while Burley has increased about 2 percent.[44] This change is largely the result of the decrease in the amount of Bright-tobacco and the increase in the amount of Burley used in filter cigarettes.

Cigarette consumption probably saved the tobacco of southern Maryland from extinction. The great growth of the Burley trade and the fact that Maryland tobacco was rather neutral in flavor drastically reduced Maryland's status as a leaf producer. In 1830 she was growing 30 percent of the nation's crop; by 1880 this rate had declined to 5 percent.[45] The inclusion of the Maryland type in blended cigarettes because of its excellent burning qualities proved to be important. The decline of "the chew" in the United States and the growing popularity of Burley and Bright-tobacco on the export market had an adverse effect, from which they have never recovered, on the dark-fired districts.

In 1965 cigarettes accounted for a little over 80 percent of the tobacco consumed in the United States, cigars approximately 10 percent, and smoking and chewing tobaccos a little less than 10 percent. Snuff production in the United States has never been very large. Although about 30,000,000 pounds of snuff is still being produced annually, this constitutes less than .015 percent of today's domestic tobacco consumption. Cigarettes account for almost 90 percent of the domestic consumption of Burley and 95 percent of the Bright-tobacco usage in the United States. Bright-tobacco types also account for over 81 percent of the total leaf exported by this country.[46] Tatham's southern states once again produce and export most American tobacco.

As a result of the expansion of tobacco culture into new areas with varied climatic conditions and soil types, hybridization and three different methods of curing new varieties and types of tobacco emerged. And as consumers came to demand distinct types of tobacco for their quid and smoke, commercial circles began to distinguish tobacco as to classes and types as well as grades. Tobacco was officially classified into classes and types for the first time in the census reports of 1880. The adaptation of tobacco for certain purposes such as cigar, smoking, chewing, or export determined the class. Type was determined by a combination of certain qualities in the leaf, such as color, strength, elasticity, body, and flavor, or the method used in curing. A particular area might produce only one class, but several types, or only one type and perhaps two classes; or a district might produce one type of one class. Tobacco was classified for the first time as shown in Table 1 (see Appendix A for a more detailed description).

Subsequent changes in the classification of to-

Table 1.

CLASSES, TYPES, AND SUB-TYPES, 1879 *

Class I. Domestic Cigar Tobacco and Smokers
Seed-leaf and Havana seed

Connecticut seed-leaf
New England seed-leaf
Pennsylvania seed-leaf
New York seed-leaf

Ohio seed-leaf
Wisconsin and Illinois seed-leaf
Florida seed-leaf

Other cigar and smoking tobacco

White Burley lugs
American-grown Havana
Perique
Common Virginia, North
  Carolina, Missouri, Eastern
  Ohio, Maryland, and Illinois
  lugs

Kentucky and Indiana cheroot
  and stogie wrappers and fillers
Fine-fibered Clarksville wrappers
Indiana Kite-foot

Class II. Chewing Tobacco
Fine-cut and plug fillers

Fine-cut Burley
Fine-cut Mason County
White Burley fillers
Red Burley fillers
Virginia sun- and air-cured fillers
Virginia flue-cured fillers

Missouri air-cured fillers
Kentucky, Indiana, Tennessee,
  Virginia, Maryland, and West
  Virginia fire-cured fillers
Tennessee and Kentucky air-
  cured filler

Plug wrappers

Virginia yellow and mahogany
North Carolina yellow and
  mahogany
Western Kentucky yellow
Hart County (Kentucky) bright
  yellow
Henry County (Tennessee)
  yellow

Missouri and Arkansas yellow
West Virginia yellow
Clarksville and Missouri dark
  and red
Mason County (Kentucky)
  Burley

Class III. Export Tobacco
English shippers

Bird's-eye cutting leaf
Brown-roll wrapper
Spinning leaf
Shag

Plug wrapper
Plug fillers
Navy leaf
Scotch Elder

Continental shippers

French Regie
Italian Regie

Switzerland:
  Swiss wrappers

Table 1. (Continued)

Austrian Regie	Swiss fillers
Spanish Regie	Holland:
Germany:	Dutch saucer
German saucer	Belgium:
German spinner	Belgian cutter
Ohio, Maryland,	Denmark, Norway, and Sweden:
and West Virginia	Heavy Tennessee and
spangled	Kentucky types

African shippers

Liverpool African	Gibralter African
Boston African	

Mexico, South America, and West Indies shippers

Baling wrapper	Baling filler
Black Fats	

---

* Source: Killebrew, "Report on the Culture and Curing of Tobacco in the United States," *Tenth Census, Agriculture,* III (Washington, 1883), 15–22.

bacco as to types and classes after 1880 tell much of the story of the growing specialization in types. In 1929 an act of Congress authorized the Bureau of Agricultural Economics, United States Department of Agriculture, to draw up a comprehensive system of standards for the classification of leaf tobacco grown in the United States. Tobaccos were divided into seven classes containing twenty-six types. Class was officially defined as "one of the major divisions of leaf tobacco based on soil characteristics of tobacco caused by differences in varieties, soil, and climatic conditions, and methods of cultivation, harvesting and curing." Classes 1, 2, and 3 were based on the three methods of curing (flue, fire, and air); classes 4, 5, and 6 (cigar types) were based on their intended use (filler, binder, and wrapper). Class 7 consisted of miscel-

laneous domestic grown tobacco not otherwise classified and produced in small quantities.

Type was defined as "a sub-division of class of
leaf tobacco, having certain common characteristics
which permit its being divided into a number of
related grades. Any tobacco that has the same
characteristics and corresponding qualities, colors,
and lengths, shall be treated as one type, regardless
of any factors of historical or geographical nature
which cannot be determined by an examination of
the tobacco." Type in most cases referred to the
region in which a particular class was produced.

The official classification established in 1929 was
essentially the formal recognition of the specialization of kinds and types that had emerged over the
decades.[47] The minor changes that have taken place
since 1929 have been summarized in tables 2 and 3
(see Appendix B for a more detailed description).

Accurate and complete production statistics of
agricultural products by individual states are not
available prior to 1839, at which time the United
States government began to promote the agricultural census. According to Tatham and others,
101,272 hogsheads of tobacco were exported in
1791.[48] The estimated domestic tobacco consumption for 1790 has been set at 22 percent of the total
production.[49] This indicates that approximately
124,000,000 pounds of tobacco were produced in
the 1790 period, 80 percent of which was grown in
Virginia and Maryland. By 1830 the average annual crop of Virginia and North Carolina combined was about 45,000 hogsheads, about 30,000 in
Maryland, and about 30,000 hogsheads in the

Table 2.

CLASSIFICATION OF TOBACCO GROWN IN THE
UNITED STATES, 1965 *

	Class	Type		States in which grown
1.	Flue-cured	11(a)	Old Belt	Va., N.C.
		11(b)	Middle Belt	N.C.
		12	Eastern Belt	N.C.
		13	Border Belt	S.C., N.C.
		14	Georgia and Florida Belt	Ga., Fla., Ala.
2.	Fire-cured	21	Virginia	Va.
		22	Eastern District	Ky., Tenn.
		23	Western District	Ky., Tenn.
3.	Air-cured			
	(a) *Light*	31	Burley	Ky., Tenn., Ohio, Ind., Va., N.C., W. Va., Mo., Kan.
		32	Maryland Broadleaf	Md.
		35	One Sucker	Ky., Tenn.
	(b) *Dark*	36	Green River	Ky.
		37	Virginia sun-cured	Va.
4.	Cigar-filler	41	Pennsylvania Seedleaf	Pa.
		42–44	Ohio filler	Ohio
5.	Cigar-binder	51	Connecticut Broadleaf	Conn.
		52	Connecticut Havana Seed	Conn., Mass.
		54	Southern Wisconsin	Wis.
		55	Northern Wisconsin	Wis., Minn.
6.	Cigar-wrapper	61	Connecticut Shade	Conn., Mass.
		62	Georgia and Florida Shade	Ga., Fla.
7.	Miscellaneous Domestic	72	Perique	La.
		77	Domestic Aromatic	Va., N.C., S.C.

* *Tobacco in the United States* (United States Department of Agriculture, Consumer and Marketing Service Miscellaneous Publication No. 867, Washington, D.C., 1966), 3.

western states of Tennessee, Kentucky, Missouri, and Ohio, most of which came from Tennessee and Kentucky.[50] (The average weight of a hogshead of tobacco had increased from 1,000 to 1,200 pounds

Table 3.

VOLUME OF PRODUCTION, DOMESTIC DISAPPEARANCE AND
EXPORTS, AND DOMESTIC USAGES IN MANUFACTURED
PRODUCTS, BY KINDS, 1965 *

Class	Typical production		Disappearance		Usage in products	
	Quantity (million lbs.)	Percent of total	Domestic	Exports†	Principal	Other
1. Flue-cured	1,225	59.2	62	38	Cigarettes	Smoking, chewing
2. Fire-cured	50	2.4	54	46	Snuff	Chewing, strong cigars
3. Air-cured:						
(a) Burley	600	28.9	90	10	Cigarettes	Smoking, chewing
(b) Maryland	35	1.7	64	36	Cigarettes	Cigar filler
(c) Dark	22	1.1	74	26	Chewing	Smoking, snuff, cigar filler
4. Cigar filler	90	4.3	99	1	Cigar filler	Scrap, chewing
5. Cigar binder	30	1.5	90	10	Scrap, chewing	Cigar binder
6. Cigar wrapper	18	.9	70	30	Cigar wrapper	
Total	2,070	100.0	73	27		

#Principal export markets (in order of importance) as of 1965:†

Flue-cured	*Burley*	*Fire-cured*
United Kingdom	West Germany	Netherlands
West Germany	Italy	France
Japan	UAR (Egypt)	Congo (Leopoldville)
Netherlands	Mexico	Belgium-Luxembourg
Australia	Portugal	
Belgium-Luxembourg	Netherlands	
UAR (Egypt)	Denmark	

* *Tobacco in the U.S.*, 8.
# *Ibid.*, 57.

by 1830.) This makes the total average annual tobacco production by 1830 approximately 126,000,000 pounds. Cigar leaf production in the northern states was just beginning.

The following tables summarize the production of the leading tobacco-producing states at ten-year intervals from 1839 to 1965. Table 4 is organized on the basis of the three major geographical areas: Eastern (east of the mountains and south of Pennsylvania), Western, and Northern, and covers the period 1839–1919. Table 5 covers the period 1929 to 1965 and is organized on the basis of classes and types as established by the United States Department of Agriculture in 1929, including the few minor modifications made since that time.

Although crop management remained largely as described by Tatham, there were some fundamental changes in the routine of tobacco culture during the nineteenth century. One of the first significant changes had to do with methods of curing. As Tatham pointed out, air-curing was the typical method used at the beginning of the nineteenth century, though small smothered wood fires were frequently used to help eliminate excessive moisture during damp or rainy periods. It had also been proven by this time that tobacco cured with the aid of artificial heat possessed better keeping qualities for the voyage across the ocean. As already noted, after the War of 1812 the foreign market showed a marked preference for tobacco possessing a smoky smell and flavor, and from about 1815 to 1840 fire-curing was quite common. By the 1830's there was growing opposition to fire-curing, and a swing back to air-curing occurred in some areas,[51] while others switched to charcoal as fuel and then went on to perfect a flue-curing system that gave this method its name. Flue-curing had only a lim-

Table 4. TOBACCO PRODUCTION, 1839–1919 *

Total Tobacco Production in 1000 lbs.
(Ranks in parentheses)

	1839	1849	1859	1869	1879	1889	1899	1909	1919
Northern									
Conn.	472 (10)	1,268 (8)	6,000 (10)	8,328 (9)	14,044 (8)	8,874 (11)	16,930 (10)	28,110 (8)	42,193 (9)
Mass.	65 (15)	138 (14)	3,233 (12)	7,313 (10)	5,369 (13)	2,704 (14)	6,406 (13)	9,549 (13)	14,282 (12)
N.Y.	1 (17)	83 (15)	5,765 (11)	2,349 (13)	6,481 (12)	9,316 (10)	13,958 (11)	5,345 (15)	3,353 (17)
Pa.	325 (11)	913 (11)	3,182 (13)	3,467 (12)	36,943 (3)	28,956 (6)	41,502 (7)	46,164 (7)	55,965 (7)
Wis.		1 (18)	87 (18)	961 (14)	10,608 (10)	19,389 (7)	45,500 (6)	46,909 (7)	52,454 (8)
Southern									
Md.	24,816 (4)	21,407 (3)	38,410 (4)	15,785 (5)	26,082 (7)	12,356 (8)	24,589 (8)	17,845 (11)	17,336 (11)
Va.	75,347 (1)	56,803 (1)	123,068 (1)	37,086 (2)	79,088 (2)	48,522 (2)	122,884 (3)	132,979 (3)	102,391 (4)
N.C.	16,772 (5)	11,984 (6)	32,853 (5)	11,150 (7)	26,986 (6)	36,375 (4)	127,503 (2)	138,813 (2)	280,163 (2)
S.C.	51 (16)	74 (16)	104 (17)	34 (19)	45 (19)	222 (19)	19,895 (9)	35,583 (6)	71,193 (5)
Ga.	162 (12)	423 (13)	919 (15)	288 (17)	228 (17)	263 (18)	1,105 (18)	1,485 (17)	10,584 (13)
Fla.	75 (14)	908 (10)	828 (16)	157 (18)	21 (20)	470 (17)	1,125 (17)	3,505 (16)	4,473 (15)
La.	119 (13)	26 (17)	39 (19)	15 (20)	55 (18)	46 (20)	102 (20)	172 (20)	221 (20)
Western									
Ky.	53,436 (2)	55,501 (2)	108,126 (2)	105,305 (2)	171,120 (1)	221,880 (1)	314,288 (1)	398,482 (1)	504,661 (1)
Tenn.	29,550 (3)	20,148 (4)	43,448 (4)	21,465 (3)	29,365 (5)	36,368 (5)	49,157 (5)	68,756 (5)	112,367 (3)
Ohio	5,942 (7)	10,455 (7)	25,093 (6)	18,741 (4)	34,735 (4)	37,853 (3)	65,957 (4)	88,603 (4)	64,420 (6)
Mo.	9,068 (6)	17,114 (5)	25,086 (7)	12,320 (6)	12,016 (9)	9,424 (9)	3,041 (15)	5,372 (14)	4,074 (16)
Ark.			990 (16)	594 (16)	970 (16)	954 (16)	831 (19)	316 (19)	267 (19)
Ill.	565 (9)	841 (12)	6,885 (9)	5,249 (11)	3,935 (14)	3,042 (13)	1,447 (16)	1,029 (18)	566 (18)
Ind.	1,820 (8)	1,945 (9)	7,994 (8)	9,325 (8)	8,872 (11)	7,710 (12)	6,882 (12)	21,387 (10)	18,752 (10)
W.Va.				960 (15)	2,296 (15)	2,602 (15)	3,087 (14)	14,356 (12)	7,587 (14)
U.S. total	219,163	199,753	434,209	262,735	472,661	488,256	868,163	1,055,704	1,371,504

* Compiled from *Seventeenth Census of the United States, 1940, Agriculture,* III, *General Report, Statistics by Subjects* (Washington, D.C. 1943), 789. Totals include data from states other than the major tobacco-producing states listed.

Table 5. TOBACCO PRODUCTION BY CLASS AND TYPE, 1929–1965 *

(in 1000 lbs.)

	TYPE NO.	1929	1935	1945	1955	1965
Class 1, Flue-cured:	11–14					
Virginia	11	75,600	74,390	117,130	130,680	
North Carolina	11	210,200	215,940	336,640	350,625	
Total Old Belt	11	285,800	290,330	422,770	481,305	355,587
Total Eastern N.C. Belt	12	249,500	297,600	395,360	516,710	
North Carolina	13	38,800	59,085	93,500	128,790	
South Carolina	13	82,460	89,760	139,520	198,900	
Total South Carolina Belt	13	121,260	148,845	233,020	327,690	225,658
Georgia	14	88,184	68,400	105,060	147,965	
Florida	14	6,155	6,020	17,169	29,751	
Alabama	14			225	654	
Total Georgia-Florida Belt	14	94,339	74,420	122,484	178,370	132,835
Total All Flue-cured Types	11–14	750,899	811,195	1,173,634	1,504,075	1,058,970
Class 2, Fired-cured	21–24					
Total Virginia Belt	21	22,800	20,445	11,760	11,193	9,576
Kentucky	22	47,460	23,850	7,800	11,745	
Tennessee	22	56,800	45,050	25,000	26,648	
Total Hopkinsville-Clarksville Belt	22	104,260	68,900	32,800	38,393	26,216
Kentucky	23	40,655	19,750	9,500	12,090	
Tennessee	23	5,880	6,075	2,940	2,572	
Total Paducah-Mayfield Belt	23	46,535	25,825	12,440	14,662	10,388
Henderson Stemming (Ky.)	24	9,492	3,025	95		
Total All Fire-cured Types	21–24	183,087	118,194	57,095	64,248	46,180
Class 3, Air-cured	31–37					
3A LIGHT AIR-CURED						
Ohio	31	17,798	6,435	18,160	15,040	
Indiana	31	14,040	4,200	13,320	12,160	
Missouri	31	4,050	3,895	6,800	3,680	
Kansas	31		225	300	115	
Virginia	31	6,950	7,140	22,185	20,670	
West Virginia	31	6,588	1,596	3,729	4,160	
North Carolina	31	4,100	4,810	20,300	21,560	
Kentucky	31	242,440	154,530	385,200	339,450	
Tennessee	31	41,600	36,120	108,000	93,000	
Total Burley Belt	31	334,566	220,923	577,994	509,835	586,299
Southern Maryland Belt	32	24,750	27,935	21,600	35,525	38,525
Total All Light Air-cured	31–32	359,316	248,858	599,594	545,360	624,824
3B DARK AIR-CURED						
Indiana	35	4,000	438	202		
Kentucky	35	21,840	10,354	20,500	15,300	
Tennessee	35	3,504	2,228	6,000	4,205	
Total One Sucker	35	29,344	13,020	26,720	19,505	11,891
Green River Belt (Ky.)	36	27,390	15,210	14,600	10,080	6,631
Virginia Sun-cured Belt	37	4,150	2,790	2,240	4,192	1,989
Total All Dark Air-cured	35–37	60,884	31,020	43,560	33,777	20,511
Class 4, Cigar filler						
Pennsylvania Seedleaf	41	48,920	28,188	45,890	43,350	51,300
Miami Valley Types (Ohio)	42–44	21,213	17,415	4,510	7,480	5,550
Georgia	45	940	420			
Florida	45	1,035	770			
Georgia-Florida Sun-grown	45	1,975	1,190			
Total Cigar Filler Types	41–45	72,108	46,793	50,400	50,830	56,850

Table 5. (Continued)

	TYPE NO.	1929	1935	1945	1955	1965
Class 5, Cigar binder	51–56					
Massachusetts	51	595	170	148	155	
Connecticut	51	11,463	10,540	13,122	12,246	
Conn. Valley Broadleaf	51	12,058	10,710	13,270	12,401	5,550
Massachusetts	52	9,211	4,225	6,750	8,507	
Connecticut	52	8,294	2,475	3,410	1,610	
Conn. Valley Havana Seed	52	17,505	6,700	10,160	10,117	1,400
New York	53	800	390	1,000	375	
Pennsylvania	53	616	300	465	315	
N.Y. and Pa. Havana Seed	53	1,416	690	1,465	315	
Southern Wisconsin	54	29,705	8,400	18,720	6,815	8,484
Wisconsin	55	18,420	6,625	17,328	12,540	
Minnesota	55	1,800	230	910	238	
Northern Wisconsin	55	20,220	6,855	18,238	12,778	10,757
Georgia	56			93		
Florida	56			93		
Georgia-Fla. Sun-grown	56			186		
Total Cigar Binder Types	51–56	80,904	33,355	62,039	42,426	24,156
Class 6, Cigar wrapper	61–62					
Massachusetts	61	1,794	1,025	1,274	2,185	
Connecticut	61	8,424	4,700	6,298	6,283	
Conn. Valley Shade-grown	61	10,218	5,725	7,572	8,468	14,576
Georgia	62	746	180	822	1,410	
Florida	62	3,880	1,890	2,820	5,343	
Georgia-Fla. Shade-grown	62	4,626	2,070	3,642	6,753	8,322
Total Cigar Wrapper Types	61–62	14,884	7,795	11,214	15,221	22,898
Total All Cigars Types	41–62	167,856	87,943	123,653	108,477	103,904
Class 7, Miscellaneous	72					
Eastern Ohio		1,942				
Louisiana Perique		378		192	150	259
		2,320				
UNITED STATES	ALL	1,524,362	1,437,100	1,997,728	2,256,087	1,854,648

* *Yearbook of Agriculture*, 1931 (United States Department of Agriculture, Washington, D.C., 1931), 701–702; *Crops and Markets* (United States Department of Agriculture, XIII, No. 12, December, 1936), 420–421; *Crops and Markets*, XXIII, No. 4 (October, 1946), 160–161; *Crops and Markets* XXXIII (Washington, 1956 edition), 33; *Agricultural Statistics* (United States Department of Agriculture, Washington, D.C., 1966), 104.

ited following before the Civil War, but spread rapidly following the end of hostilities.[52] The heavy shipping districts in Tennessee and Kentucky and other areas retained the old fire-curing method before and after the war. Thus by 1860 three distinct curing methods had evolved and came to be associated with certain geographical areas, classes, and types of tobacco.

A new method of harvesting evolved out of the Colonial practice of "priming" tobacco by the end of the nineteenth century. "Priming" tobacco was originally the task of removing several of the bottom or ground leaves that became dirty and bruised from chopping and plowing the young plant. This operation was also thought to give additional strength to the remaining leaves. This task was sometimes performed at the last cultivation, but some preferred to prime at the same time the tobacco was being topped, and others waited until the tobacco needed suckering. Some Colonial planters waited until just before the entire plant was ripe enough to cut before priming and, instead of discarding these leaves, collected and cured them for market. Many farmers continued to prime and discard the leaves, and in the 1830's and 1840's a few farmers revived the practice of collecting and curing them and offered them for sale as "lugs." The idea of profit from these previously worthless leaves encouraged the practice to the extent that by 1885 the sale of primings was described as a growing evil in some areas.

As early as the 1870's several farmers in the Bright Belt were suggesting that harvesting and curing single leaves rather than the entire plant would save time, labor, and fuel. Harvesting a few leaves from each plant as they ripened, by priming and tying the leaves on sticks with strings to be cured rather than cutting the entire stalk, was inextricably bound up with the increasing popularity of the cigarette and so was confined principally to the Bright Belt. By 1900 a sizable number of farmers in the Bright Belt were priming rather than cutting tobacco, though many clung to the older practice for another decade. Others adopted a modification of priming whereby a considerable number of leaves were removed in this manner and the remainder left on the stalk until ripe and then harvested by cutting. This procedure was thought to hasten the ripening process of those left on the stalk.[53] The rapid conversion to the priming method of harvesting came in the period of the development of the blended cigarette and the expansion of the Bright Belt. The priming method came to be used to harvest Bright-tobacco, shade-grown cigar wrapper, and Turkish tobaccos.

The "fly" (flea beetle) described by Tatham continued to be a most serious pest, destroying many seedlings in tobacco plant beds, until near the end of the nineteenth century. After over two centuries and many ineffective remedies, the "fly" menace finally was greatly reduced. In the 1870's a thin cloth cover or canvas was used successfully in Pennsylvania and Virginia to keep out the "fly." By the end of the century this simple protective covering was used in all tobacco-growing sections. In 1897 J. B. Killebrew wrote: "Nothing that has ever been invented or devised has effected so much for the tobacco grower, at such a small cost, as a canvas-covering for the seed bed." [54] The cloth covering has now been replaced by a plastic cover, which not only gives better protection against the "fly," but aids in hastening the germination of the seed and provides more protection from the elements.[55]

During the Colonial period and in the early national period the absence of commercial fertilizers to hasten the growth of tobacco and revive old worn out fields was an important factor in promoting the expansion of tobacco culture into new areas. When the era of commercial fertilizers arrived in the 1840's it soon proved to be of immense value to the tobacco industry as well as for other crops. Meyer Jacobstein wrote: "It was the use of artificial commercial fertilizer that made possible the production of a cigar leaf in the Northern states." [56] The widespread acceptance and use of commercial fertilizers after the Civil War often doubled the yield and greatly improved the quality of tobacco.[57]

The widespread use of commercial fertilizers and the dissemination of information on every facet of tobacco culture by the tobacco experiment stations, which multiplied after the Hatch Act of 1887, were also of immense value to the tobacco farmers of all sections. Perhaps the most obvious and measurable results of the total efforts of the experiment stations can be seen in the massive increase in yield per acre in the past century. Yield per acre has always varied greatly from district to district and within each district. The summary here will concern itself only with changes in the national averages.

Leading authorities agree that the average yield per acre in the period 1800–1860 ranged from 650 to 700 pounds, with only slight variations.[58] In the decade 1850–1860 the average yield was probably the maximum of the above range. The total number of acres harvested in 1859 was double that of

1839. Statistics suggest that the tobacco industry had recovered from the Civil War era by 1879, as production for that year slightly exceeded the total yield for 1859. The 1879 crop of 469,395,000 pounds was harvested from 650,000 acres, with an average yield per acre of 740 pounds. Average yield per acre passed the 800 pound mark slightly for the first time in 1904, something close to 100 pounds more than in the pre-Civil War era.

The years 1901 through 1919 were good years in terms of general demand for most of the tobacco types. Market demand was good for cigar, chewing, smoking, and cigarette tobaccos. Tobacco acreage increased from slightly over a million in 1901 to a little less than two million acres by 1919, while the average yield per acre remained rather static. The average annual per acre yield for the two decades was 818 pounds.[59] This was due partly to the fact that the major increase in tobacco acreage occurred in the Bright-tobacco Belt where the yield per acre was low.

In the last decade before the inauguration of the twentieth century tobacco production controls, beginning with the Agricultural Adjustment Act of 1933, the average annual tobacco crop harvested amounted to 1,773,800 acres, which was 260,000 acres more than the annual average acreage for the prewar decade. The average annual yield per acre in the decade 1911–1920 was 807 pounds; in the period 1921–1933 this average dropped to 770 pounds. The tobacco farmer of the pre-Depression decade simply followed the procedure of his Colonial ancestors in attempting to do something about his declining farm income—plant more tobacco.

It was not until the adoption of the policy of acreage control that the tobacco farmers as a whole really became seriously concerned about increasing their yield per acre. The tremendous increase in the national average yield per acre in the past three decades is ample evidence of this as well as evidence of the effective work of the experiment stations and other agencies. In the period from 1860 to 1933 the national average yield per acre increased little more than 100 pounds. In 1940 the average reached the 1,000 pound mark for the first time. In 1950 it reached 1,269 pounds; 1,703 pounds in 1960; [60] and in 1965 the national average yield per acre reached 1,900 pounds.[61] Since the adoption of the first acreage control program in 1933 the national average yield per acre has increased approximately 1,100 pounds. This can be attributed primarily to heavy fertilization, new high-yielding varieties, an increased number of plants per acre, pesticides, irrigation, and the widespread use of chemicals to prevent the growth of suckers.

In 1965, farmers in the Burley and Bright-tobacco belts were given the opportunity to accept or reject an acreage-poundage control program as the problem of excessive production and ineffective production controls became more acute. The acreage-poundage program was adopted for a three-year period by the farmers in the Bright-tobacco Belt, while the Burley farmers voted to retain the acreage control program and rejected poundage control.[62] The problems of overproduction and ineffective production controls are not new, as both were present in seventeenth century Virginia.

The loose-leaf auction market, which handles most of the tobacco crop today, originated in the early nineteenth century. At the beginning of that century the Colonial practice of sale by simply producing the tobacco note or receipt issued by the warehouse inspector was still in use. However, lax and sometime corrupt inspections resulted in the decline of the reputation of the inspectors and the tobacco note, and careful buyers began to demand that the tobacco be re-inspected. To avoid the difficulties of re-inspection, a few shippers began sending buyers to some of the larger inspection stations during the tobacco season. By 1810 a new system of sale began to emerge. As one or more hogsheads were opened for inspection, and upon hearing a prearranged signal, buyers present at a particular inspection warehouse approached the opened hogsheads and personally inspected them. The planter usually sold his tobacco to one of the buyers present in order to avoid another inspection. By 1820 warehouse sale was a well established practice at the principal inspection warehouses. Warehouse sale of the leaf led to the development of the auction system by the middle of the 1830's with the inspector frequently assuming the role of auctioneer.

The third feature of the major present-day marketing system was soon added—the sale of loose-leaf tobacco. Around 1830 buyers began to buy loose-leaf or unprized tobacco directly from the farmer, and this caused the practice of admitting loose-leaf tobacco at the warehouse for inspection. The purchase of tobacco prized into the traditional hoghead and branded by the inspector continued to be the general practice during the antebellum period. However, the loose-leaf auction sale at the warehouse had become firmly established and spread rapidly, especially in the Bright Belt after the Civil War.[63] By 1901 the system had been introduced in Tennessee and Kentucky, though a small quantity in the fire-cured districts is still sold directly at farms. Approximately 95 percent of the tobacco grown in the United States today is marketed by the loose-leaf auction method.[64] Since the passage of the Tobacco Inspection Act in 1935, tobacco inspection and grading has been mandatory.

The only "hogshead" market still in operation today is located at Baltimore, Maryland, and sells only the small quantity of the Maryland type still grown exclusively in that state. The tobacco is examined by state inspectors and sold at "closed bid" auction. These bids are opened at a specified time and the tobacco goes to the highest bidder, with the approval of the grower. There are no established market centers for conducting firsthand sales for the cigar leaf. Farmers contract for the sale of their tobacco at the farm, a system known as "barn-door marketing." The contract may be made before or after harvest.[65]

When the machine age began in America it barely touched the tobacco farm. One noted historian on the culture of tobacco wrote in 1949: "The routine of culture by 1940 differed in few respects from the procedure of fifty years earlier." [66] A few mechanical and chemical aids had emerged: the horse or mule and plow and occasionally a tractor had reduced but not eliminated the hoe; on the larger, flatter farms horse-drawn "tobacco setters" were used successfully, though the majority of the tobacco was planted with a hand planting instrument containing a water reservoir that eliminated many aching backs associated with the ancient peg or dibble, which was still widely used; and insecticides helped restrain the gluts of the tobacco worms so common in the Colonial period. Tobacco still had to be topped, suckered, primed or cut, and put on sticks to be cured; and later the leaves had to be taken off the sticks or stalks, if cut, and tied into hands or bundles in preparation for the market. Only the human hand could accomplish these tasks. Although destructiveness of the "fly" and tobacco worm had been greatly reduced, the tobacco farmer was now plagued with many new, serious, and destructive plant diseases.

Science and the machine age have made considerable progress in the tobacco belts since World War II. Much progress had been made in breeding disease-resistant varieties as well as varieties that have improved the quality and yield of tobacco. More effective insecticides have been developed to deal with old and new pests of the tobacco plant. Irrigation systems are now quite common and have brought an increase in production, quality, and net profit.

The majority of tobacco today is planted with mechanized transplanters that require the human hand to simply place the plants on a conveyer belt.

The machine sets and waters the plant. Cultivation is done largely by tractor and plow. The horse and hoe are disappearing rapidly from the tobacco field.

The task of "suckering," which traditionally followed the topping operation since the beginning of the culture of tobacco, has now been virtually eliminated. Sucker control experiments using several different preparations began as early as 1949. Maleic hydrozide proved to be one of the most effective sucker deterrents and was being used extensively by 1958. This chemical prevents or deters the growth of suckers to such a degree that it gives effective sucker control. Within two or three days after the tobacco is topped the upper portion of the plant is sprayed with Maleic hydrozide, better known as MH-30. With favorable weather conditions, one spraying with MH-30 eliminates hours of costly and back-breaking labor of hand-pulling suckers. When the skip-row method of planting is used (i.e., not planting every fifth row) this chemical can be applied with tractor-mounted spraying equipment. This method of sucker control not only eliminated a laborious task but tobacco experiment station tests have shown that, if properly used, it also increases the yield per acre without affecting the quality.[67]

Considerable progress is being made, at last, in mechanizing the harvesting of tobacco. The greatest progress is being made in the Bright Belt where the entire crop is harvested by priming. For more than a decade farmers in the Bright Belt have been "sitting down" to prime their tobacco. The "new tobacco harvester" does not harvest the tobacco itself. On the larger, self-propelled, four-row harvesters four men, the pickers, sit in seats only inches above the ground, and as they ride slowly past the plants, they snap off the ripe leaves and stick them into clips on an endless chain, which carries the leaves to a platform above them, where several additional laborers tie the leaves on the tobacco sticks. The sticks of tobacco are hung on racks mounted on the platform until all the available space is filled; then the harvester is driven to the tobacco barn and the sticks of tobacco are unloaded. Many farmers insist that these tobacco-harvesting machines save as much as 50 percent of harvesting labor. Agricultural engineers say that a primer can handle as much as 25 percent more leaves from a sitting position on a machine than when walking through the field. Probably the greatest advantage of the harvester is that it demands greater efficiency from the laborer. As the machines move steadily down the rows of tobacco the pickers or primers must work at a regular and constant pace from one end of the row to the other. The "stringers" up above tying the leaves on the tobacco sticks must take the leaves from the revolving chain as rapidly as they come up. The new harvester is only the beginning of the task of reducing the amount of labor required to harvest and cure each acre of flue-cured tobacco. It requires between 400 and 480 hours of man labor to produce one acre of flue-cured tobacco, 165 of which are required for the conventional method of harvest alone. The mechanical harvester has reduced this requirement to somewhere between 25 and 50 percent.[68]

By 1963 a tobacco "stitching" or "looping" machine was in use at some barns to tie (sew) the leaves on the tobacco sticks; by 1964 its use was becoming widespread. The machine is operated by a crew of three: one person spreads the leaves evenly on a conveyer belt; another puts down a stick and a second layer of tobacco, and the machine literally sews the butt end of the leaves together just above the stick; the third person operates the stitcher and removes the stick of tobacco. The tying machine has reduced labor requirements for the barn operation about 59 percent.[69]

For a century, flue-cured tobacco farmers spent many laborious hours during the winter months cutting wood for fuel to cure the coming crop. During the curing season, after the barns of tobacco had yellowed sufficiently, someone had to closely watch the fires and the temperature until the barn of tobacco was thoroughly cured. This was not a difficult task from the standpoint of physical labor but it was time consuming. As late as about 1950 it was estimated that sixty man-hours were required to cure the product of one acre of tobacco.

Experiments with other fuels and different types of heating systems were being conducted by the late 1930's; however, World War II delayed the transition to new heating systems using various products of the petroleum industry or coal. In 1946 about 10 percent of the curing barns in the Bright Belt were converted from the traditional wood furnaces to coal stokers or oil burners. By 1950, 70 percent of the farmers in one state were curing with oil burners of various types, some without use of the sheet-iron flue. By the middle of the 1950's many were switching from oil to the cleaner LP-Gas systems. The dirty coal stoker became more and more unpopular. It is now difficult to find many wood-curing barns in the Bright Belt. The great advantage of the oil- or gas-curing systems is the elimination of many man-hours of constant careful attention, both day and night, during the curing season. The heat can be regulated with greater accuracy for longer periods of time than with the old wood furnaces. Short visits to the barn to determine the stage of the curing process and to maintain the proper barn temperature are all that are necessary. More efficient and constant heating systems also shortened the curing time per barn of tobacco. In addition, many agree that these new systems have improved the quality and color of the cured product.[70]

In 1956 laboratory investigations were begun on a new method of curing Bright-tobacco, the first major change in Bright-leaf curing in more than a century. North Carolina State University and United States Department of Agriculture engineers and plant scientists discovered a method of curing involving tobacco packed loosely in crates in about one-sixth of the space normally required when leaves are hung from sticks in the curing barn. This method is known as bulk curing and opens a whole new approach to harvesting and curing. The loose leaves of ripe tobacco are placed in crates; these crates are then stacked one on top of another in a small, compact curing barn. The tobacco is then cured by forced hot air from an outside, thermostatically controlled heating system. Bulk curing is said to eliminate about 70 to 75 percent of the labor required to harvest, cure, and prepare for market by the traditional method, by eliminating stringing the leaves on sticks and unstringing them before they are tied into hands or bundles for marketing. This would be a reduction of about 140 of the approximately 200 hours per acre normally required at this stage.

The first experimental bulk curing farm unit was installed on the Stone Brothers' farm in Robeson County, North Carolina in 1960. About 300 bulk curers were in operation during the 1962 season, and many thought the new system was firmly established. However, the buying trade objected to certain characteristics that began to show up when a large volume reached the market during the marketing season for the 1962 crop, resulting generally in lower prices for the bulk-cured tobacco. The most objectionable feature was the apparent tendency of bulk-cured tobacco to "cake" or stick together when packed down after curing awaiting sale. The "caked" tobacco is difficult to separate for processing after it leaves the market. Some users were thoroughly disappointed, some were completely satisfied, and others were elated. Following the 1962 season more careful instructions were issued for users of the new curing method. In an effort to take advantage of the labor saving feature of bulk curing, some farmers attempted to make the switch from conventional curing before the product of the new system was adequately tested under normal marketing conditions.

One of the original objectives of the bulk-curing experiments was to develop a curing system compatible with mechanization of the tobacco harvest —elimination of the individual leaf-handling operations that are the major bottlenecks to mechanization. In 1954 engineers at North Carolina State University built a "tobacco picker" to pick or prime the ripened leaves from the stalk as it moved down the tobacco rows. Untouched by human hands, the leaves were dumped by the machine into crates, which were taken directly to the bulk-curing unit. A third phase of the overall scheme was to market the tobacco "loose-leaf," to eliminate the task of tying the leaves into hands in the traditional method after curing for marketing. These three developments combined would virtually eliminate 75 percent of the total labor required to produce a tobacco crop.

Several one-row automatic harvesters were constructed by at least one farm equipment manufacturer in 1961 and 1962 for demonstration purposes. In 1961 one firm demonstrated a self-propelled harvester and a bulk-curing barn. With these, two men could do the work of barning tobacco that ordinarily takes eleven hand-laborers. At least two commercial manufacturers demonstrated "tobacco combines" during the harvesting season in 1966. Neither the harvester, farmer, the tobacco marketing system, nor the tobacco manufacturer or shipper seems to be quite ready for these three related and revolutionary changes. Plant breeders may also play an important role soon by developing a variety of tobacco that will ripen more uniformly to lessen the number of times the tobacco has to be primed.[71]

The marketing system in the flue-cured belt is also in a transitional stage, the first major change in its marketing system since the development of the loose-leaf auction market system in the pre-Civil War days. Traditionally, the Georgia-Florida markets have been the only "loose-leaf" markets. Loose-leaf sales originally meant discarding the hogshead and packing the hands in neat piles on the warehouse floor, where each pile was examined and sold. Loose-leaf in the new twentieth century context means untied leaf—the elimination of the hand of tobacco on the auction floor. While interest in mechanical harvesting and bulk curing may be partly responsible for the growing demand in Virginia, North Carolina, and South Carolina for loose-leaf sales, the primary motive centers around labor and the cost of tying tobacco in bundles for marketing. By 1960 so much untied South Carolina tobacco was being sold on the Georgia markets that Georgia began requiring that out-of-state tobacco be identified with a blue tag. This law was later ruled illegal. (A 1968 Georgia law requiring the labeling of Georgia tobacco has been upheld by a United States court.) In 1961, South Carolina growers petitioned the United States Department of Agriculture for permission to allow untied sales in their markets for the first eight days of each season; this request was rejected. Mounting pressure resulted in allowing loose-leaf sales for a short period of time on all flue-cured markets outside of the Georgia-Florida belt. In 1965 the United States Department of Agriculture allowed loose-leaf sales for the first five days of the marketing season; the time was lengthened to twelve days in 1966 and nineteen days for the 1967 season. Farmers maintain that it requires around 130 hours to grade and tie an acre of tobacco, and they estimate that this operation costs from three to eight cents per pound. Marketing untied tobacco can cut the labor cost as much as 20 percent.[72]

In general, warehousemen and buyers have resisted the growing pressure for unrestricted loose-leaf sales throughout the Bright Belt. It requires more warehouse space to sell untied leaf, manufacturers insist that for the most part their processing machinery is designed to handle bundled tobacco, and exporters claim that their foreign customers do not want untied leaf. Shortage of farm labor and labor costs, however, are forcing this transition in marketing and paving the way for the day when automatic tobacco harvesters and bulk-curers will be a practical reality.

The Burley growers, the second largest tobacco producers in the United States, have not been unconcerned and idle regarding the amount of labor and the cost of stalk-cutting their tobacco. Engineers in Kentucky tested a unit handling system for manipulating the heavy sticks of stalk tobacco with machinery in 1963. They developed a portable metal frame to distribute at various points in the tobacco field. When the tobacco was cut and placed on sticks, the sticks of tobacco were hung on these frames. A tractor-mounted mechanical lift was then used to place the racks or frames on wagons to be transported to the barn. The racks of tobacco were later placed in the barn with the use of the same mechanical lift. It was estimated that the portable frames and mechanical lift cut the man-hours of labor for harvesting about 50 percent.[73]

Indications are that Burley tobacco harvesting may soon be more fully mechanized. Agricultural engineers in Kentucky have developed a new device for impaling and handling stalk-cut tobacco without damage to the leaves. On tests thus far more than 98 percent of the stalks were properly impaled and spaced on the sticks, with negligible leaf damage. Further field studies to assure satisfactory performance of all functions of this tobacco-harvesting machine will be made before the perfected harvester will be released for manufacturers. Burley growers have also expressed considerable interest in the latest Bright-tobacco harvester.[74] It is possible that efforts to mechanize the tobacco harvest may lead to the abandonment of the traditional stalk-cutting method of harvesting in the Burley belt.

Mechanically-minded William Tatham would no doubt heartily approve of the progress now being made in mechanizing the tobacco industry.

APPENDIX A

Classes, Types, and Sub-types, 1879[*]

Class I. Domestic Cigar Tobacco and Smokers

Connecticut seed-leaf. This included both the seed-leaf and the Havana seed. The seed-leaf was a large, fine-fibered, light colored leaf, soft and silky, and sweet in taste. It was used mostly as a binder, though like all cigar types it produced fillers and wrappers. Havana seed, grown from seed acclimated for four years, produced a thin, fine-textured, silky leaf with a delicate flavor.

New England seed-leaf. The tobacco of Massachusetts, New Hampshire, and Vermont, including some Havana seed. New England seed-leaf differed from that of Connecticut in that it produced a coarser and heavier leaf and fewer wrappers.

Pennsylvania seed-leaf. Dark brown in color, rich in body, and produced a larger percent of wrappers than the Connecticut product, but was inferior in flavor.

New York seed-leaf. This type was inferior to the Pennsylvania and Connecticut seed-leaf.

Ohio seed-leaf. Was noted for its exceptional dryness. While the texture was not as fine as that of Connecticut

[*] Killebrew, *Tenth Census,* III, 15–22; Killebrew and Myrick, *Tobacco Leaf, Its Culture and Cure, Marketing and Manufacture* (New York, 1909), 50–78.

or the color equal to that of Pennsylvania, the burning qualities of that produced a dark brown, fine, silky, sweet leaf. That grown in the Miami Valley usually sold for more than double the price of other seed-leaf. Some Little Dutch was grown in Indiana but classed with the Ohio product.

Wisconsin and Illinois seed-leaf. A very thin leaf, the tenderest of all seed-leaf tobaccos. Its great uniformity of color and ability to absorb and retain moisture were considered superior qualities.

Florida seed-leaf. Distinguished by the large number of white specks covering the leaf. It declined in popularity as cigar manufacturers began to demand darker and stronger tobaccos. Havana seed produced a lower yield but the superior price and the larger percentage of wrappers made it profitable to cultivate. The lower grades were used to make sweet cigar fillers.

Other cigar and smoking tobacco

American-grown Havana. That grown from seed imported from Cuba. The first year's product was small but very sweet in flavor. Florida produced a small quantity for market, though small patches for domestic use might be seen in all parts of the country. The flavor deteriorated rapidly when grown from seed matured in this country, but increased in size and in its usefulness as a wrapper.

Perique. Grown only in Louisiana and cured in its juices under heavy pressure. Was black and glossy in appearance and strong in flavor. Popular only to those habituated to its use. Some Louisiana tobacco was air-cured and used to make a very strong cigar.

Stogie wrappers and fillers. A stogie was a cigar of common quality, frequently sold in a roll-your-own package, which consisted of the proper portion of wrappers and filler tobacco. Stogie filler consisted of the same quality leaf as the wrapper, leaves that were too short to make wrappers. A short, dark, air-cured leaf was most in demand for the stogie.

Indiana Kite-foot. A broad, brown, fire-cured, short leaf tobacco used in making a common cigar known as a cheroot, which was small in size and of simple construction, open at both ends and frequently without a binder.

White Burley lugs. Light or yellowish brown, mild, trashy, and chaffy lower leaves of the plant mixed with the bright Virginia and North Carolina lugs to make an excellent mixture of smoking tobacco for pipes. Some of the brighter, thin leaves were used in making cigarettes.

Common lugs. From the heavy tobacco districts (Virginia, North Carolina, Missouri, Eastern Ohio, Maryland, Tennessee, Kentucky, Indiana, and Illinois). The lower leaves from many types: trashy, thin in body, and milder than the better grades of the type from which they came. Used mostly in making various brands of smoking tobaccos: bright and dark, brown and red, spangled and yellow, and mild and strong. Super air-cured lugs, light in color, might be used in cigarettes.

Class II. Chewing Tobacco

Fine-cut and plug fillers

Fine-cut White Burley. Thin and chaffy in body, possessed little gum and oils.

Fine-cut Mason County (Kentucky). Possessed less gum than any tobacco grown in the Burley district.

White Burley fillers. Possessed more body and was thus more elastic and softer than the cutters. Was very popular because of its ability to absorb the sauces used in making the plug.

Red Burley fillers. Lighter and more flimsy than the White Burley, dark cinnamon in color.

Virginia sun- and air-cured fillers. Grown chiefly in Caroline, Hanover, Louisa, and Spotsylvania counties. Very sweet and fragrant.

Virginia flue-cured fillers. Grown principally in Henry County. Fine in texture, oily, and elastic. Noted for its superior natural sweetness.

Missouri air-cured fillers. A tough and sweet leaf, frequently mixed with tobacco of other states.

Fire-cured fillers. Of the heavy tobacco districts (Kentucky, Indiana, Tennessee, Virginia, Maryland, and West Virginia). Used in making a coarse, strong, chewing tobacco preferred by miners, sailors, and lumbermen.

Tennessee and Kentucky air-cured fillers. Possessed good texture, a mild natural flavor, and a bright or pale-red color. Heavier than the White Burley filler and very porous, a most desirable characteristic for plug tobacco.

Plug wrappers

Virginia and North Carolina yellow and mahogany. The lemon-yellow leaf was considered the superior plug wrapper. Was very popular because it retained its golden luster when subjected to the processes of manufacturing. The mahogany was more oily, somewhat heavier, and blackened under pressure.

Western Kentucky, Hart County (Kentucky), and Henry County (Tennessee) yellow. These three districts produced a leaf unexcelled in beauty because of its yellow color. This color did not hold up under the manufacturing processes, however.

West Virginia yellow. Inferior to the Virginia–North Carolina yellow but superior to that of the above western yellow-wrappers.

Missouri-Arkansas yellow. Closely resembled the western Kentucky yellow wrapper.

Clarksville and Missouri dark and red. Heavy, strong, elastic, soft, and smooth leaf. Most popular in Canada.

Mason County (Kentucky) Burley wrappers. Noted for great elasticity, fine texture, and silkiness. Used for both plug and cigars.

Class III. Export Tobacco

English Shippers

Bird's-eye cutting leaf. A very bright, smooth, thin, and clean leaf from the lower Green River district in Kentucky, the White Burley areas, and Virginia and North Carolina. When the leaf was cut (shredded) across the stem, the cut stem surface had the appearance of the eye of a bird, hence its name. This was the only type of leaf used exclusively in English consumption.

Brown-roll wrapper. A bright red or bright leaf, thin and smooth in texture, used as a wrapper for the spun brown-roll. The brown-roll was made by spinning stemmed tobacco into a strand about one inch in diameter. It was then packed into a coil from which sections were cut for retail.

Spinning-leaf or strips (stemmed leaf). A heavy, strong, elastic, smooth leaf produced primarily in the Clarksville and lower Green River Valley districts. It was prepared in the same manner as the above Brown-roll except that the strand was smaller and the wrapper was of the same leaf as the filler. England sold much of this to Germany, Scotland, and Ireland.

Shag. A coarsely cut, cheap, English-manufactured product grown largely in Indiana and the Green River district in Kentucky.

Plug wrappers and fillers. Purchased in very small amounts since plug tobacco had a very limited market in Great Britain.

Navy leaf. Came from the best Green River and White Burley fillers and manufactured into chewing plugs for use in the English navy.

Continental Shippers

French Regie. Purchased both heavy leaf and good sound lugs for the manufacture of cigars, smoking tobacco, and snuff. Most of it came from Kentucky, Tennessee, and Maryland.

Italian Regie. Imported heavy to medium leaf types from western Kentucky, southern Indiana, and Illinois, and a small quantity of White Burley. Consumed mostly in the manufacture of cigars.

Austrian Regie. Imported only one type from the United States: a smooth, fine-textured, medium-heavy wrapper leaf for cigars. These came principally from the Clarksville district, with Virginia supplying a small quantity.

Spanish Regie. Bought common and medium lugs of all types and from all districts except the Burley and Bright-tobacco areas. Was consumed mostly as smoking tobacco.

German types. Principally the heavy bodied leaf from Tennessee and Kentucky. Germany also purchased some of the mild, sweet, yellow, spangled leaf from West Virginia, Ohio, and Maryland for rehandling and export to Russia. The saucer was treated with sauces when processed for smoking consumption. The spinner was spun into a rope-like strand.

Swiss wrapper. A long, broad, silky, elastic, dark brown leaf supplied mainly from the Clarksville district. It was used as a wrapper in the manufacture of cigars.

Holland: Dutch saucer. Bought mostly heavy tobaccos from the fire-cured western districts.

Belgium. Belgium cutter was similar to Dutch saucer except that the tobacco was of a lower grade. Belgium also bought some Burley lugs.

Denmark, Norway, and Sweden

These three countries consumed the heavy, fire-cured types prepared for their markets mainly by the Germans.

African Shippers
(shipped from Boston, Liverpool and Gibralter)

Africa, West Coast. Inhabitants here preferred the long, dark, heavy, strong leaf.

Southern and Northern Areas. Consumed a milder, medium to bright colored tobacco possessing a fine-fibered leaf.

Mexico, South America, and the West Indies

Baling wrappers. A heavy, dark, long leaf tied neatly into small hands and packed into bales weighing from 100 to 200 pounds so that two bales might be balanced across the back of a mule for transportation to inland markets.

Baling fillers. Rich heavy leaf and fine lugs.

Black Fats. Tobacco made dark by the application of water and excessive pressure. Popular in the West Indies.

APPENDIX B

Classification of Leaf Tobacco as to Classes and Types, 1929–1965 *

CLASS 1. Flue-cured types—those grown in certain areas and cured under certain artificial atmospheric conditions by a process of regulating the heat and ventilation without allowing smoke or fumes from the fuel to come in contact with the tobacco. Its name comes from the metal flues of the heating apparatus originally used in the curing barns. It normally ranges from yellow to reddish-orange in color, is thin to medium in body, and is mild in flavor. All five flue-cured types are used primarily in the manufacture of cigarettes.

> *Type 11.* Known as Old Belt flue-cured and produced in a large section of Piedmont Virginia and North Carolina. This is the oldest area of flue-cured production, produces the darkest of the flue-cured types, and has been losing ground competitively to the newer belts.

* *Classification of Leaf Tobacco Covering Classes, Types, and Group of Grades* (United States Department of Agriculture, Bureau of Agricultural Economics, Service and Regulatory Announcements No. 118, November, 1929), 1–7.

That part of the Old Belt that straddles the fall-line in these two states is often treated as a separate belt and type. It is frequently referred to as the Middle Belt and classified as Type 11b, while that produced in the "Old Belt" has been designated Type 11a. Tobacco in the Middle Belt is somewhat brighter in color and milder in flavor and seems to have a more favorable competitive position than Type 11a.

Type 12. Commonly known as eastern flue-cured, new belt of North Carolina flue-cured, or eastern Carolina's bright. It is produced principally in the coastal plains section of North Carolina, north of the South River.

This has been called by some the premium flue-cured belt, and its leaf characteristics appeal especially to British buyers. This belt frequently commands the highest average prices.

Type 13. That produced in what is commonly known as the Border Belt. This district is situated in the Tidewater area and straddles the border between North and South Carolina. The soil, topography, and tobacco of this area are very similar to those of the Eastern Belt and produces a very fine tobacco.

Type 14. Tobacco grown in the newest flue-cured belt and known as the Georgia-Florida Belt, or southern bright, and includes a small portion of Alabama. The land is somewhat more rugged than the two above belts, though the soils are very similar. Type 14 is frequently considered to be the finest for use in the manufacture of domestic cigarettes.

CLASS 2. Fire-cured types—Those cured under artificial atmospheric conditions by the use of open fires, allowing the smoke and fumes to come into contact with the tobacco.

In the nineteenth century fire-cured tobacco was the leaf most in demand for export. Only about half of the current annual production of fifty million pounds is exported. The principal domestic use of these types is in the manufacture of snuff, although it is also used for making roll and plug chewing tobacco, strong cigars, and heavy smoking tobacco.

Type 21. Known as eastern fire-cured, Virginia fire-cured, or dark Virginia. Produced principally in the Piedmont and mountain sections north and west of the flue-cured area.

Type 22. Southern fire-cured, Clarksville, Hopkinsville, and Springfield fire-cured, dark-fired or Kentucky-Tennessee broadleaf. It is produced largely in the area east of the Tennessee River in northern Tennessee and southern Kentucky known as the eastern district.

Type 23. Western fire-cured, custom dark district, or Mayfield and Paducah dark-fired. Grown principally in the area between the Tennessee, Ohio, and Mississippi rivers in western Kentucky and northwestern Tennessee.

Type 24. Henderson dark-fired or smoked, or Northern fire-cured, the stemming district. Production of this type was centered in the Henderson district of Kentucky. It is no longer listed in current statistics on the fire-cured types.

CLASS 3. The air-cured types. So called because it is cured under natural weather conditions, usually without the use of supplementary heat. This class is subdivided as follows:

Class 3a or Light Air-cured. This tobacco is usually very thin to medium in body, light yellow shading toward red and reddish brown in color, and mild in flavor. It is used primarily in the making of cigarettes, being combined with flue-cured and small quantities of imported or "Turkish" tobacco to form the blends in the manufacture of cigarettes.

Type 31. Most commonly known as Burley, Burley air-cured, or White Burley, and is produced principally in central and northeastern Kentucky, central and eastern Tennessee, southern Ohio and Indiana, western West Virginia, Missouri, western North Carolina, southwest Virginia, and, until fairly recently, Arkansas. Kansas joined the Burley ranks on a small scale in 1935.

In terms of area, Burley is the most widely grown single type. It is produced in eight states and constitutes more than one-fourth of all the tobacco grown in the United States. Cigarettes currently account for about 90 percent of its domestic consumption. It is also used in the manufacture of pipe tobaccos, chewing plugs, and twists. Once the favorite for chewing plugs, it now ranks second only to flue-cured as a cigarette tobacco.

Type 32. Commonly known as southern Maryland tobacco, Maryland air-cured, Maryland export, or Maryland Broadleaf. It is grown only in southern Maryland.

The blended cigarette brought about an increased demand for this type in the American cigarette industry. It is especially desired for its ideal burning qualities in the manufactured form.

Class 3b or Dark Air-cured. This is a medium to heavy-bodied type and varied in color from a light to a medium brown. It is used essentially in the manufacture of the same products as the fire-cured types, i.e., primarily for chewing tobacco and snuff, though some of it is used in making smoking tobacco and cigars. Annual production has declined from over forty million pounds since the end of World War II to less than twenty-five million pounds, of which about four million pounds are exported.

Type 35. Most commonly known as One-sucker, One-sucker Air-cured, Kentucky-Tennessee One-sucker, or Indiana One-sucker. Produced principally in northern Tennessee and south-central Kentucky, and in southern Indiana until recent years.

Type 36. Green River, Green River Air-cured, Henderson District Air-cured, or Owensboro District Air-cured. Produced in the Green River section of Kentucky in both the Owensboro and Henderson areas.

Type 37. Air-cured or sun-cured tobacco, most commonly known as Virginia Sun-cured, or Dark Virginia Air-cured. Produced principally in the central Piedmont section of Virginia north of the James River.

Sun-curing was originally a modification of air-curing. The freshly cut tobacco was hung on scaffolds in the field for a day or so longer before being hung in the barns to complete the curing. Exposing it to direct sunlight for a time expedited the drying of the leaf and exerted a bleaching action that tended to modify the color.

CLASS 4. Cigar-filler types. This class is air-cured and is used mainly as the core, filler, or body of the cigar. The filler is medium to heavy in body and is noted for its flavor, aroma, and burning quality.

Type 41. Pennsylvania Seedleaf, Pennsylvania Broadleaf, also known as the Lancaster and York County filler type. It is produced principally in Lancaster County, Pennsylvania, and the adjoining counties.

Type 42. Known as Gebhardt, Ohio Seedleaf, or Ohio Broadleaf, and produced in the Miami Valley area in Ohio (and at one time in Indiana). This is a derivation of the Connecticut Seed-leaf.

Type 43. Commonly known as Zimmer, Ohio Zimmer, or Zimmer Spanish. This is the common name for a Havana seed type introduced in the Miami Valley area of Ohio and extending in earlier years into Ohio.

Type 44. Dutch, Shoestring Dutch, or Little Dutch. Grown principally in the Miami Valley area of Ohio. Originally introduced from Germany around 1870.

Type 45. Known as Georgia and Florida Sun-grown, Georgia-Florida Sumatra, and Georgia and Florida filler type. It was produced in southwestern Georgia and the central part of Florida.

In 1941 it was reclassified as Type 56 (cigar-binder). In 1948, Georgia sun-grown production fell below one hundred acres and was not included in the Type 56 statistics for that year, but was included in the total binder-type production. Florida harvested only about one hundred acres in 1948, and as of 1949 it disappeared from the annual summary reports.

Type 46. Puerto Rican Sun-grown.

CLASS 5. Cigar-binder types. Used mainly for binding the bunched filler into the form and shape of the cigar. Natural leaf binders are required to have a good burning quality, aroma and elasticity. In the last decade "homogenized" or the "reconstituted" (pulverizing the entire leaf and reconstituting it into a paper-like sheet) tobacco sheet has been rapidly replacing the natural leaf as a cigar binder. As a result of this development, usage and production of these types have declined considerably, some even disappearing from the market. Scrap chewing tobacco has become the principal outlet for the binder types.

> *Type 51.* Connecticut Broadleaf, or Connecticut Valley Broadleaf. Produced in the Connecticut Valley in Connecticut and Massachusetts.

> *Type 52.* Connecticut Valley Havana Seed, or Connecticut Havana Seed. Produced principally in the Connecticut Valley section of Connecticut and Massachusetts. This Cuban strain produced a narrow, more pointed leaf than the Connecticut Broadleaf.

> *Type 53.* This is commonly referred to as New York State Tobacco, Havana Seed of New York, or New York and Pennsylvania Seed. It was grown originally in the big Flats and Onondaga areas of New York and scattered through a wide area of Pennsylvania. This was originally primarily a cigar binder and filler type, though it was being used more and more for chewing tobacco even before the reconstituted leaf began to have its impact on the cigar binder types.

In 1900 New York grew approximately 11,000 acres of tobacco; in 1955 it had dropped to less than one hundred acres and production statistics for New York were included with those of Pennsylvania. Pennsylvania Type 53 acreage dropped to about two hundred acres in 1955 and in the following year disappeared, largely a casualty of technology.

Type 54. Commonly known as southern Wisconsin Cigar leaf or southern Wisconsin binder type. It was produced originally south and east of the Wisconsin River, extending into Illinois on a very limited scale. Production is now limited to southern Wisconsin.

Type 55. Northern Wisconsin cigar leaf or binder type. Grown principally north and west of the Wisconsin River and to some extent in Minnesota. This area did not become an important tobacco producing area until around the beginning of the twentieth century.

Type 56. Cigar-binder. See Type 45.

CLASS 6. Cigar-wrapper types. Cigar wrappers are the most difficult and expensive tobaccos to grow. They are used principally for the outside cover on cigars. Such leaves must possess elasticity, be free of injury, thin and smooth, uniform in color, and have good burning qualities. In order to produce such a superior leaf, this type must be protected from the extremes of the weather. The tobacco fields are covered with a framework of screening cloth to protect the tobacco against the direct rays of the sun and the force of strong winds, and it offers some protection against overnight changes in temperature. These types are known as "shade-grown" tobacco because of the above distinctive features of its cultivation.

Type 61. Northern shade, shade of Connecticut, or Connecticut Valley shade-grown. Produced in the Connecticut Valley sections of Connecticut and Massachusetts.

Experimentation in the use of an artificial shade of cheesecloth or slats in the culture of this high grade wrapper leaf was begun in the Connecticut Valley in 1900. Before the end of the first decade of the twentieth century, this industry was established in the Valley on a firm basis.

The shade-grown wrapper of the Connecticut Valley resembles the Cuban product and is used chiefly in the manufacture of medium- and higher-priced cigars with Cuban filler.

Type 62. Southern shade, or Georgia-Florida shade-grown. Produced in southwestern Georgia and central Florida.

Tobacco growers in Quincy, Florida began experimenting with this culture in 1896, and it was soon established in this area of Florida and, principally, in Decatur County, Georgia. Southern shade-grown is used primarily on lower-priced cigars.

CLASS 7. Miscellaneous. All domestic-grown tobacco not otherwise classified.

Type 72 (originally Type 70). Perique, the most important of the "miscellaneous" types, is grown in a small area in St. James Parish in Louisiana. It is noted primarily for its pleasing aroma, and small amounts are used in fancy blended smoking tobacco. A large percentage of the annual production of around 250,000 pounds is exported.

Type 77. Includes a small quantity of "Turkish" tobacco similar to that grown in Turkey and Greece and is produced in the western sections of Virginia, North Carolina, and South Carolina. High labor requirements have been a major factor in the very limited production of this type. About 1,200 man-hours are required to produce an acre of this type, which is about three times the average requirement for the major types.

Other "miscellaneous" types are Eastern Ohio export and Rustica. It is of particular interest to note that Rustica is produced commercially on a small scale.

Rustica (*Nicotiana rustica*) is the original tobacco used by North American Indians, and it was so strong and harsh that even the Indians came to prefer the *Nicotina tobacum* developed by John Rolfe. Rustica's use today is restricted to the making of insecticides.

Notes

Chapter 1

1. Lewis C. Gray, *History of Agriculture in the Southern United States to 1860* (Washington, 1933) II, 670.
2. *Commercial and Agricultural Magazine* (London, 1800), III, 212.
3. Lyon G. Tyler, *History of Virginia: The Federal Period, 1763–1860* (Chicago & New York, 1924), II, 520.
4. Gray, *History of Agriculture,* II, 947.
5. Joseph C. Robert, *The Story of Tobacco in America* (New York, 1949), 285.

Chapter 2

1. Richmond *Enquirer,* March 2, 1819; "Colonel Tatham, formerly a Field Officer in the Service of the American Republic, and lately Supervisor of the London Docks," *Public Characters of 1801–1802* (London, 1801), 410.
2. D. G. C. Allan, "Colonel William Tatham, An Anglo-American Member of the Society, 1801–04," *Journal of the Royal Society of Arts, CVIII* (London, 1960), 229.
3. "Obituary, with Anecdotes of Remarkable Persons," *The Gentleman's Magazine and Historical Chronicle,* Pt. I (London, 1820), 376.
4. *Daily Compiler* (Richmond), February 23, 1819.
5. *Public Characters,* 408–09.
6. Richmond *Enquirer,* March 2, 1819.
7. Virginia *Gazette,* February 17, 1774.
8. *Public Characters,* 410.
9. Richmond *Enquirer,* March 2, 1819.

10. Samuel Cole Williams, *William Tatham, Wataugan* (Johnson City, 1947), 15.

11. Clarence E. Carter, ed., *The Territorial Papers of the United States. The Territory South of the Ohio River, 1790–1796* (Washington, 1936) IV, 228; *Public Characters,* 412; Williams, *William Tatham, Wataugan,* 22–23; Samuel Cole Williams, *Tennessee During the Revolution* (Nashville, 1944), 8.

12. *Public Characters,* 412.

13. "Original Records of the Phi Beta Kappa Society," *William and Mary College Quarterly,* IV, Series 1 (April, 1896), 215–21.

14. *Public Characters,* 413.

15. Williams, *William Tatham, Wataugan,* 24.

16. *Public Characters,* 413.

17. Julian P. Boyd, ed., *The Papers of Thomas Jefferson* (Princeton, 1951), IV, 240.

18. *Ibid.*

19. Elizabeth G. McPherson, ed., "Letters of William Tatham," *William and Mary College Quarterly,* XVI, Series 2 (April, 1936), 179.

20. *Ibid.*

21. *Ibid.,* 180.

22. *Ibid.*

23. *Ibid.*

24. *Ibid.,* 182.

25. Wilmer L. Hall, ed., *Journals of the Council of the State of Virginia, 1781–1786* (Richmond, 1952), III, 128, 156.

26. *Public Characters,* 414.

27. Anna Nicholas, "Conservation of Natural Resources in America," *The Journal of American History,* IV (1910), 577. This article contains excerpts from a sixty-page handwritten manuscript discovered by Don José Maria Lopez Cepero of Seville, Spain and in 1910 in the possession of Judge James B. Block of Indianapolis. The essay was entitled: "A Few Hints and Remarks for the Use of The Officers, Physicians and Students of His M.C. Majesty's Botanic Garden at Madrid," June, 1796.

28. *Public Characters,* 415.

29. *Ibid.*

30. Richmond *Enquirer,* March 2, 1819.

31. Walter Clark, ed., *The State Records of North Carolina* (Goldsboro, 1905) XX, 992.

32. Elizabeth G. McPherson, ed., "Letters of William Tatham," *William and Mary College Quarterly* XVI, Series II (July, 1936), 380–81.

33. Clark, *State Records of North Carolina,* XX, 143, 230, 402.

34. *Ibid.,* 195, 227, 238, 288, 294.

35. *Ibid.,* 166, 290–91.

36. *Ibid.,* 189.

37. This was Charles Tatham, who seems to have been largely an errand boy for William. Very little is known about Charles. He was listed in the Census of 1790 as a resident of Fayetteville, North Carolina. A sketch of William Tatham published in London referred to Charles as "A Captain in the service of the American States." Sanford, another brother, was a post-captain in the British Navy. Walter Clark, ed., *The State Records of North Carolina. Census, 1790* (Goldsboro, 1905), XXVI, 464; *Public Characters,* 409.

38. Grove was a prominent citizen of Fayetteville and served in the North Carolina legislature with Tatham. He served in the North Carolina House of Commons, 1787–1790; he was elected to Congress in 1791 and served until 1803. Blackwell P. Robinson, *William R. Davie* (Chapel Hill, 1957), 152.

39. Alice B. Keith, ed., *The John Gray Blount Papers, 1764–1789* (Raleigh, 1952), I, 379–80.

40. Boyd, *Papers of Thomas Jefferson,* XIII, 621–22; Richmond *Enquirer,* March 2, 1819.

41. Richmond *Enquirer,* March 2, 1819; *Public Characters,* 417.

42. McPherson, "Letters of William Tatham," *William and Mary College Quarterly,* XVI, 390.

43. *Public Characters,* 417; Richmond *Enquirer,* March 2, 1819.

44. McPherson, "Letters of William Tatham," *William and Mary College Quarterly,* XVI, 166.

45. William Tatham to Governor [Beverley] Randolph, April 13, 1790, William Tatham Papers, Archives Division, Virginia State Library, Richmond.

46. William Tatham to Governor Randolph, August 10, 1790, William Tatham Papers.

47. McPherson, "Letters of William Tatham," *William and Mary College Quarterly,* XVI, 167.

48. *Ibid.,* 173.

49. William W. Hening, ed., *Statutes at Large: A Collection of all the Laws of Virginia, 1619–1792* (Philadelphia, 1823), XIII, 318.

50. Thomas Jefferson to Augustine Davis, July 24, 1791, Jefferson Papers, Library of Congress.

51. David Ross had "a considerable Iron Works" on the fork of the Holston River.

52. McPherson, "Letters of William Tatham," *William and Mary College Quarterly,* XVI, 168.

53. Thomas Jefferson to Augustine Davis, July 24, 1791, Jefferson Papers, Library of Congress.

54. McPherson, "Letters of Thomas Jefferson," *William and Mary College Quarterly*, XVI, 176.
55. *Annals of The Congress of the U.S. Second Congress 1791–93* (Washington, 1849), 1333.
56. Williams, *William Tatham, Wataugan*, 38–39; McPherson, "Letters of William Tatham," *William and Mary College Quarterly*, XVI, 174.
57. Richmond *Enquirer*, March 2, 1819.
58. *Public Characters*, 420.
59. *Ibid.*
60. *Public Characters*, 421–30.
61. Frederick Jackson Turner, ed., "Documents on the Blount Conspiracy, 1795–1797, *American Historical Review*, X (January, 1905), 249–79; William H. Masterson, *William Blount* (Baton Rouge, 1954), 307–12.
62. Williams, *William Tatham, Wataugan*, 45.
63. Masterson, *William Blount*, 318.
64. *Public Characters*, 422–23.
65. Nicholas, "Conservation of Natural Resources in America," *Journal of American History*, 574, 576–77.
66. William Tatham to Don Diego de Gardoqui, Aranjuez, March 18, April 22, 1796. Archivo Historio Nacional Estado Legajo 3890. Expediente 5, Documents Nos. 20 and 62. Microfilm, Library of Congress.
67. Josef de Jaudenes to Senor D. Diego de Gardoqui, New York, August 18, 1795, *ibid.*, Document No. 5.
68. Report on William Tatham's Mission from Philadelphia to Madrid to Josef de Gardoqui & Juan Bautista Virio, June 4, 1796, *ibid.*, Document No. 42.
69. Juan Bautista Virio, Josef de Gardoqui to Manuel de Godoy, Madrid, June [6 ?], 1796, *ibid.*, Document No. 41.
70. William Tatham to His Excellency The Principe de la Paz [Godoy], Sunday, June 10, *ibid.*, Document No. 44.
71. *Public Characters*, 430.
72. Turner, "Documents on the Blount Conspiracy, 1795–1797," *American Historical Review*, X, 576; Masterson, *William Blount*, 318.
73. William Tatham to John King, November 15, 1796. Great Britain, Public Records Office, Colonial Office 42, Lower Canada—Original Correspondence—Secretary of State. Microfilm, Canadian Archives.
74. The following partial list of Tatham's writings was published in *Annual of Biography and Obituary for 1820* (London, 1820), IV, 167:

List of the Works of the late Colonel Tatham

1. A Memorial on the Civil and Military Government of the Tennessee Country, published in America.

2. A History of the Western Country, America.—N.B. The facts were furnished by Colonel Todd, of Kentuckie, and the text by Col. Tatham.

3. An Analysis of the State of Virginia. Philadelphia, 1794.

4. The Case of Kamfer against Hawkins. Philadelphia, 1794.

5. Plan for insulating the Metropolis, by means of a Navigable Canal. London.

6. Remarks on Inland Canals, the small System of Interior Navigation, and various Uses of the Inclined Plane. London, 1798.

7. *The Political Economy of Inland Navigation, Irrigation and Drainage, with Thoughts on the Multiplication of Commercial Resources.* London, 1799.

8. *Communications concerning the Agriculture and Commerce of America,* being an Auxiliary to a Report made by Wm. Strickland, Esq. London, 1800.

9. The same subject continued, with the addition of a Memorial on the Commerce of Spain. London, 1800.

10. *An Historical and Practical Essay on the Culture and Commerce of Tobacco.* London, 1800.

11. Auxiliary Remarks on an Essay on the Comparative Advantages of Oxen for Tillage in Competition with Horses. London, 1801.

12. *National Irrigation; or the various Methods of watering Meadows.* London, 1801.

13. Report on a View of certain Impediments and Obstructions, in the Navigation of the River Thames. London, 1803.

14. Navigation and Conservancy of the River Thames, London, 1803.

15. Characters of the American Indians, now published for the first time, in the present volume.

75. Richmond *Enquirer,* March 2, 1819.

76. *National Intelligencer,* January 12, 1814.

77. "Colonel Tatham," *Annual of Biography and Obituary for 1820* (London, 1820), IV, 167.

78. See William Tatham, *Communications Concerning the Agriculture and Commerce of America* (London, 1800).

79. Quoted in Allan, "Colonel William Tatham, An Anglo-American," etc., *Journal of the Royal Society of Arts,* CVIII, 232.

80. *Annual of Biography and Obituary for 1820,* IV, 157; *Public Characters,* 431–32.

81. Allan, "Colonel William Tatham, An Anglo-American," etc., *Journal of the Royal Society of Arts,* CVIII, 229–30.

82. *Ibid.,* 229.
83. William Tatham to Charles Taylor, December 16, 1801. Photocopy, American Philosophical Society Library, Philadelphia.
84. William Tatham to Charles Taylor, Esqr., January 15; January 20, 1802. Photocopy, American Philosophical Society Library.
85. William Tatham to Charles Taylor, Esqr., February 3; February 4; and April 17, 1802. Photocopy, American Philosophical Society Library.
86. Allan, "William Tatham, An Anglo-American," etc., *Journal of the Royal Society of Arts,* CVIII, 230.
87. *Ibid.*
88. *Ibid.,* 230–31.
89. William Tatham to the Duke of Norfolk, President, April 1, 1802. Photocopy, American Philosophical Society Library.
90. Allan, "William Tatham, An Anglo-American," etc., *Journal of the Royal Society of Arts,* CVIII, 231.
91. McPherson, "Letters of William Tatham," *William and Mary College Quarterly,* XVI, 176–77. Dangerfield was a recent arrival from England and resided in Alexandria, Virginia.
92. This letter is reproduced in Williams, *William Tatham, Wataugan,* 51; also in *American State Papers. Class X, Miscellaneous* (Washington, 1834), I, 461.
93. Richmond *Enquirer,* March 2, 1819; McPherson, "Letters of William Tatham," *William and Mary College Quarterly,* XVI, 177.
94. Thomas Jefferson to William Tatham, May 19, 1805. Jefferson Papers, Library of Congress.
95. McPherson, "Letters of William Tatham," *William and Mary College Quarterly,* XVI, 178.
96. *Ibid.,* 181.
97. *Ibid.,* 182.
98. *Ibid.,* 185, 190, 363, 366, 369; Elizabeth G. McPherson, ed., "Unpublished Letters to Jefferson," *North Carolina Historical Review,* XII (July, 1935), 359.
99. McPherson, "Letters of William Tatham," *William and Mary College Quarterly,* XVI, 183–85.
100. *Ibid.,* 383–85.
101. McPherson, "Unpublished Letters to Jefferson," *North Carolina Historical Review,* XII, 367–68.
102. *Ibid.*
103. McPherson, "Letters of William Tatham," *William and Mary College Quarterly,* XVI, 187, 378.
104. *National Intelligencer,* March 25, 1814.

105. McPherson, "Letters of William Tatham," *William and Mary College Quarterly,* XVI, 373.
106. McPherson, "Unpublished Letters to Jefferson," *North Carolina Historical Review,* XII, 365.
107. McPherson, "Letters of William Tatham," *William and Mary College Quarterly,* XVI, 363–65.
108. *Ibid.,* 381.
109. *Ibid.,* 383–97; Williams, *William Tatham, Wataugan,* 73.
110. *Annals of the Congress of the United States, 14th Congress, Second Session,* XXX (Washington, 1854), 935.
111. Francis B. Heitman, *Historical Register and Dictionary of the United States Army, 1789–1903* (Washington, 1903), I, 945; McPherson, "Letters of William Tatham," *William and Mary College Quarterly,* XVI, 163.
112. Heitman, *Historical Register and Dictionary of the U.S. Army,* I, 945; Williams, *William Tatham, Wataugan,* 85.
113. Hening, *Statutes at Large,* XIII, 318; Williams, *William Tatham, Wataugan,* 86.
114. *Daily Compiler* (Richmond), February 23, 1819.
115. George Wythe Mumford, *The Two Parsons; Cupids Sports; The Dream; and The Jewels of Virginia* (Richmond, 1884), 232.
116. Richmond *Enquirer,* February 23, 1819.
117. Williams, *William Tatham, Wataugan,* 88–89.
118. William Tatham to John King, Esqr., London, November 15, 1796, Great Britain, Public Records Office, Colonial Office 42, Lower Canada. Microfilm, Canadian Archives.

Chapter 3

1. William Tatham, *An Historical and Practical Essay on the Culture and Commerce of Tobacco* (London, 1800), 201.
2. Lewis Cecil Gray, *History of Agriculture in the Southern United States to 1860* (Gloucester, 1958), II, 752.
3. Tatham, *Essay on Tobacco,* 201.
4. Meyer Jacobstein, *The Tobacco Industry in the United States* (Columbia University Studies in History, Economics, and Public Law, XXVI, No. 3, New York, 1907), 28.
5. Joseph C. Robert, *The Tobacco Kingdom Plantation, Market, and Factory in Virginia and North Carolina, 1800–1860* (Durham, 1938), 128–129.
6. George K. Holmes, *Tobacco Crop of the United States, 1612–1911* (United States Department of Agriculture, Bureau of Statistics *Circular* No. 33. Washington, 1912), 8, 10.
7. *Tobacco in the United States* (United States Department of Agriculture, Consumer and Marketing Service Miscellaneous Publication No. 867, Washington, D.C., 1966), 2.

8. Joseph C. Robert, *The Story of Tobacco in America* (New York, 1949), 172. Gray estimates the per capita consumption in the antebellum period at 4.23 pounds, while Jacobstein places it at less than 2 pounds until after 1870. Gray, *History of Agriculture,* II, 753; Jacobstein, *Tobacco Industry,* 44.

9. Jacobstein, *Tobacco Industry,* 44.

10. Robert, *Story of Tobacco,* 172, 275.

11. *Tobacco Situation* (United States Department of Agriculture, Economic Research Service, March, 1967), 8.

12. Holmes, *Tobacco Crop,* 8; *Tobacco in the U.S.,* 8.

13. J. B. Killebrew, "Report on the Culture and Curing of Tobacco in the United States," *Tenth Census, Agriculture,* III (Washington, 1883), 29; Wightman W. Garner, *The Production of Tobacco* (New York, Philadelphia, and Toronto, 1951), 37; Gray, *History of Agriculture,* II, 756.

14. Killebrew, *Tenth Census,* III, 82.

15. Robert, *Tobacco Kingdom,* 142.

16. *United States Census of 1860, Agriculture* (Washington, 1864), 189.

17. Percy W. Bidwell and John I. Falconer, *History of Agriculture in the Northern United States* (New York, 1941), 132, 183; Killebrew, *Tenth Census,* III, 94.

18. Harlow Lindley, ed., *Indiana As Seen By Early Travelers, A Collection of Reprints from Books of Travel, Letters, and Diaries Prior to 1830* (Indianapolis, 1916), 151; Emma Lou Thornbrough, *Indiana in the Civil War Era, 1850–1880* (Indianapolis, 1965), 373; Killebrew, *Tenth Census,* III, 32.

19. Killebrew, *Tenth Census,* III, 25.

20. *Ibid.,* 25; Bidwell and Falconer, *History of Agriculture,* 246.

21. Stevenson W. Fletcher, *Pennsylvania Agriculture and Country Life, 1640–1840* (Harrisburg, 1950), 166.

22. Garner, *Production of Tobacco,* 37.

23. Garner, *Production of Tobacco,* 37; Killebrew, *Tenth Census,* III, 103.

24. *Ibid.;* Killebrew, *Tenth Census,* III, 231.

25. Garner, *Production of Tobacco,* 24, 32, 40.

26. Nannie Mae Tilley, *The Bright-Tobacco Industry, 1860–1929* (Chapel Hill, 1948), 11–20.

27. *Ibid.,* 21–31.

28. Robert K. Heinmann, *Tobacco and Americans* (New York, Toronto, and London, 1960), 118; Robert, *Story of Tobacco,* 102. Jacobstein claims that pipe tobacco was the principal form of tobacco consumption (p. 42).

29. Heinmann, *Tobacco,* 119.

30. *Ibid.,* 133.

31. J. B. Killebrew and Herbert Myrick, *Tobacco Leaf: Its*

Culture and Cure, Marketing and Manufacture (New York, 1909), 291.

32. Jacobstein, *Tobacco Industry,* 40.
33. Tilley, *Bright-Tobacco,* 34; Heinmann, *Tobacco,* 148.
34. Garner, *Production of Tobacco,* 40; Heinmann, *Tobacco,* 133.
35. Jacobstein, *Tobacco Industry,* 39.
36. Based on the comparison of cigar leaf production with the total tobacco production for the United States.
37. Holmes, *Tobacco Crop,* 10.
38. Heinmann, *Tobacco,* 173.
39. *Ibid.,* 100, 105, 266.
40. Robert, *Story of Tobacco,* 121; Heinmann, *Tobacco,* 160.
41. Heinmann, *Tobacco,* 266.
42. *Tobacco in the U.S.,* 45.
43. Tilley, *Bright-Tobacco,* 123, 391, 395.
44. *Tobacco in the U.S.,* 45.
45. Heinmann, *Tobacco,* 178.
46. *Tobacco in the U.S.,* 4, 8, 45, 54.
47. *Classification of Leaf Tobacco Covering Classes, Types, and Group of Grades* (United States Department of Agriculture, Bureau of Agricultural Economics, Service and Regulatory Announcements No. 118, November, 1929), 1–7.
48. Tatham, *Essay on Tobacco,* 201; Gray, *History of Agriculture,* II, 1035.
49. Holmes, *Tobacco Crop,* 8.
50. Robert, *Tobacco Kingdom,* 142.
51. Robert, *Tobacco Kingdom,* 41.
52. *Ibid.,* 46.
53. Tilley, *Bright-Tobacco,* 71–81.
54. Killebrew and Myrick, *Tobacco Leaf,* 156.
55. *Progressive Farmer* (January, 1963), 61.
56. Jacobstein, *Tobacco Industry,* 39–40.
57. Killebrew, *Tenth Census,* III, 201.
58. Robert, *Tobacco Kingdom,* 18.
59. Holmes, *Tobacco Crop,* 10–11.
60. *Agricultural Statistics, 1962* (United States Department of Agriculture, Washington, 1963), 125.
61. *Tobacco in the U.S.,* 15.
62. *Tobacco Situation* (United States Department of Agriculture. Economic Research Service, June, 1967), 3.
63. Robert, *Tobacco Kingdom,* 94–110.
64. *Tobacco in the U.S.,* 28.
65. *Ibid.,* 34, 36.
66. Robert, *Story of Tobacco,* 217.
67. *Agricultural Research Report of the Agricultural Experiment Station, July 1, 1953—June 30, 1957* (Virginia Poly-

technic Institute, Blacksburg, Virginia, November, 1957),
115; "Chemical Sucker Control for Flue-Cured Tobacco,"
University of Florida Agricultural Experiment Stations,
Circular S-93 Gainesville, August, 1956; *The Tobacco Leaf,*
XCVI, No. 4982 (August 6, 1960), 14; *Progressive Farmer*
(January, 1960), 23; *Progressive Farmer* (July, 1961), 19;
Progressive Farmer (January, 1963), 52.

68. *The Tobacco Leaf,* XCI, No. 4690 (January 1, 1955), 79;
Robert Wilson, "Mechanizing Flue-Tobacco Harvest," *Agricultural Engineering,* XXXVII, (June, 1956), 407; Progressive Farmer* (May, 1955), 163; *Progressive Farmer* (August,
1955), 114; *Progressive Farmer* (February, 1961), 36.

69. J. S. Chappell and W. D. Toussaint, *Harvesting and Curing
Flue-Cured Tobacco with Automatic Tying Machines, Bulk
Curing and the Conventional Method: Labor Requirements;
Cost and Prices Received* (Agricultural Experiment Information Series No. 123, Department of Economics. North
Carolina State University, August, 1965), 3; *Progressive
Farmer* (February, 1961), 36; *Progressive Farmer* (July,
1962), 20; *Progressive Farmer* (November, 1962), 6.

70. O. A. Brown and N. W. Weldon, "Engineering Phases of
Curing Bright-Leaf Tobacco," *Agricultural Engineering,*
XXIX (January–December, 1948), 109–111; *Tobacco Production Practices and Costs, Lower Coastal Plains Georgia
Station of the University System of Georgia,* Mimeo Series,
(1950), 5; *Georgia Progress,* III (June, 1957), 3; *Progressive Farmer* (June, 1955), 34; *ibid.,* 27.

71. Wilson, "Mechanizing Flue-Cured Tobacco Harvest," *Agricultural Engineering,* XXXVII, 408–410; *The Tobacco Leaf*
XCVI, No. 4951 (January 2, 1960), 33; *Progressive Farmer*
(February, 1961), 36, 120; *Progressive Farmer* (September,
1961), 34, 90; *Tobacco,* CLXIV (April 28, 1967), 36; *Tobacco,* CLXVIII (November 15, 1968), 9.

72. *Progressive Farmer* (August, 1961), 22; *Progressive Farmer*
(November, 1961), 30; *Progressive Farmer* (July, 1962),
23; *Tobacco,* CLXIV (April 28, 1967), 34.

73. Elmon Yoder and E. M. Smith, "Handling Stalk-Cut Tobacco on Portable Frames," *Agricultural Engineering,* XLVI
(December, 1965), 27.

74. *Tobacco,* CLXIII (July 1, 1966), 25; *Tobacco* (December 16,
1966), 27.

Glossary

to Tatham's *An Historical and Practical Essay on the Culture and Commerce of Tobacco*

Aseribed. Printing error. This should read ascribed.

Breaking bulk. Breaking open a hogshead or cask of tobacco.

Cape merchant. The person in charge of the company magazine established by the London Company of Virginia at Jamestown.

Carrot (also carotte). A sweet leaf formed in long thin rolls and cut like the modern pigtail twist.

Commissio specialis concernens le garbling herbae Nicotianae. Special commission concerning garbling tobacco.

Communibus annis. Common annual or the usual annual.

Conveyance by Canoes. The practice of fastening two canoes together to transport tobacco on the inland waterways above the Falls was supposedly begun by the Reverend Robert Rose of Albermarle County, Virginia, around 1740. This became known as the "Rose Method."

Corps Diplom. Jean Dumont, *Corps Universal Diplomatique Du Droit Des Gens.* 8 vols. Amsterdam, 1726–1731.

Cut Up the Plant. To harvest the plant of tobacco by cutting the stalk off just above the ground and below the lower leaves on the plant.

Cow-Penning on the Sward. Penning the cattle on a particular field to be planted in tobacco. This eliminated the necessity of having to spread the barnyard manure by hand. Cow-penning involved little additional labor since crops were fenced in to keep the cattle out.

Damage Feasant. Doing damage. A term applied to a person's cattle or beast found upon another's land, doing damage by treading down the grass, grain, etc.

De Concessione demiss, Edwardo Dichfeild and Aliis. Concerning the revoked concession to Edward Ditchfield and others. The Ditchfield contract of 1625 concerned a monopolistic privilege in marketing tobacco, which failed because of determined opposition by the Virginia planters.

De Commissione speciali Georgio domino Goring et aliis Concessa concernente venditionem de Tobacco absque licentia regia. Concerning the special commission granted to George Lord Goring and others concerning the sale of tobacco without royal license. Negotiations for the Goring contract in 1638 included an attempt to revive the Virginia Company.

De Proclamatione de Signatione de Tobacco. On the proclamation concerning the labeling of tobacco.

De Proclamatione pro Ordinatione de Tobacco. On the proclamation for regulating tobacco.

Distraining. To constrain by seizing and holding some item in order to obtain satisfaction of a claim.

Dray. A strong, low cart or wagon, without permanent sides. Used for carrying heavy loads.

Drawback. Remittance of duties (partial or total) previously paid on imports upon their being exported.

Drinking Tobacco. Smoking tobacco. The term probably had reference to the popular habit of inhaling (apparently swallowing) the smoke.

Dum armes silent leges. When laws are suspended by war, or, while arms suspend the law.

Engrossing. Monopolizing the supply of a marketable product.

Eye of the Hoe. The hole in which the handle is inserted.

Fewel. Fuel.

Firing. Virtually all diseases of the tobacco leaf were called "firing" throughout the Colonial period and in the first half of the nineteenth century. The most common "firings" were probably mosaic and frenching.

Flook Plough. More commonly known as the fluke plough. Fluke evidently refers to the shape of the bit, which was in the form of a fluke or flounder. A light plough designed to be used in light soils or soil that had already been cut or turned by a heavy plough.

The Fly. Now known as the tobacco flea beatle. It was a serious pest capable of destroying the young seedlings in the seedbed or plant bed. It was not until the perfection of a cloth cover or thin canvas for the tobacco plant bed in the latter part of the nineteenth century that the "fly" ceased to be a serious menace.

Forestalling. Buying up or monopolizing the market in advance of the trade generally. To intercept and buy products before they reach the normal or usual marketing channel.

Garbling. In 1619 two royal commissions were issued providing that no tobacco should be sold in England until the duties on it were paid and until it was officially inspected and sealed. The sealing of the tobacco implied a guaranty of its quality. This inspection for the purpose of insuring the sale of a commodity of good quality was known as "garbling."

Groundsel. Groundsill; the lowest horizontal timber of a frame or building lying next to the ground.

Ground-Worm. More commonly known today as the "cutworm."

Half-Sledge. A short sleigh on which the butt ends of logs were placed to facilitate the movement of these long heavy objects.

Helve. Handle of a hoe, axe, hatchet, hammer, etc.

Hoe Up. To make hills or small mounds of earth for the reception of the tobacco plant at planting time.

Inured to the Open Air. After the tobacco seeds were sown in the plant beds, the plant bed was covered with leaves or straw. Oak boughs were then placed on top of the leaves or straw and left there until the frosts were gone in the spring to protect the young seedlings. When the last frosts were gone this cover was removed so that the young tender plants were exposed to the elements to allow them to grow strong and large enough to be transplanted.

Irishism. Idiom or slang expression peculiar to the Irish.

Isthmus of Darien. The former name of the Isthmus of Panama.

Kite-foot Tobacco. An early Maryland-grown bright or yellow leaf tobacco. The best grade of Oronoko tobacco cured to a bright color became universally known as Kite-foot by the end of the eighteenth century.

La' Bat, Mr. P. (also referred to as Pere La Bat and Peere La' Bat). Jean Bapiste Labat, the French Dominican missionary sent to the West Indies. He explored the islands, founded the city of Basse-Terre, and defended Guadeloupe against the English. He wrote several volumes on his travels in Europe and America.

Lady Day. Annunciation Day, March 25th; a day observed in the honor of the Virgin Mary. In England it was one of the quarter days when quarterly payments were due.

"Land When Hired. . . ." This is a misprint. It should read, "Land when tired. . . ."

Little Frederic. One of several strains or varieties of tobacco that had evolved during the eighteenth century. Different soil types and inevitable hybridization resulted in the emergence of several different varieties. These varieties came to acquire the names of individuals or were given names indicating some distinctive characteristic, such as Frederick, Little Frederick, Thick-Joint, Shoe-String, and Blue Pryor.

Nippling. Nipping frost; a frost severe enough to damage vegetation susceptible to frostbite.

One Hand. Monopolistic control.

Oronoko (Orinoco or Aranoko). The most common type of tobacco grown during the Colonial period. It is thought by some to have orginated in the vicinity of the Orinoco River valley in Venezuela. It grew a large porous leaf and was stronger in taste than the famous Sweet-scented type. As Tatham pointed out, all tobacco by the end of the eighteenth century tended to be classified as Oronoko.

Pitching the Crop. Planting tobacco in the field.

Posse commitatus. A body or force armed with legal authority.

Priming. Removing the bottom leaves from the stalk. The bottom three or four leaves were usually battered, broken, and bruised from the several hoeings in the course of the growing season. Priming also permitted a larger mound or hill of earth to be drawn up around the stalk at the final hoeing, or when the crop was "laid-by." These leaves were usually considered worthless and discarded.

Proclamatio de herba Nicotiana. Proclamation concerning tobacco.

Quo warranto. A writ of right by which one was required to show by what right he exercised any office, franchise, grant, or liberty.

Roll Tobacco. Tobacco twisted on a small hand-spinning machine to produce a thick rope of spun leaf weighing from one to thirty pounds. The spun rope of tobacco was then wound into a roll, wrapped in a heavy canvas, and bound.

Rood or Pole of Land. A square measure equal to about one-fourth acre or forty square rods.

Rump Parliament. Also known as the Long Parliament, 1640–1660. It met on November 3, 1640, declared the House of Lords to be useless, and passed a bill that no authority but Parliament itself could dissolve Parliament. The Long Parliament came to an end when it dissolved itself on March 16, 1660.

Rushworth. John Rushworth, *Historical Collections of Private Passages of State, Weighty Matters in Law, Remarkable Proceedings in Five Parliaments. . . .* 6 vols., London, 1703–1708.

Rym. Thomas Rymer, *Foedera* (see Bibliography of Published Works Used by William Tatham).

Scobell's Acts. Henry Scobell, *A Collection of Several Acts of Parliament in the Years 1648 . . . 1651. . . .* London, 1651.

Sells. Sills; the horizontal timber serving as a foundation of a wall, doorway, etc.

Shag Tobacco. A coarse strong or rough type of tobacco finely shredded or cut.

Shelving. Slanting or sloping.

Short-cut Tobacco. A type of manufactured tobacco. A carrot or roll of tobacco cut up into short lengths for the retail trade.

Smart Hooping. Putting thicker and stronger hoops around the hogshead of tobacco to enable the hogshead to withstand the strain of being rolled to market.

Somer Islands. The Bermudas.

Sweet-scented. One of the two types or varieties of tobacco that emerged in early seventeenth century Virginia. It was grown principally in the sandy loam soil between the York and James rivers. It is thought by some to be one of the earliest and most definite evidences of the evolution of dark tobacco toward the brighter variety. It produced a very mild and fine fibered leaf.

Tare. The weight of the empty hogshead or cask. In determining the total price for a hogshead of tobacco, the tare was always deducted from the gross weight.

Taking Off. The task of physically transferring the hogsheads of tobacco from the inspection warehouse to the oceangoing vessel for exportation.

Thorow. Through.

Thurl. *Thurloe Papers. Collection of the State Papers of John Thurlow.* Edited by Thomas Birch. 7 vols., London, 1742.

Tlascalians. Indians of the Nahuatlan tribe that originally occupied the state of Tlaxcala, Mexico. They were defeated by Cortez and later joined him in the conquest of Mexico.

Told Off. Tobacco transferred from the inspection warehouse to the vessel for exportation.

Topping Tobacco. Removing the blossoms and sometimes several of the top leaves in order to permit greater growth of the desired number of leaves left on the plant to be harvested.

Upland Warehouses. Tobacco inspection warehouses above the Fall Line. After 1730 all tobacco exported from the colony of Virginia was required by law to be inspected at one of the public inspection warehouses (Maryland and North Carolina soon followed suit). The public inspection warehouses in Virginia were restricted to the Tidewater area until after the Revolution. By 1820 about half of the inspection warehouses were above the Fall Line.

Weare for Fish. Weir; a fence of stakes, brushwood, etc., set in a stream for taking fish.

Wiatt, Sir Francis. Sir Francis Wyatt, the first royal governor of Virginia, 1625–1626. He served a second term, 1639–1642.

Bibliography

of the Published Works Used by William Tatham

Anderson, Adam. *An Historical and Chronological Deduction of the Origin of Commerce, from the Earliest Accounts to the Present Time; Containing an History of the Great Commercial Interests of the British Empire.* 4 vols. London, 1787–1789.

Catesby, Marc. *The Natural History of Carolina, Florida, and the Bahama Islands . . . with Remarks upon Agriculture, etc.* 2 vols. London, 1731–1743.

Chalmers, George. *An Estimate of the Comparative Strength of Britain during the Present and Four Preceeding Reigns; and the Losses of Her Trade from Every War Since the Revolution.* London, 1794.

Hall, William Henry. *The New Royal Encyclopedia; or Complete Modern Dictionary of Arts and Sciences, on an Improved Plan. Containing a . . . Display of the Whole Theory and Practice of the Liberal and Mechanical Arts, etc.* 3 vols. London, [1788].

Hakluyt, Richard. *Divers Voyages Touching the Discoverie of America, etc.* London, 1582.

Harriot (or Hariot), Thomas. *A Brief and True Report of the New Found Land of Virginia, of the Commodities, and of the Nature and Manners of the Natural Inhabitants. . . .* London, 1588.

Hazard, Ebenezer. *Historical Collections; Consisting of*

State Papers and other Authenic Documents, intended as Materials for an History of the United States of America. 2 vols. Philadelphia, 1792–1794.

Jefferson, Thomas. *Notes on the State of Virginia.* London, 1787.

Jones, Hugh. *The Present State of Virginia.* London, 1724.

Keith, Sir William. *The History of the British Plantations in America, etc.* London, 1738.

Labat, Jean Baptiste. *Nouveau Voyage aux isles de l' Amerique: contenant l' historie naturelle de ces pays, l' origine, les moeurs, la religion, & le gouvernement des habitans anciens & modernes, etc.* 6 vols. Paris, 1722.

The Level of Europe and North America: or the Observer's Guide. Philadelphia, 1795. A periodical in English and French.

Mascall, Edward James. *Consolidation of the Customs and other Duties. Tables of the Net Duties Payable, and Drawbacks Allowed on Certain Goods . . . Imported and Exported, or Carried Coastwise, etc.* London, 1787.

"Method of Raising and Curing Tobacco, communicated to the Committee on Agriculture in Boston and Published by Them, 1786," *American Museum,* I (February, 1787), 135–36.

Morse, Jedidiah, Compiler. *The American Geography; or, A view of the Present Situation of the United States. . . .* London, 1792.

Parker, Richard. "An Account of the Culture of Tobacco," *American Museum,* V (June, 1789), 537–40.

Rymer, Thomas. *Foedera, Conventiones, Litterae et Cujuscunque Generis Acta Publica, inter Reges Angliae et Alios Quosvis Imperatores, Reges, Pontifices, Principes, vel Communitates. . . .* 20 vols. London, 1704–1735. Volumes XVI–XX, edited by Robert Sanderson.

Smith, Adam. *An Inquiry into the Nature and Causes of the Wealth of Nations.* 3 vols. Dublin, 1776.

Steel, David. *Steel's Table of the British Custom and Excise Duties, with the Drawbacks, Bounties, and Allowances, etc.* London, 1799.

Wafer, Lionel. *A New Voyage and Description of the Isthmus of America, Giving an Account of the Author's Abode There . . . with Remarkable Occurrences in the South Sea. . . .* London, 1699.

Weld, Isaac, Junior. *Travels Through the States of North America, and the Provinces of Upper and Lower Canada during the Years 1795, 1796, and 1797.* 2 vols. London, 1799.

Wheeler, James. *The Botanist's and Gardener's New Dictionary; in which is also comprised, a Gardener's Calendar . . . and to which is prefixed an Introduction to the Linnaean System of Botany.* London, 1763.

Whitworth, Charles. *State of the Trade of Great Britain in its Imports and Exports Progressively from the Year 1697 . . . with a Preface and Introduction Setting Forth the Articles whereof each Trade Consists.* London, 1776.

General Bibliography

Manuscripts

Archivo Historio Nacional Estado, Legajo 3890, Expediente 5, Madrid, Spain. Microfilm copy in the Library of Congress.

Papers of Thomas Jefferson, Library of Congress.

Great Britain. Public Records Office, Colonial Office 42, Lower Canada—Original Correspondence—Secretary of State, 1796–1805. Canadian Archives, Ottawa, Canada.

Correspondence of Members of the Royal Society of Arts, London. Microfilm copy of the correspondence of the American members in the American Philosophical Society Library, Philadelphia.

William Tatham Papers, Archives Division, Virginia State Library, Richmond.

Newspapers

Daily Compiler (Richmond), 1819.
National Intelligencer, 1814.
Richmond *Enquirer,* 1819.
Virginia *Gazette,* 1774.

Periodicals

Agricultural Engineering, 1956–68.
The Burley Tobacco Farmer, 1965–68.
The Flue Cured Tobacco Farmer, 1960–68.

Georgia Progress, 1955.
Progressive Farmer, 1955–68.
Tobacco, 1960–68.
The Tobacco Leaf, 1960.

Articles

Allan, D. G. C. "Colonel William Tatham, An Anglo-American Member of the Society, 1801–1804," *Journal of the Royal Society of Arts,* CVIII (London, 1960), 227–34.

"Colonel Tatham," *Annual of Biography and Obituary for 1820,* IV (London, 1820), 149–59.

"Colonel Tatham, formerly a Field Officer in the Service of the American Republic, and lately Supervisor of the London Docks," *Public Characters of 1801–1802* (London, 1804), 408–33.

McPherson, Elizabeth G., ed. "Unpublished Letters to Jefferson," *North Carolina Historical Review,* XII (July and October, 1935), 252–83, 354–80.

McPherson, Elizabeth G., ed. "Letters of William Tatham," *William and Mary College Quarterly,* XVI, Series 2 (April and July, 1936), 162–91, 362–98.

Nicholas, Anna. "Conservation of Natural Resources in America," *The Journal of American History,* IV (1910), 572–80.

"Obituary, with Anecdotes of Remarkable Persons," *The Gentleman's Magazine and Historical Chronicle,* Pt. I (London, 1820), 375–76.

"Original Records of the Phi Beta Kappa Society," *William and Mary College Quarterly,* IV, Series 1 (April, 1896), 213–41.

Turner, Frederick J., ed. "Documents on the Blount Conspiracy, 1795–1797," *American Historical Review,* X (January, 1905), 574–606.

Federal and State Publications

Agricultural Statistics. United States Department of Agriculture. Published annually.

Agricultural Research Report of the Agricultural Experiment Station, July 1, 1953—June 30, 1957. Virginia Polytechnic Institute, Blacksburg, 1957.

Beal, George M. and Summer, Paul F., Jr. *Marketing Maryland Tobacco.* Maryland Agricultural Experiment Station Bulletin 451. College Park, 1954.

Bufton, V. E., *et al. Wisconsin Tobacco Production and Marketing.* Wisconsin Department of Agriculture Bulletin 305. Madison, 1951.

Chappell, J. S. and Toussaint, W. D. *Harvesting and Curing Flue-Cured Tobacco with Automatic Tying Machines, Bulk-Curing and the Conventional Method: Labor Requirements; Cost and Prices Received.* Agricultural Experiment Information Series No. 123, Department of Economics, North Carolina State University. Raleigh, 1965.

Chemical Sucker Control for Flue-Cured Tobacco. University of Florida Agricultural Experiment Station, Circular S–93. Gainesville, 1956.

Classification of Leaf Tobacco Covering Classes, Types, and Group of Grades. United States Department of Agriculture, Bureau of Agricultural Economics, Service and Regulatory Announcements No. 118. Washington, 1929.

Cockroft, Lindon U. and Brown, J. W. H. *Developing and Market Testing an Improved Looseleaf Tobacco Package.* Marketing Economics Research Service, United States Department of Agriculture. Washington, D.C., 1964.

Crops and Markets. United States Department of Agriculture. Publication ceased in 1956.

Everette, George. *Harvesting, Curing, and Preparing Dark-Fired Tobacco for Market.* Kentucky Agricultural Extension Service Circular 555. Lexington, 1958.

Gage, C. E. *American Tobacco Types, Uses and Markets.* United States Department of Agriculture Circular No. 249. Washington, 1942.

Holmes, George K. *Tobacco Crop of the United States,*

1612–1911. United States Department of Agriculture, Bureau of Statistics Circular No. 33. Washington, D.C., 1912.

Killebrew, J. B. "Report on the Culture and Curing of Tobacco in the United States," *Tenth Census, Agriculture,* III. Washington, 1883.

Kincaid, Randall R. *Shade Tobacco Growing in Florida.* Florida Department of Agriculture Bulletin 136. Tallahassee, 1960.

Mathews, G. R. *Growing Sun-Cured Tobacco.* Virginia Polytechnic Institute Agricultural Extension Service Circular 653. Blacksburg, 1959.

McMurtney, James E. *Tobacco Production.* Agricultural Research Service, United States Department of Agriculture. Washington, D.C., 1962.

Seventeenth Census of the United States, 1940. Agriculture, III, General Report, Statistics by Subjects. Washington, D.C., 1943.

The Tobacco Situation. United States Department of Agriculture. Washington, D.C., issued quarterly.

Tobacco in the United States. United States Department of Agriculture. Consumer and Marketing Service Miscellaneous Publication No. 867. Washington, D.C., 1966.

Tobacco Production in Kentucky. Kentucky Agricultural Extension Service Circular 482. Lexington, 1954.

Tobacco Production Practices and Costs, Lower Coastal Plains Georgia Experiment Station of the University System of Georgia, Mimeo Series. Tifton, 1950.

Books

Annals of the Congress of the United States. 42 vols. Washington, D.C., 1834–1856.

Bidwell, Percy W. and Falconer, John I. *History of Agriculture in the Northern United States.* New York, 1941.

Billings, E. R. *Tobacco, Its Culture, Manufacture and Use.* Hartford, 1875.

Boyd, Julian P., ed. *The Papers of Thomas Jefferson.* 17 vols. Princeton, 1950–

Brooks, J. E. *The Mighty Leaf*. Boston, 1952.

Carter, Clarence, ed. *Territorial Papers of the United States*. 17 vols. Washington, D.C., 1934–1950.

Fletcher, Stevenson W. *Pennsylvania Agriculture and Country Life, 1640–1840*. Harrisburg, 1950.

Garner, Wightman W. *The Production of Tobacco*. New York, Philadelphia and Toronto, 1951.

Gray, Lewis C. *History of Agriculture in the Southern United States to 1860*. 2 vols. Gloucester, 1958.

Heinmann, Robert K. *Tobacco and Americans*. New York, Toronto, and London, 1960.

Heitman, Francis B. *Historical Register and Dictionary of the United States Army, 1789–1903*. 2 vols. Washington, D.C., 1903.

Hening, William W., ed. *Statutes at Large: A Collection of All the Laws of Virginia, 1619–1792*. 13 vols. Richmond, 1809–1823.

Jacobstein, Meyer. *The Tobacco Industry in the United States*. Columbia University Studies in History, Economics, and Public Law, XXVI, No. 3. New York, 1907.

Jahn, Raymond. *Tobacco Dictionary*. New York, 1954.

Keith, Alice B. and Masterson, William H., eds. *The John Gray Blount Papers, 1764–1802*. 3 vols. Raleigh, 1952–1965.

Killebrew, J. B. and Myrick, Herbert. *Tobacco Leaf. Its Culture and Cure, Marketing and Manufacture*. New York, 1909.

Lindley, Harlow, ed. *Indiana as Seen By Early Travelers, A Collection of Reprints from Books of Travel, Letters, and Diaries Prior to 1830*. Indianapolis, 1916.

McDonald, A. F. *The History of Tobacco Production in Connecticut*. New Haven, 1936.

McIlwaine, H. R. and Hall, Wilmer L., eds. *Journals of the Council of the State of Virginia, 1776–1781*. 3 vols. Richmond, 1931–1952.

Masterson, William H. *William Blount*. Baton Rouge, 1954.

Mumford, George Wythe. *The Two Parsons; Cupids*

Sports; The Dream; and the Jewels of Virginia. Richmond, 1884.

Robert, Joseph C. *The Story of Tobacco in America.* New York, 1949.

Robert, Joseph C. *The Tobacco Kingdom: Plantation, Market, and Factory in Virginia and North Carolina, 1800–1860.* Durham, 1938.

Robinson, Blackwell P. *William R. Davie.* Chapel Hill, 1957.

Tatham, William. *An Historical and Practical Essay on the Culture and Commerce of Tobacco.* London, 1800.

Tatham, William. *Communications Concerning the Agriculture and Commerce of America.* London, 1800.

Tennant, R. A. *The Rise of the Cigarette Industry.* New Haven, 1950.

Tilley, Nannie Mae. *The Bright-Tobacco Industry, 1860–1929.* Chapel Hill, 1948.

Thornbrough, Emma Lou. *Indiana in the Civil War Era, 1850–1880.* Indianapolis, 1965.

The Tobacco Institute, Inc. *Tobacco—A Vital U.S. Industry.* Washington, D.C., 1959.

The Tobacco Institute, Inc. *The Tobacco Industry—Six Factual Reports* (tobacco, the industry story, and separate reports on the cigarette, cigar, smoking tobacco, chewing tobacco, and snuff industries). Washington, D.C., 1959.

Williams, Samuel Cole. *Tennessee During the Revolution.* Nashville, 1944.

Williams, Samuel Cole. *William Tatham, Wataugan.* Johnson City, 1947.

Index